SOCIALISM AND THE WORKERS

Socialism and the Workers in Massachusetts, 1886-1912

HENRY F. BEDFORD

THE UNIVERSITY OF MASSACHUSETTS PRESS

AMHERST, MASSACHUSETTS   1966

FOR MY MOTHER AND FATHER

Preface

After several years in the vanguard of American socialism, the Massachusetts socialists quite suddenly lost momentum in 1903. Elsewhere in the nation the movement developed and occasionally prospered during the following decade. But support in Massachusetts dwindled. Growth and slump were partly the product of political conditions in the Bay State. Shrewd local leadership, a close alliance with the Boot and Shoe Workers' Union, and the disenchantment of many voters with established political institutions contributed to early success. An effective anti-socialist crusade led by former party leaders, the mounting opposition of the Roman Catholic Church, and the major parties' practice of appropriating parts of the socialist program helped check the advance.

Socialists themselves were partly responsible for their failure. Internal quarrels, more often the result of personality than of ideology, alienated idealists and the rank and file. Elected Socialists could not produce a child labor law, let alone the promised workers' utopia. Radical rhetoric drove away middle class reformers; workers who bothered to listen found Socialists theoretical, tiresome, and often irrelevant. The laborers' problems were specific and immediate; the Cooperative Commonwealth was only cheap prophecy.

"Socialist movement" is defined to include both the refined reformers who followed Edward Bellamy and the more orthodox Marxists who followed Daniel DeLeon. The socialists of Massachusetts inherited the ideals of Nationalists and Christian Socialists, the reform program of the Populists, and much of the vocabulary of the Socialist Labor party. All agreed that the present was not ideal, that the state should help the less fortunate, that various schemes of collective ownership would promote these ends. They used radical terminology to present their program; semantic confusion, which may perhaps be dignified as "ideology," was the product.

By 1912, constant discouragement had made hesitation a habit. Socialists failed to derive any political advantage from the Lawrence textile strike and seemed uneasy at the practice of militance they had only preached for so long. For years socialists had claimed to be a revolutionary political organization. When circumstance showed the impossibility of being both "revolutionary" and "political," socialists discovered they were neither.

Almost without exception Massachusetts socialists had placed politics first. They borrowed a few Marxist slogans for campaigns but left the intellectual content of socialism virtually undisturbed. However much they posed as radicals, this emphasis made them reformers in fact. This book reflects their own consuming interest in reform politics. It is not a social history of the workers or an institutional history of organized labor in the Commonwealth. Nor is it a political history of Massachusetts in the early twentieth century; there is no need here to duplicate Richard M. Abrams' *Conservatism in a Progressive Era* (Cambridge: Harvard University Press, 1964), which treats the politics of the period at length. Finally, this study deals only tangentially with the national movement already analyzed in several books. Since the national electorate was not homogeneous in 1900, a detailed study of socialists in a single state both confirms and modifies the

PREFACE

insights of scholars who have worked with a larger focus. In the preparation of this book, I have had the willing cooperation and warm encouragement of many interested people, and the generous financial support of the Phillips Exeter Academy, which aided my research with grants for summer work and a sabbatical in 1963–1964.

Two articles based on research for this book have previously appeared. Portions of these articles are here used with the permission of the editors of *Labor History* ("'The Haverhill Social Democrat': Spokesman for Socialism," II, Winter, 1961) and *Essex Institute Historical Collections* ("The Socialist Movement in Haverhill," XCIX, January, 1963).

Mentioning a library is an inadequate method of acknowledging the help of the people in it. The Davis Library at the Phillips Exeter Academy has for years tolerated my whims and promptly fulfilled them with good humor. Curators at Duke University, the State Historical Society of Wisconsin, the Tamiment Library of New York University, and the Yivo Institute for Jewish Research guided me through their extensive collections of socialist materials. The Goodell Library at the University of Massachusetts found items that I had despaired of locating. For a year I used the Converse Memorial Library at Amherst College, and for a whole summer and parts of others, the Haverhill Public Library made me welcome. The Massachusetts State Library and the New England Deposit Library made special arrangements for my use of their newspaper collections. The Library of the College of the Holy Cross also made newspapers available.

Roland Sawyer gave most freely of his time on several occasions and lent me his personal scrapbooks and the records of the Ware local which he had preserved. Ralph Gardner and Mrs. Glenroy Colby both gave me cordial and informative interviews. John E. Mara, President of

ix

PREFACE

the Boot and Shoe Workers' Union, permitted me to use materials in the Union's archives. William N. Scanlan of the Union's staff gave me much helpful counsel.

Several scholars have read and criticized the manuscript, sometimes in more than one draft. Professor Howard Quint lent me his extensive collection of microfilm and gave me the benefit of his sure editorial hand. This book is the revision of a doctoral dissertation prepared under his direction at the University of Massachusetts. Professors Milton Cantor and Gerard Braunthal suggested revisions that have improved the book. My colleague Donald B. Cole gave a thoughtful and exacting critique.

Several people have been indispensable in transforming my handwriting into print. Mrs. Grace Casey turned an illegible draft into finished copy. John Williamson disrupted his schedule to do some photography at my convenience.

Finally, my sons, Hank, Billy, and Jeff, all of whom have lived with this project since it began, warrant their father's warmest thanks for usually trying to be quiet while he was working. Their mother too has cheerfully tolerated history in her house; she has more of a share in this book than she will let me acknowledge.

Exeter, New Hamphire
September, 1965

Contents

ABBREVIATIONS

Bulletin	*Daily Evening Bulletin* (Haverhill, Massachusetts).
DeLeon Papers	Daniel DeLeon Papers, State Historical Society of Wisconsin.
Gazette	*Haverhill Evening Gazette* (Haverhill, Massachusetts).
HSD	*Haverhill Social Democrat* (Haverhill, Massachusetts).
Hillquit Papers	Morris Hillquit Papers, State Historical Society of Wisconsin.
ISR	*International Socialist Review* (Chicago).
Kangaroo *People*	*The People* (New York). When the Socialist Labor party split in July, 1899, both factions published a weekly called *The People*. This abbreviation refers to the paper that opposed Daniel De-Leon.
People	*The People* (New York). This abbreviation refers to DeLeon's weekly, the official organ of the Socialist Labor party. In June, 1900, the title was changed to *Weekly People*.
Sawyer Scrapbooks Sawyer Papers	Roland D. Sawyer Papers, in the possession of Rev. Sawyer, Kensington, New Hampshire. The collection consists largely of scrapbooks.
SDH	*Social Democratic Herald* (Milwaukee).
SLP Papers	Socialist Labor Party Papers, State Historical Society of Wisconsin.
SP Papers	Socialist Party Papers, Duke University Library, Durham, North Carolina.

Prologue:
January 4, 1903

William Mailly, the secretary of the Socialist party of Massachusetts, was quietly and justifiably pleased. A Socialist by conviction as well as by profession, Mailly knew that economic and social injustice persisted throughout the nation in January, 1903. But Massachusetts, he thought, had stepped toward a more humane society in the year he had guided Socialists there. They had registered spectacular growth in the elections of the previous fall: some 36,000 voters—one in every eleven—had supported the party's ticket. If rising political strength did not prove that a growing number of Massachusetts residents was adopting Socialism, it nevertheless provoked comment.

One such comment explained William Mailly's satisfaction on January 4, 1903. The Boston *Sunday Herald* for that morning devoted five full pages and a long editorial to the state's Socialist movement.[1] Though disagreeing with details, the party's secretary believed the article "carefully prepared," and was cautiously happy about its publication.[2]

Mailly was too restrained. An unusually thoughtful piece of reporting, the feature was balanced and factual.

1. Unless otherwise noted, the prologue is based upon material in this issue of the *Sunday Herald*.
2. *Worker* (New York), January 11, 1903.

1

SOCIALISM AND THE WORKERS

While noting the large percentage of Socialists of foreign birth or parentage, the *Herald* did not editorialize about un-Americanism. There was no strident defense of private property or public morality. The paper was informative, not hysterical, and its circulation was about three times the Socialist vote. William Mailly liked that kind of audience.

"No feature of the last state election in Massachusetts," began the *Herald*, "has created more widespread comment than the vote cast by the Socialist party." Its total in 1902 was larger than that of any third party since the days of the Know-Nothings; its percentage of the electorate represented the best showing by a minor party since Wendell Phillips ran on a Labor ticket in 1870. Most observers (including the writer of the day's editorial) maintained that Socialists had temporarily captured the popular resentment of capitalists stirred by the recent national coal strike. The article furnished material for a more informed opinion.

Questions demanded answers: Was "anything peculiar about Massachusetts which . . . provoked the growth of Socialism . . . ?" Was it just coincidence that the movement seemed strongest where the shoe industry predominated and weakest in the textile towns? Did the votes signify support for collectivism, or merely a temporary dissatisfaction with candidates and programs of other parties? Did the movement consist of Yankees or immigrants? How were other institutions—trade unions, churches, political parties—reacting? Who controlled the party? Just what did Socialists believe?

A reporter, identified only as "the Herald man," sought answers in William Mailly's office in Boston, in the lobbies of the legislature, in the Emergency Hospital located in Boston's sixth ward, and in conversation with a group of local cigarmakers. He interviewed shoe workers in Brockton, Haverhill and Lynn; textile workers in Lawrence,

2

Lowell, Fall River and New Bedford; a minister, two merchants and a printer in Fitchburg; clergymen, doctors, and trade union officials; Republicans, Democrats and Prohibitionists; Swedes, Germans, French Canadians and the ubiquitous Irish; and people he could describe only as "Americans." The reporting was good; "the Herald man" deserved a by-line.

Scattered through the article were photographs of a dozen party leaders. Their names gave no indication that the socialist movement had once been almost entirely German-speaking; the large Scandinavian segment was also unrepresented. While the portraits of Patrick Mahoney and James F. Carey indicated an Irish element, other leaders bore "American" names like Billings or Chase or Bingham. Four men were members of educated professions: two were physicians, one a dentist, and one a Unitarian minister. Nor were the others plain proletarians; union officials, proprietors of small businesses, professional lecturers and party managers guided the Socialists.

The past political affiliation of both leaders and led depended partly upon nationality. Swedes and Germans had probably been Republicans; Irish had almost certainly been Democrats. The Socialist surge in Haverhill, Brockton, and Rockland had come at the expense of the Democrats. In Fitchburg, on the other hand, Republican converts outnumbered former Democrats. Some Socialists had once been Prohibitionists. Perhaps more had belonged to the People's party. Many prominent Socialists had served their political apprenticeship and gained a popular reputation as Populist candidates. Early Populist platforms constantly reappeared in the guise of Socialist campaign proposals. The link between Populism and Socialism was so apparent that "the Herald man" lumped the Populist vote with that of the Socialist Labor party to establish a statistical base for comparison.

The determined "Herald man" sought more information

about the ethnic background of the membership. He divided a list of 457 Socialist candidates along ethnic lines and discovered an overwhelming preponderance of "Americans." Trailing 272 "Americans" were 64 of Irish extraction, 54 identified as German or Jewish, 16 each French and Swedish, a lone Italian, and 34 who could not be identified. German, Swedish, and English immigrants seemed most receptive to the Socialist message; the Irish showed some interest in areas where control of the Democratic machine had eluded them; French Canadians and Italians proved indifferent when not actively hostile.

Still a final conclusion was impossible. Both Haverhill and Brockton had relatively small numbers of immigrants; these were the Socialists' banner cities. Fall River's population was overwhelmingly of foreign origin; usually persistent Socialists had practically given up there. While many Americans, including "the Herald man," believed most Socialists were no more than a generation removed from Europe, the impression was not demonstrable. Even had it been proven, the same statement described the entire population of Massachusetts, and consequently was hardly restrictive.

For want of a photograph of an "average Socialist," an impression of the two thousand men and women who crowded a rally in Brockton might serve. They looked intelligent, earnest, scrubbed. Mostly working people, they were respectably dressed, attentive, and enthusiastically responsive. The reporter thought the same crowd would look at home at a Republican rally in Boston. The affair was "plainly not a gathering . . . to be dismissed with a sneer as a lot of cranks and anarchists. . . ."

The party claimed a close link with trade unions. Not all members of labor organizations were Socialists, but most Socialists were members of labor organizations. Cooperation between the party and the shoe unions of Haverhill and Brockton strengthened both groups. The chief representative of the Boot and Shoe Workers' Union in Haverhill, for instance, was a former Socialist office-holder and chairman of the party's city committee. In a Socialist stronghold, his political prestige and connections helped the union. At the same time, tracts and posters turned his office into an unofficial campaign center. Socialists believed the calculated appeal of the major parties to the labor vote in Lynn retarded progress there. In Springfield, the local Socialist leader was a cigarmaker who was also the district organizer for the American Federation of Labor. In the textile centers, where struggling trade unions matched employers' hostility to Socialists, the party made little headway. Socialists claimed that their following in the unions was evidence that their doctrine appealed to the most intelligent members of the working class. The *Herald* did not dispute the boast: "Our analysis shows that the Socialist party in this state draws its chief strength from the highest grade of wage-earning labor, . . . the aristocracy, as it were, of labor. . . ."

Massachusetts Socialists had one political advantage denied their comrades elsewhere in the nation. Every winter from the State House came reams of newspaper copy about two honest, noisy, and interesting Socialist representatives. James F. Carey and Frederic MacCartney publicized the Socialist program when they introduced bills; they publicized it again in hearings and debates; and they publicized it yet once more when the legislature killed most of their proposals. One of MacCartney's constituents remarked that his district had regularly sent a Republican to Boston and never heard of him again until the following election. Now, he said, "we have got a representative who makes himself heard and that's the kind of representative we like." Though the Socialists' campaign oratory irritated other legislators, it began to have an effect. The charge that a measure was "socialistic" was not enough to deny it some public exposure. Legislators gave the party an aura of success and respectability; they were an invaluable campaign asset.

Service in public office at any level added to the party's political skill. Socialists readily admitted that a few leaders controlled their organization and that a Socialist "machine" dictated platforms, nominations, and tactics. Shrewd judges of the local situation, these leaders chose their issues well. Politicians in Haverhill, for instance, knew that James Carey was the key to the local movement. While they thought him a demagogue, they respected him as "a crafty politician," who would have to be "met on his own ground and beaten for office" if his party were to be checked.

To secure an authoritative statement of Socialist ideology, "the Herald man" went to see William Mailly. Socialism, suggested the reporter, was supposed to be an imported doctrine, but Massachusetts had a tradition of hospitality to strange ideas. Was Socialism, he continued, more than unorthodox? Was it revolutionary?

William Mailly replied that it certainly was. Of course, he added carefully, "revolutionary" did not imply violence; the transition from capitalism to socialism would be "revolutionary" but peaceful. Socialists incited workers, but only to get them to the polls. The party opposed neither private property nor the individual ownership of homes. Rather, said Mailly, "the modern Socialist movement . . . demands the collective ownership of the means of wealth production and distribution. . . ."

An editorial writer on the *Herald* either did not believe Mailly or failed to read his statement, for the day's editorial suggested that the party would equalize wages, an anti-Socialist cliché that was not part of Mailly's program. The editorial also observed that the party's astounding political showing had not been "due to the discovery . . . of the merits of the Socialist methods of reform, but to . . . disgust at the seeming unwillingness of the older political parties to . . . handle certain great industrial and social problems" facing the state and nation. And that observation was correct. The reporter made the same point differently: ". . . the Socialist party in this state, perhaps more than in some other states, has been a party of opportunism. It has laid more emphasis on practical Socialism than upon ideal Socialism, believing that while waiting for the era of complete Socialism, it has been good policy to take everything it could get. . . ."

"The Herald man" had peeled back radical rhetoric and uncovered plain, old-fashioned reform. The Massachusetts Socialists did shoulder some of the handicaps of doctrinaire Marxist language. They talked about class stratification when the prevailing belief was that the classless society was already fact. They suggested that America's equality of opportunity was only a folk fable.[3] They seemed sometimes to oppose the general American faith that industrialization was desirable, or at least worth the social cost. They advocated revolution, but they did not really want a new society. They did not, as Mailly noted, oppose private property; they wanted more of it for those who had too little. They did not propose to break up the home, as the anti-Socialists insisted; they wanted to give the working man a chance to own one.

Along with the vocabulary, the Massachusetts Socialists accepted some dubious radical assumptions. Workers were invariably "wage slaves"; labor created all value and never received full compensation; working conditions in factories, mines, and mills always bordered on the desper-

3. See Sidney Hook, "The Philosophical Basis of Marxian Socialism in the United States," in Donald D. Egbert and Stow Persons, ed., *Socialism and American Life* (Princeton, 1952) I, 450–451.

ate. The pathetic Socialist faith that these oppressed workers would soon vote for their emancipation survived constant demonstrations to the contrary.

"The Herald man" thought radical trappings were a device to attract attention; moderation did not rouse passion. He was partly right. The combination of radical rhetoric and a moderate reform program was also a central ambiguity that American Socialists never completely resolved. How could a party operating within the context of American institutions stand for revolution? Did relief of labor's distress through legislation really bring the proletarian upheaval closer? In spite of all their ranting about class consciousness, the Socialists of Massachusetts never decided which class they favored. They hoped to win labor without alienating anyone else. They tried in practice to blur the very class distinctions they decried. They acted, in this respect, like other politicians.

The party could respond to local crises and local opportunity. The Haverhill Socialist movement grew out of one strike, turned another to advantage, and gained votes from such local matters as unprotected railroad grade crossings and the arrogance of a gas company. The issue in Brockton was temperance. In Rockland, a Republican state senator opposed hunting on Sunday and thus helped bring success to the Socialists. "The Herald man" also found local circumstances at the root of the party's relative failure in Chicopee, Holyoke, and Lynn. Composed of loosely connected local organizations, the Massachusetts Socialists were instinctively behaving like the established political parties.

Opportunism, defined as freedom to respond to events without the limitation of a confining ideology, was a game the major parties could join to draw off Socialist strength. The *Herald*'s editorial thought the Democrats "the only real opportunist party." They could "have the government undertake . . . what the government could do best" and yet "leave the individual or corporation" alone if other citizens were unharmed. Such a balance would enable "the citizen as an individual to uphold his independence against both the despotism of corporations and the tyranny of government."

In Haverhill, where the Socialist party was a fact of life rather than a subject for investigation, the editor of the local paper, the *Gazette*, urged Republicans to overthrow the bosses and confront pressing economic issues. The G.O.P. could wipe out Socialism in an instant if only it would alleviate industrial hardship with legislation that rank-and-file Republicans everywhere would support.[4] The same idea had occurred to a prominent Bay State Republican legislator, who saw MacCartney as "nine-tenths Good Republican. . . ."

Both parties were already discussing programs and candidates to regain defecting workers and reformers, and Socialists were unlikely to win such a competition. While "the Herald man" was not explicit, his article implied that the Socialist party had more past than future. Where trade union support was lacking, party efforts were futile; unskilled workers were also uninterested. The American Federation of Labor frowned on Socialism and help from craft unions might dwindle. In some places, Roman Catholic priests actively opposed Socialism, though in others the clergy was benevolently neutral. Yet the Church, like the A.F. of L., was officially hostile, and a determined anti-Socialist effort could cut deeply into Socialist ranks. The party's victories were often related to local conditions not duplicated in other communities. Only a major crisis discrediting both established parties could spread a promising local movement across the state. Present Socialist leadership was unquestionably able, but the firm author-

4. *Gazette*, January 10, 1903.

ity of a few did not encourage the development of new leaders. The party's publicity and record, dependent on a few strategically placed office-holders, might not survive their defeat. "Reform" and "opportunism" were hardly fighting faiths likely to command loyalty in adversity.

"The Herald man's" perceptive article had a few surprising omissions. He ignored the national Socialist party and the inspirational leadership of Eugene V. Debs. While alluding to the factionalism that had long kept the Socialist movement in turmoil, he suggested that maturity had eliminated such growing pains. He ignored the anti-Socialist charge that Socialists favored moral as well as economic innovation. And in five solid pages of newsprint about the Socialist party of Massachusetts, he mentioned Karl Marx only once. In the party's Springfield office, "the Herald man" had observed a picture of the Socialist prophet hanging on the wall.

CHAPTER I

Nationalism, Populism, Socialism

Before 1887, Edward Bellamy was as obscure as the hamlet of Chicopee Falls, Massachusetts, where he lived. Still a quiet community in the 1880's, industrialization had not transformed Chicopee Falls into a Holyoke or a Springfield or a Worcester. But industry had made changes that a sensitive observer like Edward Bellamy could hardly fail to notice. He used some of these impressions in a utopian romance called *Looking Backward*, which he published in 1887, and which turned obscurity to fame.

Briefly summarized, *Looking Backward* described the society of 2000 A.D. as a golden age in which cooperation had replaced competition at the core of the economic and social system. Human and economic waste was eliminated; industry was a blessing, not a menace; production was for use, not for profit; humanity enjoyed peace, plenty, leisure, freedom and beauty. Refined, idealistic people of taste, not frothing radicals, had promoted the evolutionary change to the perfect society. In the twentieth century, when control of the nation's economy had become lodged in progressively fewer hands, the government had assumed the right to manage the economy in the interest of the public. The state became the last great trust. "Nationalism"—state ownership of the means of production and distribution—was accomplished peace-

11

fully and by majority will. And thereafter the populace lived in harmony and contentment.

Edward Bellamy had not read the standard socialist texts and did not like what he knew of Socialist activity in the United States. But his Nationalism did share with "scientific" socialism the goal of an abundant cooperative commonwealth. The immense sale of *Looking Backward* gave collectivism an American audience of which more orthodox Socialists had only dreamed. The assured respectability of Nationalism, however, contrasted sharply with radical militancy. And Bellamy was not one to give practical form to his ideas. Yet the history of modern American Socialism really begins with the publication of *Looking Backward*.[1] Bellamy's ideas, which his admirers gave instititutional expression in Nationalist clubs, mingled with other contemporary currents of reform in Populism. Both Nationalism and Populism, in turn, profoundly influenced American Socialism, as first expounded by the Socialist Labor party and subsequently by the Social Democracy and the Socialist Party of America.

Founded in the late 1880's by proper Bostonians, the Nationalist movement was soon preaching public ownership well beyond Massachusetts. Bellamy himself did not join immediately, but the founders consulted the prophet and received his blessing. Though other states had more than the eleven clubs chartered in Massachusetts, the Bay State remained the heart of the movement. The official journals, one of which Bellamy edited, were published in Massachusetts. Nationalists in the Commonwealth were active and articulate, and soon resolved themselves into a political pressure group that served as an example for their fellows elsewhere.

1. Howard H. Quint, *The Forging of American Socialism* (Columbia, S.C., 1953), 77–78; vii.

The Nationalists of Massachusetts were respectable reformers of middle class or patrician stock. A Boston newspaper remarked that the "Brahmin caste of New England" dominated the local Nationalist Club. The *Nationalist,* the first journal of the movement, proudly claimed that members were "men of position, educated, conservative in speech, and of the oldest New England" families. Reform-minded businessmen signed Nationalist petitions for municipal ownership or helped shape a proposal for a municipal fuel distribution center. David Goldstein, a fervent disciple of Bellamy, hoped to work for the Nationalist cause. But he knew instinctively that a young Jewish cigarmaker would be out of place among the "'high brows' and 'literati.'" Instead David Goldstein joined the Socialist Labor party, which was more in keeping, he thought, with his social standing.[2] Advertisements attest the middle-class circulation of Nationalist periodicals. Displays promoting lawn tennis shoes, typewriters, custom tailors, trains to Saratoga, sheet music and summer resorts all appeared in the columns of the *New Nation,* which succeeded the *Nationalist.* Patent medicine advertisements, the staple of the popular press, were rare. The *New Nation* itself, noted the New Bedford *Mercury,* was not in any way "coarse."[3] Nationalists feared coarseness more than capitalism.

No matter what the social rank of the members, their collectivist ideas were unconventional. While Nationalists carefully distinguished their variety of Socialism from others, they believed that most Socialists also disdained bomb-throwing radicalism. "Anglo-Saxon Socialists," they held, had wholly discarded such lunacy, and even "their continental brethren very generally" sought the end

2. The *Nationalist* (Boston), December, 1889, 38; *New Nation* (Boston), January 31, 1891, 12; February 14, 1891, 43; David Goldstein, *Autobiography of a Campaigner for Christ* (Boston, 1936), 4–5.
3. Quoted in *New Nation,* May 9, 1891, 230.

"through gradual and peaceful methods." Anarchists, advocating violence and revolution, admittedly did not believe in a state or God. But Christian Socialists preached the brotherhood of man under God. Nationalists found Marxian Socialism difficult to define. They guessed that Marxists sought "a sort of confederation of industrial guilds, each controlling for its own benefit some province of industry." If their impression of Marxism was hazy, Nationalists knew exactly what they themselves stood for. Their American brand of Socialism was an advanced, more complete, more practical, and more specific form of Christian Socialism. Having no bias in favor of the industrial proletariat, Nationalists stood for the equality of all men of whatever class. When some trade unionists announced their support of the Nationalist program, the Bellamyites feared that "the extreme activity of their labor allies" would make their movement seem "only another 'labor scheme.' " Nationalists hoped "to keep the labor interests in the background or as subordinate."[4]

Nationalists did not, in fact, emphasize industrial oppression or labor's demands. They considered the usual labor program insufficiently inclusive. The eight-hour day was "only a palliative measure"; trade unions could never provide a lasting solution to industrial problems; "struggles for mere wages" were "only transitory in their results." Other proposals were "deficient in Yankee shrewdness" and therefore "un-American." Only Nationalism offered a complete cure for social ills. Nationalists deplored competition among men and among classes. They decried also the maldistribution of wealth, discrimination against women, control of government by private interests, unemployment in the midst of need, and the wasting of

4. *Ibid.*, May 28, 1892, 341; September 12, 1891, 527; December 12, 1891, 725–726.

national resources. In the "new nation," foreseen by Edward Bellamy, all these evils would vanish.

Nationalists advanced several methods of promoting social equality and economic cooperation. A "more radical" variety of civil service reform would constitute a "first step toward nationalism. . . ." The initiative, referendum, and recall would make government more responsive to the people. Cooperative marketing would aid both consumers and producers. The eight-hour day for public employees was legislatively possible and would set a good example. A municipality should hire its own maintenance and construction crews, thereby avoiding the corruption that often resulted from the letting of city contracts. Equalized educational standards would raise everyone to a new level of refinement.[5]

Still more important was the demand for an expansion of public services through government ownership by city, state, or nation. Nationalists saw no need to wait; the need was evident and it was time to begin. In a speech in Boston late in 1889, Bellamy said the nation was about ready to own and operate the railroads. Public ownership of coal mines, telephone and telegraph facilities, and city utilities were, he said, logical sequels. About two months later, the *Nationalist* reported that at least 200,000 signatures now accompanied several petitions for municipal gas plants in various cities in the Commonwealth. Monopolistic gas utilities had long been a political target, and legislation already permitted regulation of rates. Nationalists wanted more than regulation; they demanded municipal ownership, not only of gas and water, but also of transportation and lighting facilities, and public distribution of fuel and milk.

5. *Ibid.*, August 22, 1891, 479; January 31, 1891, 10–11, 13; March 1891, *passim;* April 11, 1891, 179.

Propaganda brought response. From a modest start in Lynn in 1889, agitation for municipal fuel yards spread to New Bedford, Boston, Worcester, Weymouth, and Haverhill. Terrence V. Powderly, leader of the Knights of Labor, endorsed the project. Once more petitions began to circulate around Massachusetts; one report had 40,000 signatures secured early in 1892. But the Supreme Court of Massachusetts throttled the proposal with an advisory opinion that such facilities would be an illegitimate use of tax funds.[6]

A campaign for municipal ownership of lighting facilities was more successful. First efforts seemed crushed early in 1891 when the Massachusetts Senate defeated a bill the House had passed. By the middle of the year, however, Governor William E. Russell signed a bill that crowned Nationalist efforts. In 1892, several communities voted to construct their own street lighting facilities; some soon expanded their operations to offer power to consumers. In 1893, the *New Nation* cited annual reports that proved municipal ownership would reduce costs.[7] Nationalism, at least in Massachusetts, was a practical program, not an idle dream.

Nationalism also generated a discussion that spread greater understanding of municipal ownership. Collectivism might not be entirely acceptable, but it showed signs of popularity. In 1891, the mayor of Boston proclaimed the right of the city "to undertake for itself, if financial and other conditions" allowed, "all functions of a public character now commonly intrusted to private enterprise." While this affirmation was carefully qualified, it was made. Not long after, mayors of Chicopee, Newton, Everett, Fall River, and Holyoke were all advocating munici-

6. This campaign can be traced in the *New Nation* throughout 1891; see also May 14, 1892, 306 ff.
7. *Ibid.*, March 4, 1893, 117.

pal ownership of at least one utility. More significantly, the Massachusetts House resolved that the national government should take over the telephone and telegraph facilities. The Boston *Record*, in mid-1893, predicted that within five years socialism would become "more firmly engrafted in the laws of this state than anywhere else in the nation," and warned the "great corporations doing business" in the Commonwealth that they might as well prepare for the inevitable.[8]

The *Record's* prediction assumed a political activity beyond the early efforts of the Nationalists as a pressure group. A tiny third party, advocating similar reforms, was at hand, and in 1893, Nationalists took control of the People's party of Massachusetts.

Nationalists, in Massachusetts and elsewhere, were well acquainted with the People's party. Bellamyites from around the country had participated in conferences in Cincinnati and St. Louis that prepared for the Populist convention in Omaha in 1892. Although most Populists thought of the industrial East as "enemy country," a few hardy Nationalists tried to preserve the reform movement from agrarian parochialism. The influence of Nationalism was visible in Populist demands for government ownership of railroads and telegraphs, and in the composition of the national committee, several members of which belonged to Nationalist clubs. After the Omaha convention nominated James B. Weaver for President, the *New Nation*, gratified that the platform had "done so well by . . . our cause," urged Nationalists to work for Populist victory.[9]

Bellamy's supporters in the Bay State, cooperating with

8. *Nationalist*, February, 1891, 488; *New Nation*, April 1, 1893, 173; June 3, 1893, 281.

9. *New Nation*, July 9, 1892, 440; see also J. Martin Klotsche, "The United Front Populists," in *Wisconsin Magazine of History*, XX (1937), 378–377.

Greenbackers, Christian Socialists, independent labor organizations, and Grangers, had helped launch the Massachusetts People's party in June, 1891. The Boston *Herald*
accused the new party of promoting too many reforms, a
criticism, Nationalists retorted tartly, that would never be
made of major political groups. In more than twenty
planks, the platform set forth the ambitions of the People's party, ambitions that were to be echoed by reform
groups for two decades. The proposals were familiar; the
editor of the Springfield *Republican* had read "so many
platforms of much the same purport . . . in recent
years" that he was neither frightened nor impressed. The
Populists demanded first that government solve the
"money question" by reasserting its exclusive right to coin
money. Tax reforms should include a graduated inherit-
ance tax and equalize the burden on farmer and urban
resident. Woman suffrage, civil service legislation, elective railroad commissioners, carefully scrutinized public
works contracts, and continued annual election of state
officers would help secure honest, democratic government. A program of state insurance, an eight-hour day,
abolition of leased convict labor, and raising the age at
which children could legally leave school were planks
that appealed to labor. The Nationalist wing of the party
wrote proposals for public ownership of telephone and
telegraph facilities, municipal transit franchises, "oppres-
sive" corporations, fuel yards, and the liquor business.
The Boston *Advertiser* observed that the new party had
overlooked very few possibilities.[10]

The ticket emphasized respectability. Major Henry
Winn, the candidate for governor, was a product of both
Yale and Harvard, and had been a Republican with unim-
peachable credentials. His primary interest was tax re-

10. *New Nation*, June 6, 1891, 300; September 5, 1891, 508–9;
August 29, 1891, 485–486; see also April 11, 1891, 162.

form, and his main appeal was to farmers. In second place on the slate was William J. Shields, an official of the Carpenters' Union of the American Federation of Labor. Completing the ticket were a former Greenbacker with extensive fraternal connections, a manufacturer who had once been a partner of Alexander Graham Bell, a Civil War veteran, and a school teacher-turned-lawyer. Major Winn, the chief campaigner, subordinated other issues to advocate tax reform at county fairs and urban rallies. The *New Nation* reported that Winn spoke to large crowds, but in a total vote of nearly 320,000 he polled only 1,749; he ran more than 7,000 votes behind the nominee of the Prohibition party. In the following spring, when the Populists elected delegates to the Omaha convention, the Boston *Herald* suggested archly that the entire membership could make the trip and "the wagon wouldn't be crowded." [11]

Even before the Omaha meeting, Massachusetts Populists shared the national concern about the currency. The keynote speaker at the state convention subordinated the Nationalist program to his emphasis on "an improper, unhealthy circulation" of the nation's "life blood—its money." While the platform called currency the "leading political question," Populists extended "the hand of fellowship to every reform," and invited a "union of forces" to secure "public control of public utilities for the public benefit." A Bay State member of the party's National Committee said the "key to the whole situation" was to be found "in this measure of values called money." While Bellamy was less emphatic, he too underscored currency reform. [12]

Major Winn, once more heading the state ticket, tucked free silver into his standard campaign speech for tax re-

11. *Ibid.*, September, October, 1891, *passim;* April 2, 1892, 216.
12. *Ibid.*, March 5, 1892, 146–147; April 9, 1892, 230–232.

form. The platform added the initiative and referendum to earlier proposals without attracting many more voters. Edward Bellamy received 3,204 votes, about one per cent of the total, as an elector for James B. Weaver. Major Winn fell short of 2,000 ballots. Walter Raymond, a correspondent of the Chicago reformer Henry Demarest Lloyd, scanned the returns and lost his illusions about Boston. Once, Raymond recalled in a letter to Lloyd, he had longed to visit the birthplace of the Nationalist movement.

I took the New Nation from the first issue until its suspension, and as I read it week after week I thought: "Boston must be near the kingdom of heaven; everybody there is a nationalist." Imagine my rude awakening when the returns in the last presidential election showed that Boston had given Weaver and Field electors only five hundred votes! . . . Theologically Boston is advanced enough. Every Bostonian I meet is an out and out heretic in religion, but so narrow in economics . . . ! His cant about an "honest dollar" is downright fatiguing.[13]

Probably election returns were no more accurate a measure of reform in Boston than were the columns of the *New Nation,* but the figures were undeniably discouraging.

Hope revived when a coalition of reformers elected Winn mayor of Malden. The Boston *Herald* glanced through the inaugural address and decided the new mayor was "a conservative citizen first and a populist afterward," a description that would have been equally valid before the inauguration. In a special Congressional election in 1893, the Populist vote tripled. The onset of the depression of 1893 promised reformers a broader audience in the fall elections. But the Populist tendency toward complete concentration on currency reform disturbed the Nationalists. At the Populist state convention, Nationalists

13. Walter Raymond to Henry D. Lloyd, March 1, 1895, Lloyd Papers, State Historical Society of Wisconsin.

for the first time dominated the party machinery. Henry R. Legate, a member of the staff of the *New Nation*, chaired the assembly; Mason Green, another Nationalist, headed the Resolutions Committee. The currency plank was no more prominent than it had been in earlier platforms. Public ownership, a labor program, political democracy, and tax reforms remained among the party's demands. Bellamy thought the party would obtain 10,000 votes, but the new directorate could not work miracles. The count for George Cary, the candidate for governor, did not quite reach 5,000.[14]

Having secured their own organization, Massachusetts Nationalists joined Populists beyond the Bay State who hoped to save the national party from the silver monomania. Henry Legate planned strategy with Henry Demarest Lloyd, who led a group of Chicago supporters of the broad Omaha Platform. Henry Winn commended Lloyd's "great service" in keeping "the People's Party train from derailment," and pledged his active support to Lloyd's continued efforts. Harry Lloyd, a Bostonian and sometime recruiter for various labor bodies, also liked the Chicago platform for its steadfast refusal to make concessions to "time-servers." Nonetheless, he found himself "drifting nearer to Socialism daily."[15]

Still others who leaned toward Socialism were gently nudged by *Merrie England*, a collection of essays by Robert Blatchford, a popularizer of British Fabian Socialism. Blatchford's wit and simplicity soon found a wide audience in the United States. At a Labor Day outing in Haverhill in 1895, the local Socialist Labor party sold 138 copies of *Merrie England*. One former Populist in the city reported that he alone had sold three hundred additional

14. *New Nation*, January 14, 1893, 26; July 22, 1893, 358; September 9, 1893, 420–421.
15. Legate to Lloyd, December 19, 1894; Winn to Lloyd, February 14, 1895; Harry Lloyd to Lloyd, March 9, 1895, Lloyd Papers.

copies and estimated that others had distributed at least two hundred more.[16] Four years later, when the Haverhill Socialists were riding the crest of political success, *Merrie England* became the text for the local Socialist women's discussion group.

Blatchford's description of contemporary conditions was convincingly realistic, for he did not make the workers into "wage slaves" or automatons controlled by cosmic historical forces. His workers were people—workers to be sure—but recognizable human beings. They lived in tenements that needed repair, not in hovels. They were not starving, but lacked a nourishing and varied diet. Nor was Socialism "a perfect system of life"; misguided Socialists erred when they sought "to prove that Socialism and Heaven" were "the same thing." All Blatchford claimed was that Socialism would provide a better, fuller life for more people than did the capitalism he saw in England in the 1890's. He predicted no seizure of the property of the rich and no distribution among the needy. Rather, Socialism was a "kind of national scheme of co-operation, managed by the state." Socialists had one demand: "the land and other instruments of production shall be the common property of the people and shall be used and governed by the people for the people." [17]

Like Edward Bellamy, Robert Blatchford looked backward. He longed for a life of uncluttered, pre-industrial simplicity, of open spaces, of fresh air, of leisurely contemplation. *Merrie England* called for no Marxian revolution. Karl Marx, indeed, went unmentioned, even in Blatchford's informal bibliography, which recommended John Ruskin, William Morris, Henry David Thoreau, Henry George, Thomas Carlyle, Thomas More, Cicero, and Walt Whitman. But not Karl Marx.

16. P. C. Beal to Daniel DeLeon, September 10, 1895, DeLeon Papers.

17. Robert Blatchford, *Merrie England* (London, 1895), 185, 21–22; 99–100.

And it was precisely the absence of Marxian complexity that appealed to American readers. For years the Socialist Labor party had espoused a rigid, orthodox, and militant variety of socialism. Yet American workers had consistently spurned it, and Daniel DeLeon and other party directors had to find consolation for political futility in doctrinal purity. Rarefied Marxist theory appeared in the *People,* the party's polemical weekly newspaper, and brought a remonstrance from a New England shoe worker in 1897. "I claim," he wrote, "that the common herd cannot understand such stuff."

. . . we must use plain language, yes very plain language. The masses are not at present educated in such a manner as to understand Karl Marx, but they can very *easily* understand Merrie England.[18]

Nothing, however, baffled the Reverend William Dwight Porter Bliss, a refined Episcopalian from Roslindale. A Christian Socialist, he also warmly endorsed the specific reforms of the Socialist Labor party. Although he had once preferred Populism, by 1895 Bliss had decided to start an independent labor party based on domesticated socialist principles. Every nation, Bliss held correctly, developed an indigenous shoot from the socialist seed. He established the *American Fabian* to broadcast his variety.

Socialism was "more than a soothing syrup," Bliss explained. It aimed "gradually" to remove "the causes of suffering." Socialists were sensitive Christian gentlemen and hoped, through the eight-hour day and the initiative and referendum, to alleviate existing conditions. The long-term goal required study, and Bliss proposed a course of instruction with a four-page bibliography and a syllabus based on the works of three English Fabians—Blatchford,

18. E. Payne to "To Whom it May Concern" November 21, 1897, SLP Papers.

George Bernard Shaw and Sidney Webb—with Bellamy and Bliss himself included for variety. Marx, Bliss held, was not a reliable theorist; English socialists, he noted, were suspicious of his economics. Though not politically inclined, Fabians believed that eventually all socialists would "naturally vote for the Socialist Labor party." No need to take the plunge all at once; the People's party would serve as a way station on the road to full-fledged political socialism. Bliss admitted that even the most dedicated Fabian had reservations about the "unnecessarily censorious and vindictive" tone of the official weekly of the S.L.P. While he hesitated "to speak ill of brother Socialists," he could find "very little good" to say of the leadership of the S.L.P. Bliss admired the party's program, but no gentleman could swallow Daniel DeLeon. [19]

Bliss expected to generate labor support for Fabian Socialism through the National Economic and Educational League. He hoped to persuade wealthy backers to put Harry Lloyd, the labor lecturer from Boston, on the road preaching independent political action to trade union audiences. Bliss was momentarily shaken when Henry D. Lloyd expressed misgivings about the convictions of Harry Lloyd, the prospective travelling salesman, who had opposed both the S.L.P. and a Socialist-sponsored resolution for collective ownership at a national convention of the A.F. of L. Perhaps, Henry Lloyd suggested gently, the credulous clergyman was being deceived. Undaunted, Bliss went ahead with his scheme to use a non-Socialist front organization to solicit funds to explain Socialism. Harry Lloyd, indeed, was already "teaching Socialism among the conservative trade unionists. . . ." Still skeptical, Henry Lloyd wrote a friend that Bliss was "a good fellow; one of the best." But when it came to politi-

19. *American Fabian* (Boston), May–June, 1895, 5; July–August, 1895, 8–16; December, 1895, 1, 6; July 1896, 8–9.

cal agitation, Lloyd added sadly, the clergyman was "a mere child." [20]

Long before Bliss sent Harry Lloyd on his mission, the shoe workers of Haverhill had heard about independent political action. Workingmen's parties appeared on the ballot occasionally during the 1880's. In 1891, the *New Nation* reported three hundred Populists in the city, and Major Winn received 93 votes there, a total that put Haverhill behind only Boston and Lynn on the puny Populist roll of honor. In 1892, the Populists sent a speaker to the Labor Day picnic that annually inaugurated Haverhill's political season. About a month later, they flooded a caucus of the local Labor party and committed it to the program and candidates of the People's party. "The Labor party in this city," commented a local paper, "must feel something like Jonah when he encountered the whale." [21]

The People's party in Haverhill lacked the proportions of a whale, but it had ambitious leadership, the possibility of broad labor support, and hopes of becoming "the banner populist town of the state." The party's leadership had come to Populism through Nationalism. A local daily, reporting a campaign rally, could not decide whether to refer to the sponsors as Populists or Nationalists. James F. Carey, the young shoe worker who presided as the Populists absorbed the Labor party, had been a member of the local Nationalist club. Charles Bradley, who would be an attractive nominee on the Socialist as well as the Populist ticket, had also learned his collectivism from Bellamy.

Organized labor's role in the Haverhill Populist movement, while not always avowed, was never disguised. A printer told an inquiring reporter that the Haverhill Cen-

---

20. Bliss to Lloyd, March 19, 1895; April 16, 1895; Lloyd to Bliss, May 4, 1895; Lloyd to Thomas Morgan, July 11, 1895, Lloyd Papers.
21. *Bulletin,* September 6, 1892; October 1, 1892.

tral Labor Union was paying for Populist campaign material. The Cigarmakers officially endorsed the People's party and T. T. Pomeroy, business agent of the local shoe union, doubled as the chairman of the Populist city committee and unofficial campaign manager. Individual union members proselyted in the shoe factories. John C. Chase and Louis M. Scates, both local shoe workers, joined Carey on the Populist slate. Effort returned a small reward when in 1893 the party's vote jumped to nearly five hundred ballots.[22]

The *New Nation* had once described Carey as "a man able and willing to give a reason for the faith that is in him," and he was soon bearing the brunt of the Populist work in the area. He upheld the Populist cause against representatives of four other political groups including Henry Cabot Lodge, the Republican champion. The Populist platform, Carey said, was "drafted by the labor unions . . . to redress the wrongs inflicted upon the working people by the corrupt and partial legislation of both the republican and democratic parties." The Populists demanded control of railroads that had become "instruments of tyranny." They called for a redistribution of the national wealth and a "money system of the people, by the people, and for the people." They would enact legislation to establish the initiative and referendum. Carey pointed to the industrial conflicts at Homestead and Pullman, asserting that such strife was the logical result of the labor program of both major political parties. In rebuttal, the young politician made Lodge a particular target in a "bright and witty" effort that was "continually interrupted with laughter and applause." Carey's speech helped dispel the notion that Populists advocated "the burning of build-

22. *New Nation,* November 5, 1892, 667; *Bulletin,* October 10, 21, 1893; November 8, 1893; December 6, 1893.

ings and the murdering of everyone who owned a home," as one editorial put it.[23]

Late in 1894 there was speculation that Carey might lead a reform coalition of Populists, Socialist Laborites, Prohibitionists, and other progressives in the municipal election. The alliance was eventually formed, though Samuel L. Jewett, a businessman and former alderman, was the candidate for mayor. Michael T. Berry, a Socialist Laborite, co-ordinated the campaign; John C. Chase and other Populists had places on the ticket. Backed by several clergymen, Reform candidates harvested votes from liquor scandals that had plagued the incumbent Republican administration. Democrats decided against an independent nomination, and enough disgruntled Republicans deserted to elect Jewett by more than 400 votes. The stunned chairman of the Republican city committee had no explanation.

Nobody caught James Carey at a loss for words. The Haverhill *Gazette* now referred to him as "the leader of the socialistic movement." He was learning the politician's language: his friends, said Mr. Carey, "were looking for no office at City Hall"; they were "only working for the good of the city." [24] He and his colleagues were learning more than conventional responses. None of them won office in 1894; Democratic candidates below the head of the ticket split the vote and Republicans generally triumphed. But the reformers learned techniques of practical politics and kept their names before local voters. And they saw that a hard-hitting campaign, directed at recognized local problems, might undercut the major parties. Better yet, it could succeed.

23. *New Nation*, October 21, 1893, 469; Haverhill *Weekly Bulletin*, October 19, 1894; *Bulletin*, October 13, 1894; *Gazette*, October 13, 1894.
24. *Gazette*, December 4, 5, 1894.

Shortly after the municipal election, a bitter dispute in Haverhill's shoe industry made political problems seem trifling. Earlier in 1894 management had imposed a reduction in wages. Labor also resented a mandatory contract which specified output and required that part of each week's pay be left with the employer until $50 was on deposit. This sum became an informal bond to be forfeited in the event the worker left his job without notice. Everyone understood that management would confiscate the deposit in the event of a strike.

A week before Christmas small groups of shoe workers began to walk out of the factories. On the day before the holiday, employers retaliated with a partial lockout (though everyone still called the struggle a strike). Strikers were not all union members; union officials organized rallies and parades to recruit, to discourage scabbing, and to demonstrate labor's determination. The press, the public, and the municipal government thought labor had the better case, especially after employers refused to refer the dispute to arbitration. Both daily papers evoked the American revolution in editorials; the virtue of the Continentals was with the workers. "The strike is, of course, a hardship to those engaged," said the *Bulletin,* "but so was Valley Forge."

Once the dispute broke, James F. Carey became one of the busiest men in Haverhill. During January, when the struggle was most intense, he spoke again and again, urging union membership, discouraging violence, and pleading with audiences outside the city for funds to continue the battle. Carey also introduced a political note when he asked labor to develop a political arm as well as economic unity. The strike, at the moment, was the best available weapon; ultimately "the place to strike was the ballot box." The contract system, he said, was "the outcome of a long series of legislation in favor of the other fellow. . . ."

Labor must sink internal differences and combine "for all time" in a "fight against a common enemy."

Industrial conflict need not mean destruction. On the day the lockout occurred, the *Gazette* reported that labor leaders, anxious to prevent trouble, were earnestly seeking arbitration. A week later, when employees of a factory that had remained open forfeited their deposits by walking out, there was no disorder. The resulting demonstration, however, had "never had a parallel in Haverhill." Employers complained that parades endangered property and the lives of workers who remained on the job, but the city marshal did not agree. Labor leaders, he said, were also interested in preserving law and order.

Good intentions did not preserve the peace. Tempers flared and an assault case got into the local police court. The judge in the case delivered a little speech about strikes and strikers, who, he said, were led "by . . . men who hate the flag. . . ." About the same time, when blood was spilled as strikebreakers attacked pickets, a state court issued the inevitable injunction.

James F. Carey dismissed the judicial pronouncements as the law of Pontius Pilate. He knew that the local judge had called him a Socialist, and he welcomed the epithet. He was a Socialist, Carey said, because he had sought "right and law and justice." Perhaps, he added, the judge would be better for knowing "more about socialism and less about things less to his credit." Within the week, Martha Moore Avery, considered by the Massachusetts Socialist Labor party its most lucid teacher of Marxism, was lecturing to strikers in Haverhill.[25]

By spring, when the hungry shoe workers finally capitulated, the People's party in Haverhill was as dead as the

25. *Ibid.*, December 17, 1894–January 23, 1895; the Haverhill Public Library has clipped the accounts of this and other local strikes in a volume entitled "Haverhill Labor Problems."

strike. When earlier press reports had referred to Carey as a Socialist, the reference was to his Nationalist ideology, not to his political affiliation. After the strike, "Socialist" would serve both purposes. Bay State Populists recognized the importance of the struggle in Haverhill, and hoped, as one Bostonian wrote Henry Demarest Lloyd, that "the three thousand starving people involved" would "open the eyes of a large number of people." But Lloyd's correspondent wanted those open eyes to see "the value of trade unions and of Boards of Conciliation and Arbitration." [26] The view from Haverhill differed from that of polite Bostonians. James F. Carey saw those "three thousand starving people," and, at second glance, he saw the Socialist Labor party.

In April, about a month after the shoe workers in Haverhill had surrendered, Carey went to Boston to attend a meeting of independent shoe unions. His prestige in the craft was evident when delegates representing over 100,000 shoe workers in seventy-three cities selected him to preside. Leaders of the convention hoped to convince local unions to combine in one industry-wide organization. The assembly represented all shades of political opinion from Socialist Laborite to Republican. The balance was left of center. Scattered through the convention were men already convinced that socialism was the long-range solution to industrial problems. John F. Tobin, from Rochester, New York, who would become the first president of the union, had been a Socialist Laborite for years. Michael Berry, also a Socialist Laborite, had managed the Reform campaign in Haverhill in 1894. At the convention, he sat on a committee that considered "secret work." On the same committee was Carlton Beals, whom the first Socialist mayor of Brockton would appoint city marshal. Fred Carter, an official of the Lynn Lasters' Union, joined

26. Mrs. Anne Fields to Lloyd, February 14, 1895, Lloyd Papers.

Tobin at the deliberations of the vital committee that wrote the first constitution. Carter would later cause President Tobin no end of trouble and try to take the Lynn group into Daniel DeLeon's Socialist Trade and Labor Alliance. Fred G. R. Gordon, from Manchester, New Hampshire, was elected secretary of the assembly. Gordon, who had been a Populist, was in 1895 a Socialist Laborite. Later he would become a Social Democrat and a member of the Socialist party. In 1902 he began a new career—as a professional anti-socialist.

The Boston press expected the Socialist cabal, "headed by Delegate Carey of Haverhill," to include in the union's constitution an endorsement of government ownership. But Tobin could not persuade a majority of his committee, and Carey and Tobin together could not persuade the convention to adopt a minority report calling for government ownership. A reporter asked why the convention had selected Carey to preside, while rejecting his Socialist program. One delegate answered: "Carey is a good fellow, very popular, but we ain't quite willing to give him all we've got. . . ." A similar reply might well have explained the election of John F. Tobin to guide the newly-formed Boot and Shoe Workers' Union.[27]

About the time the convention of shoe workers adjourned, the Socialist Labor party granted a charter to a new local in Haverhill. By fall, many former Populists had joined. An early S.L.P. manifesto, signed by John C. Chase, showed the persistence of the Populist heritage.

. . . the time has arrived [for] the voting masses of this district, . . . the toilers of the earth in the workshop, on the railroad and on the farm, the only creators of wealth and ever the defenders of liberty, to assert . . . a protest to the present industrial system . . . ; a system that in the last quarter of a

27. This account of the convention is based on accounts in the Boston *Herald, Globe, Journal,* and *Post,* April 11–14, 1895, and *Bulletin,* April 16. 1895.

century has made more millionaires and tramps than . . . in a like period since the dawn of creation; a system that makes honest industry the synonym of poverty and indolence and usury the sure road to wealth.[28]

Michael Berry thought the strike of 1894–5 would boost the party's vote, but the immediate improvement was negligible. For the first time, however, the Socialists outpolled the Populists and topped other minor parties as well. Nationalism seemed to be emerging as Socialism in Haverhill. Time would demonstrate that the core was still Bellamy's gentle, reforming creed; only the veneer had changed.[29]

28. The *People* (New York), April 21, 1895; *Bulletin,* September 5, November 20, 1895.

29. Lyman Abbott, himself a Socialist of this persuasion, wrote in 1900, when the Massachusetts Socialists had achieved promising success, that Bellamy's books were probably "largely responsible for the growth of the Socialistic sentiment." The Socialist movement of 1900 was, "clearly the logical development of an earlier and vaguer Populist movement." See "The Socialist Movement in Massachusetts," *Outlook* (New York), February 17, 1900, 411.

CHAPTER II

Trials and Errors of the Socialist Labor Party

For about a decade before 1895, when it welcomed a new section in Haverhill, the Socialist Labor party had professed to be the political spokesman for the American working class. Any set of election returns rendered the claim preposterous; the presidential candidate in 1896, for instance, polled less than three-tenths of one per cent of the total vote. Eventually, the party stopped looking to the ballot box for vindication. If workers did not recognize their true interest in the present, they surely would in the future. American capitalism, the S.L.P. held, was producing an oppressed industrial proletariat. Consequently, if the party adhered strictly to the principles of scientific socialism and correctly educated the working class, ultimate success was inevitable. Positive of its doctrine, secure in its knowledge of the course of history, the Socialist Labor party could afford to be patient.

When native workers did not respond during the 1880's, German-speaking immigrants became the core of the party. German was the normal method of communication among members; the party long maintained a newspaper in the German language. Henry Kuhn, an important S.L.P. official from 1890 to 1906, later thought the party of the early '90's "must have looked rather quaint" to English-speaking recruits. Only two members of the central hierarchy could speak English; "correspondence in that 'foreign' tongue, unless dealing with simple matters, had to be 'explained'" to others on the National Executive Committee. The committee included many excellent men, Kuhn recalled, but most of them "were strangers in a strange land." [1]

In 1888, *Der Socialist,* then the official newspaper of the S.L.P., reached about forty isolated subscribers in Yankee Massachusetts.[2] Considerable optimism was required to see these forty comrades, some of whose accounts were far from current, as the nucleus of a mass political movement. Yet, in 1888, socialism began to seem less alien in the Bay State. *Looking Backward,* published the year before, was not "scientific socialism," but it was eloquent and written in English. By 1893, *Vorwaerts,* the successor to *Der Socialist,* went to about 200 addresses in Massachusetts.[3] The circulation of the German press, moreover, was no longer an accurate measure of the Bay State's interest in socialism.

Some English-speaking converts joined the party in order to lead it. David Goldstein, who enlisted in 1895, thought the S.L.P. a natural haven for young workingmen seeking a quick reputation. The tiny organization lacked native leadership and thus gave the new recruit, "small though he be intellectually and culturally, a chance to play a big part. . . ." Workers who would otherwise never achieve public recognition, Goldstein calculated, could rapidly become known as "'labor leaders,'" and gain a notoriety they mistook for importance.[4]

The party hoped to minimize friction between old and new Socialists by chartering "foreign" and "American"

1. Henry Kuhn, "Reminiscences of Daniel DeLeon," in *Daniel De-Leon: The Man and His Work* (New York, 1934), 4.
2. Account book, SLP Papers.
3. "Report on the condition of Vorwaerts," SLP Papers.
4. David Goldstein, *Autobiography of a Campaigner for Christ* (Boston (1936), 5.

sections. Boston, for instance, had German, Jewish, American, and Flemish sections at various times during the '90's. This solution was not completely successful, since separate sections gave jealousies an official, institutional recognition. Rarely could Boston's Socialist organizations work together. As early as 1893, a member of the German section protested that "grossly illegal" proceedings had given the American group disproportionate representation at a party convention. Carrying their grievance to the national convention, the foreign sections maintained that they were victims of a parliamentary shell game. The protest, written in broken English, recalled the days when Socialists had gotten together for companionship rather than for political action. Now, the American faction's "insatiate ambition to dominate" had sapped the party's old-time spirit. The curiously punctuated protest went on: "They do force their rule upon the party, hence we must protest, I see it is too vain an element it will destroy all friendly relations within the ranks of the Boston Socialists." [5] Significantly, the Americans most resented by the foreign sections included Simon Wing, the S.L.P. presidential candidate in 1892; Martha Moore Avery, soon to be a salaried lecturer for the state organization; and Thomas C. Brophy, a dominant figure in the hierarchy and a frequent candidate for office during the decade. The old order was changing; *gemütlichkeit* was giving way to politics.

When campaigns were not imminent, Socialist meetings retained a fraternal air. A May Day celebration in Holyoke in 1894, for instance, featured music by the German *Turnverein*, followed by a dance to which local labor organizations were invited. But when elections approached,

5. Carl Friede to National Convention, June 29, 1893; Friede to P. O'Neil, June 28, 1893; see also L. Eisner to Convention, June 28, 1893, SLP Papers.

music and good fellowship were subordinated to formal political activity. A minuscule treasury and the lack of a widely-circulating propaganda organ dictated the party's campaign tactics. Candidates were usually chosen before other parties held their conventions. By launching the political season, Socialists could monopolize the early part of the campaign and gain publicity that might otherwise have been lost. When the major parties became active, Socialists challenged their opponents to debate. These challenges invariably went unanswered, since other parties were reluctant to share their press coverage and their audiences. Socialists then trumpeted that their rivals feared the incontestable logic of socialism. Any public meeting served as a potential forum. Socialists might enter the hall, fan out through the audience to give the illusion of greater numbers, and ask questions that turned into speeches expounding the party's doctrine. A strike was a particularly prized opportunity for demonstrations replete with red banners and parades. When the budget would not support a hall and no suitable public occasion presented itself, the street corner was always available. If a municipal ordinance perchance limited such agitation, so much the better. An imprisoned orator furnished a splendid opportunity to champion free speech, and Socialists were quick to exploit an arrest and the resulting trial.[6]

In 1892, when they decided to test tactics and support for the first time in a presidential contest, the party's leaders turned to Massachusetts. Although 1892 was a good year for political protest, the 21,164 votes cast for Simon Wing, the Boston manufacturer of photographic equipment who bore the S.L.P. standard, were a microscopic two-tenths of one per cent of the national total. Wing ran about as well in his own state as he did in the rest of

6. Holyoke *Labor*, April 28 1894; Goldstein *Autobiography*, 9–13. The newspaper is cited hereafter as *Labor*.

the nation. Of the 391,000 votes cast in Massachusetts, he received 659, less than a tenth of the support given the Prohibition candidate.

Two years later, the Massachusetts S.L.P. nominated a ticket that balanced three German immigrants with two English-speaking comrades who might attract more general support. And if the party was to make a significant political impression, it surely needed such support. The convention consisted of nineteen delegates representing fourteen sections. These sections claimed a total membership of 650, a figure that may well have been inflated in order to increase representation at the convention. The sections varied in size from the Jewish organization in Boston, which reported one hundred members, to the tiny local in Webster, which numbered five. The S.L.P. in Massachusetts was able to collect less than a dollar per year per member to finance the end of capitalism in Massachusetts. The treasurer's report showed receipts of $514.83 and expenses of $545.79.[7]

The delegates hardly paused to consider the significance of these figures. Confident of the direction of social change, they adopted a platform, resolved to establish a daily newspaper, and adjourned to agitate for the coming cooperative commonwealth. The platform advocated a mixture of political, social, and economic reforms that reflected Populist ancestry. The most radical planks echoed the Nationalists: public ownership of transportation and public utilities. Other economic demands were beamed directly at the working class: reduction in the hours of labor; abolition of convict labor; more strict legislation to prevent industrial accidents; state-financed public works projects for the unemployed; legislation requiring that wages be paid in lawful currency. The Socialists also took the Populists' solution to the "money question" with a

7. *Labor*, June 2, 1894.

plank declaring that only the federal government could constitutionally coin money. They advocated more hospital facilities, abolition of capital punishment, administration of justice without charge, and free, universal education through secondary school. Finally, government must become more democratic through adoption of the initiative, referendum and recall, and extension of the franchise without regard to race or sex.[8]

For the Socialist Labor party, in Massachusetts as elsewhere, a political campaign served a dual purpose: in the immediate present, it attracted support for the party's candidates; in the long run, the constant exposure to socialist teaching prepared the proletariat for its historic destiny. Campaign oratory blended promises, economic theory, and denunciation of exploiting capitalists. In the same campaign, two of the party's most prominent spokesmen could define Socialism with an engaging and misleading simplicity, or with a baffling, pseudo-academic complexity. Herbert Casson, pastor of the Labor Church in Lynn, told a Holyoke audience that Socialism meant "a bit of Yankee shrewdness, coupled with honesty, put to work at full force." On the other hand, Martha Avery, whom the national party had occasionally paid to enlighten labor gatherings, began a paper on "The Philosophy of Socialism" with this sentence: "From opposite directions, the human mind and the human consciousness have been slowly gathering facts of demonstration and facts of revelation that have at last satisfied men that, stated in the language of philosophy, Divine Economy, and, in scientific terminology, Universal Economy, exists." [9] Mrs. Avery, who usually did not speak as badly as she wrote, was the unchallenged favorite of many of the

8. *Ibid.*, June 9, 1894.
9. *Ibid.*, September 3, 1894; Socialist Labor Party, *Socialist Annual for 1894* (Boston, 1894), 8.

state's Socialists. Yet only a literate and alert listener could unscramble her murky, Germanic word order.

Moritz Ruther, a genial Holyoke cigarmaker who almost always had a place on the party's ticket, kept his program and prose well within the intellectual limits of his audience. Capital, for instance, was a simple concept. Borrowing a definition from a local laborer, Ruther said that capital was "like a heap of manure in a farmer's barn yard. . . . By itself it is a stinking nuisance and of no earthly use to anyone, but spread out over the land where it belongs, it performs its natural functions and becomes a blessing to all."

Ruther tackled economic problems such as real estate speculation with equal ease. Owners of land, owners of street railways, owners of newspapers, and politicians conspired to fleece the worker who aspired to have his own home. Inevitably an industrial crisis enabled the "philanthropic land speculator" to repossess his houses from bankrupt laborers. The moral? "Happy homes . . . are only possible under the Cooperative Commonwealth. Therefore all of you, who want a home of your own, join hands with the Socialist Labor party." And what did the Socialist Labor party stand for? ". . . shorter hours, full pay, enough air and room for every honest individual, comforts, pleasure, and luxury for the workingman, health and happiness for everybody, good fellowship, good citizenship, good government, good education, and everything that is good and tends to make life pleasant and long." [10]

The dual view of campaigns as educational as well as political efforts helped the Socialist Labor party avoid potentially discouraging statistics. As one Socialist candidate observed of a subsequent campaign, "Although . . . we were ignominiously defeated. . . , the victory was con-

10. *Labor,* April 21, 1894; June 9, 1894; November 3, 1894.

sidered to be ours from a propaganda standpoint. . . ."
Political results could be read in quantitative terms; the
S.L.P. candidate for governor in 1894 received exactly
3,104 votes, an unimpressive performance even when
compared to the 9,954 cast for the Prohibition party. But
Socialists were consoled by their faith that the vote was
miscounted, or by their conviction that the educational
effort had been a success. In 1895, for instance, Moritz
Ruther was certain that Socialist propaganda had made
"half the American people . . . Socialists at heart." His
evidence was hardly convincing: one woman commented
favorably on the party's local newspaper; a local politician
had even bought a subscription; a second woman wished
her work in the mill were easier.[11] On such trifles was the
hope of Socialists nourished. Three isolated omens became a more accurate measure of popular sentiment than
any set of election returns.

Similar intellectual sleight-of-hand could turn a broken
strike into an occasion for cheer. The workers, it was argued, had been taught some basic economic principles.
The report of the disastrous strike in Clinton, then, subordinated present defeat to certain vindication in the
future. "Although the strike is lost, yet the workers have
received a lesson . . . . The spirit of Socialism has been
instilled into the minds of the strikers to such an extent
that it is only a matter of time until it will assert itself in
unmistakable tones."[12]

Complementing the Socialist Laborites' dual view of
their own political activity was an ambivalent attitude
toward other organizations that advanced competing solutions for the economic and political problems of the day.
While the national party was unsparingly critical of Popu-

11. Goldstein *Autobiography*, 11; *Labor*, March 30, 1895; May 18,
1895.
12. *Labor*, September 14, 1895.

40

lists, hope persisted that their errors would be corrected. Bay State Populists, many of them acknowledged Nationalists, seemed especially likely recruits. The manual for the Massachusetts campaign of 1894 boasted that the S.L.P. was the only organization pledged to enact Nationalism. When Populists did not immediately change parties, Socialists lamented their obtuseness. Moritz Ruther told farmers in western Massachusetts that advancing capitalism had made the Populist program a "delusion." Characteristically, he added that Socialism was the sure cure for agrarian distress. Would the farmer "be obliged to give up his homestead and land?" No sir; his only loss would be the mortgage.[13]

The prospect of converting a Populist leader, even if ideological deficiencies remained, warranted a special report to the S.L.P.'s national office in New York. And the prospect that Henry Legate might adopt the whole Socialist program occasioned cautious exhilaration. "In a conference of leading Populists here, . . . H. R. Legate who is their chief man in Massachusetts and a member of their national committee, told his brethren . . . that the trend of the voters is overwhelmingly towards the S.L.P., and that if the Populist leaders continue the 'money' campaign, he will join the S.L.P. himself. . . . The game is in our own hands if we toe the line. . . ."[14]

That ideological "line" was drawn in New York. There, at national headquarters, Henry Kuhn, the party's secretary, tried to maintain contact with organizations scattered across the country; only the one in New York seemed more promising than the struggling party in the Bay State. And in the New York editorial offices of the *People*, Daniel DeLeon, the party's chief theoretician, applied Marxism to American conditions.

---

13. *Socialist Annual for 1894*, 4; *Labor*, June 23, 1894.
14. W. L. Sawyer to DeLeon, March 2, 1895, DeLeon Papers.

Once a lecturer at Columbia Law School, DeLeon had become interested in the labor movement during the 1880's. He flirted briefly with Henry George's single tax movement, lectured on Bellamy's *Looking Backward*, read some Marx and Engels, and was converted to social-ism by Lewis H. Morgan's *Ancient Society*. An English-speaking intellectual in the days when the S.L.P. had few members who could handle the language and almost no intellectual leadership, DeLeon was a prize convert in 1889. In 1891, he made a national tour for the party; late in the year he became editor of the *People*. Gradually, in pamphlets, editorials, and speeches, DeLeon revealed his version of Marxism. As his control over the party tight-ened, he tolerated no deviation, no questioning of his au-thority, his tactics, or his doctrine. As a result, the Socialist Labor party became almost a mystic cult rather than a po-litical party, a cult whose chief prophet was DeLeon as often as Marx and whose Holy Writ was the *People* as often as *Das Kapital*. The party underwent a constant round of trials for heresy, as "compromisers" were driven from the temple. The faith remained uncontaminated, even though progressively fewer shared it. DeLeon did not establish an unquestioned hegemony because he sought power or office, but because he sought to serve his ideal. This dedication to the coming socialist utopia so distorted his perspective that he lost contact with the real world and real people, thereby forfeiting any chance of bringing his dream to pass. His political party consisted of zealots without followers and became a case study in fu-tility.[15]

DeLeon mistrusted the Massachusetts S.L.P. as early as 1894 when Moritz Ruther established the Holyoke

15. Though reached independently, this interpretation of DeLeon parallels that of Howard Gitelman very closely. See chapter 9 of his unpublished doctoral dissertation, "Attempts to Unify the American Labor Movement, 1865–1900" (University of Wisconsin, 1960).

Labor. A local edition of a national socialist paper printed in St. Louis, *Labor* combined a core of features and editorials with a page or two of locally-edited material. So popular was the scheme and so optimistic were the Socialists in Massachusetts that, by 1895, five separate editions of *Labor* appeared weekly from offices in Holyoke, Lawrence, Boston, Adams, and Worcester.[16]

Ruther knew that the proliferation of *Labor* editions would arouse suspicion, perhaps even jealousy, in New York. In the very first issue of his paper, Ruther reassured nervous national officials. The new publication, he said, would not hurt the circulation of the *People*. On the contrary, it would "broaden the field for that excellent journal." Shortly after *Labor's* first anniversary, DeLeon accused Ruther of neglecting the *People* to promote his local paper. The outraged Ruther replied that DeLeon's charge was unjust. The contempt that "the leading spirits of New York's Socialists" had for comrades outside "the city limits of New York" saddened Ruther. Natural phenomena, he explained, not local sabotage, had undermined the *People* in Holyoke. Some of DeLeon's readers had not renewed their subscriptions because of illness, unemployment, or death; one had been drunk for some months and was not doing much reading. "There is no one who is willing to work harder . . . for Socialism," Ruther concluded, "but I can't do impossibilities." [17]

Ruther knew his own locale. He cooperated with the local labor movement, tailored his Socialism to local conditions, and eventually saw his efforts achieve some success and recognition. The paper that he edited in his spare moments became self-sustaining, though its circulation probably never reached two hundred copies per week. Holyoke

16. *Labor*, February 2, 1895.
17. *Ibid.*, April 7, 1894; Ruther to DeLeon, April 30, 1895, DeLeon Papers.

Labor passed a second anniverary and expired only when a decision of the national party struck it down. Though Moritz Ruther protested vigorously, and though the party directorate never completely trusted him, he stayed in the Socialist Labor party.[18]

Not every member of the Massachusetts S.L.P. displayed Ruther's loyalty. Immigrants and natives constantly squabbled over control of the movement in Boston. The local edition of *Labor* suffered from the factionalism that plagued the movement in the city, and its editors complained that "the Boston Socialists do not pull together." Representatives of the American and Jewish sections tried in 1895 to agree on a comprehensive program of propaganda. The effort was neither united nor comprehensive, and the vote in the city fell. Squire Putney, the state secretary, appealed for yet another reorganization of the Boston locals. One skeptical Bostonian thought the party was entitled to a new explanation.[19]

Daniel DeLeon already had his explanation. Under the heading "Fakedom," DeLeon reported that Patrick O'Neil, a prominent member of the Boston local, had been plotting a coalition of Socialists, Prohibitionists, and Populists. Any such action, of course, constituted treason, and the *People* resorted to the usual invective. Some "Republican Tricksters" had promoted the "Bogus Convention of Miscellaneous Fakirs" for their own purposes. True Socialists had nothing to do with the scheme. Squire Putney protested that the case was by no means proven. Though O'Neil might have erred in detail, Putney was sure he remained a convinced Socialist. "If our members need discipline," Putney wrote haughtily, "the section can be

18. *Labor,* May 19, 1894, June 16, 1894; Ruther to DeLeon, January 19, 1895, April 30, 1895, DeLeon Papers.
19. *Labor,* August 18, 1894, December 28, 1895, January 11, 1896; Badger to Kuhn, January 21, 1895, SLP Papers.

trusted to institute proceedings at the proper time."
Henry Kuhn, the party's national secretary, prodded the
Bostonians; the organization's constitution, he claimed,
obligated the section to expel O'Neil immediately.[20]

Surgery was neither quick nor easy. In January, one of
DeLeon's correspondents wrote that "lots of bad blood"
fairly bubbled in Boston. Later in the month one of
O'Neil's supporters blackened the eye of an opponent at
an unruly meeting of the American section. The section
eventually voted a formal censure of O'Neil and repudi-
ated Putney's defense of him. The storm in Boston, wrote
the section's organizer to Daniel DeLeon, would probably
result in a healthy split. The rebels were likely to establish
"a pietistic, evangelistic, Socialistic society of intense
mutual admiration . . . for these very good people are
not happy in the company of devilish Socialists." [21]

O'Neil was not the only target. A second expulsion case
arose almost simultaneously in Massachusetts. In October, 1895, DeLeon wrote Putney that the *People* would
soon report that the Lynn section had suspended Herbert Casson, the pastor of a Labor Church where reform
and Christianity were twin articles of faith. A young
idealist whose convictions would lead him from the S.L.P.
to Bryan and finally into anti-Socialist activity, Casson
had campaigned across Massachusetts for the S.L.P. in
1894. The party had asked him to undertake a similar tour
in 1895. Acting on information from Casson's own local,
DeLeon informed Putney that the minister was a disguised Populist, who had denounced the *People,* rejected
the party's platform, and refused to make an unqualified

20. *People,* November 24, 1895; December 15, 1895; Putney to De-
Leon, n.d., DeLeon Papers.
21. G. Mollenberg to DeLeon, January 6, 1896; Badger to DeLeon,
January 28, 1896; February 6, 1896, DeLeon Papers; *People,* February
2, 1896.

endorsement of the S.L.P. Surely, DeLeon thought, the report that the state committee had again engaged Casson was a mistake.[22]

The Massachusetts organization had in fact once more appointed the Lynn pastor and hoped to avoid a disruption of its campaign arrangements. On the very day the *People* announced Casson's suspension, Putney sent a twenty-page document to New York defending the committee's decision. Investigation, Putney wrote, had turned up only one imperfection in Casson's conduct: the minister believed that municipal campaigns ought to be waged on purely municipal issues. While such an idea might not be "scientific," the committee was unwilling to call it heresy.[23]

The hierarchy in New York was adamant. Kuhn curtly informed Putney that the National Executive Committee had forbidden publication of the state organization's elaborate rebuttal. But the state committee, which also served as the party's Grievance Committee, officially branded the charges against Casson "frivolous" and ordered him reinstated. DeLeon still had the last word. The party's national convention overruled the Grievance Committee and reimposed Casson's suspension. Casson promptly found a new cause. Free silver, he said in the fall of 1896, was the impoverished worker's natural response to industrial conditions.[24]

Divided, disheartened, undisciplined, the Massachusetts Socialists obviously merited Daniel DeLeon's personal attention. He left New York in January, 1896, to give the wrangling Bostonians the word. His speech, en-

22. DeLeon to Putney, October 10, 1895, DeLeon Papers; *People*, October 20, 1895, December 8, 1895.

23. Putney to Kuhn, October 18, 20, 1895, SLP Papers. See also Putney to DeLeon, October 20, 1895, DeLeon Papers.

24. *People*, December 8, 1895; *Proceedings of the Ninth Annual Convention of the Socialist Labor Party* . . . (New York, 1896), 49; *American Fabian*, December, 1896, 2.

titled "Reform or Revolution," remains an S.L.P. classic. It contained DeLeon's formula for a socialist organization that would inevitably achieve success.[25]

If the Boston Socialists expected DeLeon to provide a concrete program to eliminate their internal quarrels and to afford instant political advantage, they misjudged their man. As was his habit, DeLeon talked about principles, not tactics. The message was simple: a Socialist organization must adhere absolutely to the tenets of revolutionary Socialism. Lacking such a creed, no organization could be effective. Socialists demanded nothing less than a complete reorientation of society; capitalism had to be replaced, not reformed. Under no circumstances could Socialists cooperate with reformers, because their presence in the Socialist movement could only produce confusion and weaken the effort to abolish capitalism. DeLeon did not specifically mention O'Neil and Casson. But, should anyone miss the point, he spelled it out in detail:

. . . load your revolutionary ship with the proper lading of science; . . . try no monkeyshines and no dillyings and dallyings with anything that is not strictly scientific, or with any man who does not stand on our uncompromisingly scientific platform. . . . I call upon you . . . to organize, here in Boston, upon the genuine revolutionary plan. . . . Tamper with discipline, allow this member to do as he likes, that member to slap the party constitution in the face, yonder member to fuse with reformers, . . . and you have stabbed your movement at its vitals. With malice toward none, with charity to all, you must enforce discipline. . . .

Although DeLeon's message was clear, his speech was nonetheless curious. The target was the reformer—the Populist, the labor leader, the proponent of the single tax. The capitalist, by comparison, was scarcely mentioned.

25. Daniel DeLeon, *Reform or Revolution* (New York, 1961), xii. The pamplet is also the source of subsequent quotations from this speech.

Probably most of DeLeon's audience had already decided that capitalism was outworn, but his conclusion that the reformer, rather than the outright advocate of the *status quo,* was the Socialists' most formidable enemy must have seemed strange to the uninitiated. DeLeon was so completely involved in his S.L.P. that he had lost contact with the rest of the world. The laborer who was not a dedicated Socialist simply did not see the American Federation of Labor as a rapidly dying "tapeworm"; nor would the workingman who had bothered to read the Populist platform have described it as "reactionary."

As DeLeon viewed the contemporary scene from his own peculiar vantage point, so he viewed history. He argued, for instance, that the development of manufacturing in the North had been responsible for the abolition of northern slavery. Northern masters, he said, self-righteously sold their Negroes to plantation owners, and then transformed free northern whites into "wage slaves." This interpretation, similar to that of John C. Calhoun and other ante-bellum defenders of southern rights, may have been good economic determinism. But in dating the development of northern industry before the abolition of northern slavery, DeLeon's chronology was erroneous.

DeLeon's logic was hardly better than his history. The S.L.P. might be proud of its stern logical consistency, but many of DeLeon's premises and definitions were at best dubious, and his deductions were often asserted, rather than proved. His lecture had the trappings of logical prose—"therefores," "thuses," and "hences" abound—but his logic was unique.

The higher the economic plane on which a class stands, [began one assertion] and the sounder its understanding of material conditions, all the broader will its horizon be, and, consequently all the purer and truer its morality. Hence it is that, to-day, the highest moral vision, and the truest withal, is found in the camp of the revolutionary proletariat. Hence, also, you will perceive the danger of the moral cry that goes not hand in hand with sound knowledge. The morality of *Reform* is the corruscation of the *Ignis Fatuus;* the morality of *Revolution* is lightened by the steady light of science.

The distinction between reform and revolution was vital, and DeLeon was master of the fine distinction. He ridiculed Populists because they wished to nationalize the railroads, "but only as a reform"; Socialists proposed "nationalization as a revolution." Mere reform would never improve the lot of the employees. Socialism would abolish the wage system by paying to workers the full product of their labor. Would not such a payment constitute wages in another form, asked a skeptical listener. DeLeon was impatient: "If you choose to call water Paris Green that's your business," he snapped. No economically literate individual would equate wages with the proceeds of labor. Capitalism would perish, he held, only if the Socialist Labor party, unyielding as truth and logical as science, avoided the perils of meaningless reforms.

The Bostonians applauded and filed out. DeLeon went back to New York and published his speech in the *People.* But organization, discipline, harmony, and success were more easily discussed than achieved.

While controversy boiled around Herbert Casson, who was supposed to be the Massachusetts party's chief political spokesman, the Socialist Labor party mounted another unsuccessful campaign. Moritz Ruther, nominee for governor in 1895, declared bravely that the S.L.P. would "surely win." Yet even he had misgivings. The party's effort must be "persistent and untiring," and "courage, tact, judgment, and above all—patience" were essential. Finally, said the candid Holyoke cigarmaker, ". . . the masses . . . are still unaware that we are fighting their battle and consequently treat us with suspicion." In November Ruther had 3,249 votes to show for his pains.[26]

One campaign over, another began. Most S.L.P. sections did not bother to put up candidates for the December municipal elections. But Ruther was running for alderman in Holyoke, and, characteristically, he told the Holyoke *Democrat* that he expected to win. He was, he explained to his interviewer, different from his opponents who were "handicapped by selfish interests"; he simply wanted to serve. Specifically how would he serve? Ruther stood for clean streets, for better parks and schools, for lectures and public entertainment, for better housing for workers, for an eight-hour day, for a municipal electric plant, and for public works projects to aid the unemployed.

Ruther lost by only forty votes, but J. H. Connors, a young cigarmaker running for the Common Council, the larger branch of city government, gave the S.L.P. its first victory in the Commonwealth. The local Socialist paper thought Ruther's unremitting propaganda effort had achieved a measure of success for the party. Connors, however, brought to the campaign a personal resource that no amount of Socialist propaganda could provide. He was the president of the Holyoke Central Labor Union, and the personification of the Socialist Labor party's dream: a *bona fide* official of a labor union who would run on the Socialist ticket. No wonder his election elated the *People*.[27] For most union officials were suspicious of Socialists, and Socialists reciprocated by denouncing any labor organization that would not endorse the S.L.P.

From 1891 to 1895, Daniel DeLeon had worked to commit the Knights of Labor to Socialism. Socialists gradually

26. *Labor*, October 5, 1895; December 7, 1895.
27. *Ibid.*, November 23, 30, 1895; December 14, 1895; *People*, December 8, 1895.

increased their influence within the K. of L. until, in 1894, the Grand Master of the Knights, James R. Sovereign, found it expedient to bargain for Socialist support in union affairs. DeLeon demanded the right to name the editor of the official journal of the order; Sovereign met DeLeon's terms, but never fulfilled the bargain. The Grand Master simply postponed the appointment until he was able to control the K. of L. without Socialist help. DeLeon, naturally, was disgusted.[28]

The American Federation of Labor was even more hostile to Socialists than were the Knights. In general, the craft unions that made up the A.F. of L. tried to gain immediate economic advantages for their members; Socialist schemes for a future workers' utopia rated well below shorter hours and higher wages on the A.F. of L. priority list. The name of Samuel Gompers, the perennial president of the organization, became an epithet in the vocabulary of the S.L.P. Gompers was the model of the "labor fakir"— the union official who supported capitalism and deceived the working class. In 1893, Socialists had a moment of triumph when they succeeded in committing the A.F. of L. to an eleven-point program, the tenth of which called for "the collective ownership . . . of all means of production and distribution." A year later, Socialists helped John McBride defeat Samuel Gompers for the Federation's presidency. But the victory was hollow, for if Gompers was beaten, the Federation simultaneously discarded the Socialist program, including "Plank 10," and Gompers reclaimed his office in 1895.[29] Socialists in the A.F. of L. regrouped, determined to try again.

One trade unionist who attracted DeLeon's attention

28. Henry Kuhn and Olive M. Johnson, *The Socialist Labor Party During Four Decades* (New York, 1931), 16–17; Howard H. Quint, *The Forging of American Socialism* (Columbia, S.C., 1953), 156–157.
29. Nathan Fine, *Labor and Farmer Parties in the United States, 1828-1928* (New York, 1961), 140–146.

was John F. Tobin, a shoe worker from Rochester, New York, and a party to the scheme to capture the Knights of Labor. An energetic Socialist campaigner and propagandist, Tobin was also a delegate to the A.F. of L. convention of 1894, where he was among the most conspicuous of Gompers' opponents. Tobin's courage, his politics, and, eventually, his labor union impressed the Socialist Laborites in Massachusetts. A correspondent from Lynn wrote that Tobin's opposition to Gompers had pleased Socialists in the city's shoe factories. Ruther's Holyoke *Labor* publicized Tobin's efforts to establish the Boot and Shoe Workers' Union at the Boston convention in 1895, and applauded when the convention completed its work successfully.[30]

The Socialist Labor party might well rejoice. While the shoe workers had rejected a socialistic declaration of principles, they had elected an avowed Socialist to lead them. The production of shoes was the major industry in Haverhill, in Brockton, in Lynn, in Marlboro, and in other centers scattered around the Bay State. As the union grew, the opportunity of the Socialist Labor party might grow in proportion.

And the Boot and Shoe Workers' Union did grow. By the end of 1895, Marlboro alone reported nearly 1,800 members. More than 1,300 shoe workers in Lynn had joined; the rolls exceeded 800 in both Haverhill and Brockton. The annual report for 1895 showed more than 7,300 organized shoe workers in the Bay State. In the next twelve months, the total climbed to over 10,000. The figures were somewhat inflated; not all members paid dues regularly. By 1897, the union reported a more realistic

30. Daniel DeLeon to Kuhn, October 4, 1894, DeLeon Papers; *Labor*, November 3, 24, 1894; December 22, 1894; March 16, 1895; April 6, 27, 1895.

6,700 members in Massachusetts.[31] Whatever the precise figure, the Socialist Labor party scented votes.

And, though John F. Tobin worked cautiously, he tried to deliver the vote. He did not conceal his own sympathy for the Socialists. But in harmony with the policy of the American Federation of Labor, with which his union was affiliated, Tobin made no official endorsement of the Socialist Labor party. During the presidential campaign of 1896, the union's *Monthly Report* avoided a political position that might divide the organization. Workers, it said, should grasp the opportunity to use the ballot in their own interest, but the importance of the vote must not be overemphasized. Above all, the union's leaders hoped that political discussion would not "be allowed to absorb the entire attention of members to such an extent as to cause any of the interests of our organization as a trade union to be neglected." [32]

While wary non-partisanship was the official watchword, both the rhetoric and the content of the union's published reports betrayed a leaning toward Socialism. The union invited "all the down-trodden wage workers . . . to join . . . in a class effort" to obtain better conditions in the trade. At the same time, shoe workers must realize that their efforts, "in the economic field" had to be supplemented by "an intelligent use of their weapon in the political struggle for the establishment of the Co-operative Commonwealth." The successful labor organization consisted of men who understood "the true relations of capital and labor," and who were aware of "the inexorable laws governing the price of commodity labor."

In his report to the union's second convention, Tobin

31. Boot and Shoe Workers' Union, *Monthly Report*, December, 1895, 9 ff; December, 1896, 14 ff; December, 1897, 14 ff.
32. *Ibid.*, June, 1896, 3; July, 1896, 5.

hoped his first year in office had dispelled the apprehensions of those who had feared he might lead the union "into a political quagmire." He remained, he said, absolutely convinced that the trade union movement must operate politically if it were to succeed. He urged the convention to approve a new constitutional preamble advocating "the intelligent use of [the] right of suffrage in the interest of our class and independent of all capitalistic influence and interests." The amendment ultimately lost, but Tobin had not concealed his own continued acceptance of the Socialist faith. He was, he said, "at all times a Socialist, and was ever ready to advocate" the cause.[33]

Horace Eaton, a former shoe operative from Lynn who became Tobin's close associate as secretary of the union, did not formally join the S.L.P. because he would not pledge himself to vote a straight ticket. An occasional Populist, Eaton thought, might merit his support, though in general he preferred the S.L.P. But Tobin and Eaton kept Socialism constantly before their union. The occasion might be a letter from one of Tobin's friends, reprinted in the *Monthly Report,* and signed, "Yours for peace and prosperity, i.e. Socialism." Or the appeal might be made more boldly with a reminder that the ballot should be used "in the interest of the working class" and "against the idlers." At the union's convention in 1897, some Socialists decided the time had come to press for an outright endorsement of the Socialist Labor party. While Tobin favored such a motion, he also believed it unnecessary. Not even the most partisan Socialist Laborite wanted votes, he said, unless the voter was completely convinced of the validity of the Socialist program. The resolution

33. *Ibid.*, December, 1895, 14–15, April 1896, 2; *Report of Proceedings of the Second Convention of the Boot and Shoe Workers' Union . . .* (Lynn, Mass., 1896), 2, 90, 92, 94.

binding the union to the S.L.P. might bring the party votes cast in ignorance, which the party did not want.[34]

Amid Tobin's hedging, there was one forthright statement: "Seven years ago, . . . I became convinced that the entire abolition of the present wage system was necessary, and . . . it did not take me long to find the political party that stood for [my] principles. . . ." He had "no doubt" that political action must accompany trade union work if the demands of labor were to be achieved. He left equally little doubt that the Socialist Labor party was the preferred political instrument. In spite of Tobin's support, however, the amendment committing the union to the party lost 17-59.

If the Boot and Shoe Workers' Union refused to endorse the Socialist Labor party, it would endorse part of the Socialist program. Secretary Eaton prodded the organization for an unqualified declaration "for the ultimate abolition of competition" and the "wage system" and for "the establishment of the Co-operative Commonwealth." A proposed amendment pledged the union to the goal of "government ownership of industry," a step that the union held "would remove the fierce competition and establish production for use instead of sale. . . ." The margin was a slim three votes, but Tobin, Eaton, and the Socialists carried the motion.[35]

Eaton did not propose to allow the membership to forget its political duty. In his annual report for 1897, he promised to remind the membership that employers controlled the government. "We," he wrote, "the many poor," must "wrest the control of government from the few rich" through "an intelligent use of . . . suffrage. . . ." The

34. John Finn to N.E.C., December 14, 1896, SLP Papers; *Monthly Report*, January, 1897, 8, 19; *Proceedings* . . . , 31–34.
35. *Proceedings* . . . , 33, 117, 42, 108.

union's constitution demanded " 'government ownership of industry,' " he continued, which could "be obtained only at the ballot box." [36]

While the Boot and Shoe Workers flirted with Socialism, the Socialist Labor party preferred marriage to a prolonged courtship. In December, 1895, some of DeLeon's cohorts in the earlier effort to capture the Knights of Labor voted to establish a new labor organization. The new Socialist Trade and Labor Alliance was to work with the Socialist Labor party to emancipate the working class. The S.T. & L.A. would lead the workers to economic security; members would learn economics from tried and true Socialists. The S.L.P., for its part, would become an even more vigorous political organization as a result of its connection with the union. No labor fakirs here; the S.T. & L.A. was ideologically correct, the perfect helpmeet for the S.L.P. In July, 1896, the party's leaders demanded formal endorsement of the new union.[37]

Some Socialists were no less committed to existing trade unions than was DeLeon to the S.T. & L.A. DeLeon's opponents protested that the new organization would divide organized labor into competitive groups, that dual unionism, with its jealousies and jurisdictional disputes, was hardly the way to unify the working class. The S.L.P., they argued, would lose support. DeLeon counted such Socialists "unscientific" and a weakening element in the organization. Frank Sieverman, a close friend of John Tobin and a member of the Boot and Shoe Workers' Union, led the futile effort. When the votes were in, DeLeon won 71–6.

The thirteen-member delegation from Massachusetts represented the second or third largest group in the national party. Momentarily, Moritz Ruther, the delegate

36. *Monthly Report*, October, 1897, 19–20.
37. Kuhn, "Reminiscences," *loc. cit.*, 8–12.

from Holyoke, hesitated when asked to endorse the S.T. & L.A. The delegation was otherwise docile. DeLeon got Ruther's vote as well as those of the others in the delegation. The one exception was James F. Carey, a delegate from Haverhill, who ducked the crucial roll call, and also missed most of the rest of the convention.[38]

Carey's diplomatic absence was an early sign that the convention's decision was disruptive. Shortly after adjournment, Ruther's *Labor* published the resignation of an active Maplewood Socialist who heartily disapproved of the S.T. & L.A. A few months later, a Socialist, struggling to maintain a branch of the Alliance among waiters in Boston, begged DeLeon for half an hour of inspirational oratory. The need was urgent. "Half of the S.L.P.," he reported, opposed the Alliance; Boston's Jewish section openly derided it. A boycott of S.T. & L.A. Bakers endangered the continued existence of that organization, and the failure of the Bakers "would kill the Alliance in this city." Native-born workers resisted affiliation with immigrants. All in all, the situation was disheartening.[39]

Meanwhile there was the usual political campaign to prepare, and a sadly disorganized effort it turned out to be. As early as April, 1896, the national S.L.P. office had a hint of the ineptitude of the Massachusetts organization. Lucian Sanial, a speaker working for the National Executive Committee, wrote Henry Kuhn that a meeting in Rockland was "a failure," a harsh word that Socialist lecturers rarely applied to their work. But Sanial had chosen his word aptly. He spoke in a hall with a capacity of 1,500; his audience "was barely 50." Sanial could list the apparent causes for the disappointing evening: rain, and the local industry's twenty-four hour schedule, which left half

38. *Proceedings of the Ninth Annual Convention* . . . , 30, 32, and *passim.*
39. Henry Wehner to DeLeon, March 8, 1897; see also Wehner's earlier letter, March 4, 1897, DeLeon Papers.

the working population exhausted and required the other half to be at work at the time he was speaking, figured prominently. Yet "the . . . real cause," he observed, "is that the working class is helpless and hopeless. It may at times wake up a little and listen to a speaker, but it soon sinks back into apathy." [40]

Nor did the state convention pull the party together. It nominated a ticket, prepared a platform, and, according to the *People*, endorsed the Alliance. The candidates had familiar names: Thomas Brophy, a faithful follower of DeLeon, was the nominee for governor; Moritz Ruther was his running mate; a new name was that of John Chase of Haverhill, candidate for attorney-general. The platform contained the usual mixture of a conventional Socialist preamble and immediate demands for reform: reduction in the hours of labor, better educational opportunities, free public baths, and various schemes for a more democratic governmental process. Yet platform and candidates were only the trappings of political organization, and within a few days, if DeLeon could puzzle out some unconventional spelling, he could tell that the convention had not been an unqualified success. "I will say," wrote a correspondent from Somerville, "that the Socialist Labor Party is poory organiced in Mass and husling is requrit to organise the Hub for practical work. . . ." [41]

Dissension was by no means restricted to Boston; prospects were universally bleak. A party functionary wrote Kuhn that the Pittsfield movement was very weak. The party in Adams, once "one of the best," was "smashed in pieces." Activity in Holyoke was of the "wrong kind." Springfield comrades were despondent. Carey had moved there and promised "a great deal." Still, the report went

---

40. L. Sanial to Kuhn, April 29, 1896, SLP Papers.
41. *People*, May 24, 1896; *Labor*, June 6, 1896; M. Loven to DeLeon, May 26, 1896, DeLeon Papers.

on, "Jim wears green glasses yet, and much need not be expected until he has got rid of them." Worcester was badly split over Casson's expulsion. Lynn was the only bright spot in a dismal picture. There meetings were scheduled every week, and only Socialists with "clear heads" were permitted to speak. Even Moritz Ruther could not muster his habitual optimism. "What in h—," he wondered, "is the matter in Adams, Greylock, etc." He had heard that whole sections were deserting the party; "too much fire water up there," he supposed.[42]

While local organizations went to pieces, Squire Putney, the harassed state secretary, tried to coordinate the campaign effort. His task was complicated by the temporary disappearance of the standard bearer, for Brophy's local reported that he had not been seen for some weeks. Brophy's vanishing act typified a comically mismanaged campaign. Early in August, Putney asked national headquarters about the plans to send out-of-state speakers through Massachusetts. More than a month later, he knew only that Matthew Maguire, the party's vice-presidential nominee, would tour the state at some unspecified time. Then, just prior to Maguire's arrival, the state committee of New Jersey demanded a share of his time, thereby transforming Putney's careful schedule into a tour that Maguire complained was badly arranged, unnecessarily hectic, expensive and inconvenient.[43]

Maguire's tour was only one of Putney's problems. When he asked for a German lecturer, the national office booked one on a date that conflicted with a previously arranged English campaign effort. When correspondence did not immediately resolve the impasse, Putney was

42. Badger to Comrade [Kuhn], June 14, 1896; Ruther to Kuhn, July 26, 1896, SLP Papers.
43. Goldstein to Kuhn, August 28, 1896; Putney to Kuhn, September 19, 1896; October 6, 1896; Maguire to Kuhn, October 19, 23, 1896, with enclosed clipping, SLP Papers.

petulant: "Are you," he asked Kuhn, "ready to answer my letters on this matter?" When the national office wanted to send Charles Matchett, the presidential candidate, into the Bay State, local arrangements again conflicted. When Worcester requested a Swedish speaker, Kuhn offered a French-speaking spellbinder. When Putney politely declined the offer of a Polish organizer, since the state organization "knew of very few Poles," Kuhn persuaded the committee to reverse its decision.[44]

William Fiszler, the unwanted Polish recruiter, arrived in Massachusetts and promptly reported that his task would require at least two weeks instead of the one that had been planned. His reports of the tour blend cancelled meetings and missed connections with a pathetic desire to justify his salary. Rowdies broke up his first rally in Holyoke. The section in Worcester failed to make any arrangements; Fiszler acknowledged that there were few Poles in Worcester anyhow. Scheduled meetings in Boston, Lowell, and Lawrence never took place, though Lawrence later staged a rally. In spite of this consistently dreary reception, Fiszler reported that the Poles in Massachusetts were eager for organization. He managed to establish small sections in Boston, Lawrence, and Northampton. He also sold a few subscriptions to a Polish-language Socialist newspaper and a few dollars' worth of Socialist tracts.[45] The *People* wisely did not call attention to the trip.

Through it all, some Socialists, mistaking energy for accomplishment, maintained their optimism. The results, as usual, disappointed. Although Brophy received over 4,500 votes, only about 2,000 Bay State voters supported

44. Putney to Kuhn, September 20, 1896; October 9, 1896; A. Kesseli to Kuhn, October 18, 1896; Putney to Kuhn, August 22, 26, 1896, SLP Papers.
45. Fitszler to Kuhn, September 26, 1896; October 10, 1896, SLP Papers.

Charles Matchett, the S.L.P.'s presidential nominee. Nearly everyone thought that William Jennings Bryan and "free silver" had attracted many workingmen to the Democrats. Early in the campaign Putney had twice written for literature to counter the Democratic stress on silver. So pressing was the need that when Kuhn offered to send the plates of a pamphlet to Boston, Putney hastily accepted, though the arrangement forced the Massachusetts S.L.P. to pay the printing costs. In October, Putney needed a similar pamphlet in Hebrew, and eventually more than 5,000 copies were distributed.[46] Just before the election, a correspondent in North Adams told Kuhn that the Socialist vote there would increase substantially "if the Devil had free silver." And the post-election report from Lynn was succinct: the working class there "went Bryan mad and silver crazy." [47]

Perhaps Democratic competition was a major reason for the disappointing showing of the S.L.P. But the party could blame only itself for the persistent internal quarrels and the abiding division over the proper form of labor organization. Both had sapped the patience of potential Socialist supporters. And the party could blame only itself for a sorry, mismanaged campaign.

The Socialists had another, yet more fundamental, deficiency. The root of the Socialist Labor party's failure to attract substantial support was the Socialist creed. The American workingman in 1896 did not recognize himself as a wage slave, nor did he pay much attention to orators who so described him. A reporter covering Maguire's speech in New Bedford sat next to a laborer who drifted into the hall, listened for a few moments, then nudged his

46. Putney's orders for campaign literature are in the SLP Papers; see also H. King to Kuhn, August 15, 1896, and N. Rabinoff to Kuhn, October 13, 1896, SLP Papers.
47. Philip Connor to Kuhn, November 2, 1896; C. Wentworth to Kuhn, November 8, 1896, SLP Papers.

neighbor and asked what sort of a rally he was attending. Told it was a Socialist affair, the listener guessed he was not interested, and wandered out of the hall to smoke his pipe.[48] That cooperative commonwealth was a misty unreality far off in the future. To many workingmen, the Socialist view of the present was equally unreal, and some found more comfort in tobacco than in fantasy.

In January, 1895, William Seymour, a Cambridge laborer, wrote Daniel DeLeon a thoughtful letter. Seymour suggested that Socialists ignore peripheral issues—religion, education, even government—and concentrate on economic matters. Above all, he counselled patience.

> I would . . . suggest that Socialists not be too hasty in condemning workingmen for not embracing socialism. Generally speaking, the social life of workingmen in America commences in the workshop in the morning and ends there in the evening. This unnatural condition makes them not only indifferent to the low financial return for their services, but also unfits them for any mental effort whatever. Ten or more hours in the workshop, the rest of the day in bed, makes twenty-four happy hours for the average workingman in intellectual America. So you see, Mr. Editor, you must not expect too much brightness from us workingmen.
> The veil of inheritance must be lifted slowly; inherited creeds, politics, obedience, submission, make people afraid and suspicious of all modern and advanced reforms no matter how beneficial and uplifting the reform may be, or how simple and clear it may be. . . .[49]

There is no evidence that DeLeon acknowledged Seymour's letter, nor that Seymour ever wrote him again. But William Seymour, who knew that the American workingman was a weary laborer and not a class-conscious, educated revolutionary, had an insight that the ideologically rigid DeLeon lacked.

48. Clipping enclosed in Maguire to Kuhn, October 19, 1896, SLP Papers.
49. William Seymour to Mr. Editor, January, 1895 [?], SLP Papers.

Haverhill: Shoes, Schism, Success

Massachusetts Socialists expected great things from the movement in Haverhill. In the discouraging campaign of 1895, the party's vote there had quadrupled and Holyoke *Labor* noted that Haverhill was "pushing forward in fine style." A year later, Matthew Maguire reported that the comrades in Haverhill were "made of the right stuff." They would, he thought, "push the movement as hard as possible." Yet in spite of rallies, speeches, and special shipments of Socialist pamphlets, the Socialist vote in 1896 declined, even for John C. Chase, the local organizer who ran for attorney-general.[1]

The undaunted Haverhill Socialists nominated candidates for the municipal race in December. Their choice for mayor, James F. Carey, was well known. The S.L.P. actively sought support through a careful canvass of the shoe factories, and Carey received six hundred votes, about ten per cent of the total. The Haverhill *Gazette*, previously unimpressed by the Socialists, took a second look. Carey's showing, it decided, was "significant." Six months later, in a special mayoral election, the Socialist tide was still running. Again the S.L.P. standard bearer, Carey once more had nearly 600 votes. But the total vote

1. Holyoke *Labor,* November 16, 1895; Maguire to Kuhn, October 19, 1896, SLP Papers.

dropped from about 6,000 to 4,400, and the Socialist percentage consequently rose.[2]

While the outlook in Haverhill was promising, the state S.L.P. was in bad repair. The party secretary estimated that there were about 580 members in forty local sections, about half of which contained fewer than a dozen members. The treasurer's report revealed correspondingly limited financial resources. A majority of the locals in 1895-1897 contributed less than $20.00 to the state party's budget; two sections in Haverhill, for instance, remitted a total of $15.10. In May, 1897, the Massachusetts S.L.P. had a cash surplus of precisely $17.55.[3]

Socialists in Boston, more numerous and more prosperous than most other sections, dissipated their energy in internal feuds. In May, Thomas Brophy wanted to expel the entire Jewish section. The Jewish Socialists, for their part, kept up their hostility to the S.T. & L.A. Some members, anxious to keep Boston's perpetual intramural struggles from infecting the rest of the party, sought to move state headquarters to Holyoke, which would then supply the executive officers. Divided on other matters, Boston Socialists united to oppose any attempt to diminish their influence. When a referendum of the party favored Holyoke, Martha Avery, an important Boston Socialist, prophesied an inefficient administration. The Boston organization, she added, would spend in Boston any funds it could raise.[4]

Not that anyone had much money. The new state committee, headed by Moritz Ruther, hired Fred G. R. Gor-

2. *Gazette*, December 7, 9, 1896; June 1, 2, 1897.
3. The estimate of membership is undated, but probably for 1897, SLP Papers; Financial Report of Massachusetts S.L.P., DeLeon Papers.
4. Brophy to DeLeon, May 18, 1897; Harry Wehner to DeLeon, July 13, 1897 with enclosed clipping; Martha Avery to DeLeon, September 7, 1897, DeLeon Papers; William Edlin to Leon Malkial, October 18, 1897, SLP Papers.

don, a shoe worker and a rousing speaker, to spark the campaign. His salary and expenses put a severe strain on an impossibly restricted budget. An October fund drive brought in over $200, but the state committee then hired more speakers and overdrew the treasury again. Before the end of November, the party had borrowed $50 from Ruther, and it was more than $200 in debt.[5]

While the campaign rolled on, Ruther had ideological as well as financial headaches. Fred Gordon had barely appeared on the payroll when reports sifted into New York that he was flirting with a rival Socialist group, the Social Democracy of America, which Eugene V. Debs and others had established in the summer of 1897. The formation of a competitive radical organization had provoked DeLeon to warn Socialist Laborites against such misguided schemes as "the Debs plan." Although he respected Debs's good intentions, DeLeon condemned both the program and the judgment of his rival.[6]

Partly because Debs and DeLeon differed, their organizations differed. DeLeon's preoccupation with ideological principles made the S.L.P. a narrow, intolerant sect. He contended that objective, verifiable evidence supported both his view of contemporary America and his dream for the future. In fact, DeLeon knew little of the working class he wanted so passionately to lead; and most of the working class knew nothing at all of Daniel DeLeon and the S.L.P.

Eugene Victor Debs, by contrast, had earned a reputation as labor's champion in a decade and a half of union leadership. The Pullman Strike and a subsequent term in prison had broken his American Railway Union while hardening his convictions and enhancing his standing

5. Ruther to Kuhn, September 17, 1897, SLP Papers; *People*, November 21, 1897.

6. *People*, June 13, 27, 1897.

among restless working men. Although Debs sometimes expressed those convictions in the jargon of the socialist intellectual, he was less interested in concepts than in people. While DeLeon lectured the working class, Debs talked with workers. DeLeon, the cold, impersonal editor, worked with words and abstractions; Debs, the sentimental labor leader, worked with men.

The Social Democracy of America reflected Debs's lack of concern with ideology. Composed of remnants of the American Railway Union and a group of non-partisan socialists, the organization had an ideological diversity the S.L.P. never had. One wing of the Social Democracy believed the organization's major effort ought to be directed toward establishing a cooperative community. The inevitable success of this experiment, so the faith went, would inspire imitation until a whole state had resolved itself into a socialistic polity. The other faction of the organization held that political action would spread socialism more effectively than utopian colonization. Believing that men of good will could work together in spite of minor disagreements, Debs saw no reason to choose between the two factions.

The interest Fred Gordon had shown in the Social Democracy was only one ideological lapse of which S.L.P. purists accused him. A second charge was that he preferred the *Appeal to Reason,* a non-partisan socialist weekly, to the S.L.P.'s official *People.* The *Appeal,* shrewdly edited by Julius Wayland, championed socialism to more readers than any other radical paper in the nation. Wayland, who preferred Debs to DeLeon, had asked several Socialist Laborites in Massachusetts to serve as agents for his paper. One of those approached conceded that the *Appeal* contained "very much . . . good propaganda," but refused to enlist in the "Appeal army" of subscription agents unless Wayland would specifically endorse the S.L.P. Fred Gordon was less demanding. In a letter to an official of the New Hampshire S.L.P., he admitted promoting the *Appeal*, which he preferred to "any Socialist paper in America." Though still employed by the Massachusetts party, Gordon explicitly declared war on DeLeon—"Great Jehovah Daniel," he called him. He also opposed the S.T. & L.A. and guessed he did not give a "dam" [*sic*] if these convictions led to his expulsion. Gordon was confident that the state committee would support him, for he interpreted the shift of party headquarters to Holyoke as a repudiation of the DeLeon-Avery wing of the party.[7]

Nor was Gordon's confidence misplaced. When Ruther heard that Gordon had presided at a meeting during which Debs spoke, the state secretary showed little concern about doctrinal contamination. "I feel that it would be better to fight the common enemy than to be ever watchful to discover the splinter in the neighbor's eye," he wrote a tattling comrade. What if Gordon did serve as chairman at a Debs meeting? Ruther himself would have been pleased to do so if asked. Debs had once spoken for the S.L.P. in Holyoke, and Ruther thought the party had gained 300 votes as a result. Debs was "a wonderful Socialist educator, and anyone who throws a stone in his way is doing us a wrong."[8]

Moritz Ruther might defend both Gordon and Debs, but the final decision was not his to make. DeLeon's relatively mild criticism of Debs would soon become more severe. And the New Hampshire S.L.P., of which Gordon was technically a member, was soon to expel him. This

7. M. D. Fitzgerald to DeLeon, February 10, 1897, DeLeon Papers; Arthur Keep to Kuhn, October 4, 1897; Gordon to Whitehouse, October 20, 1897, SLP Papers.

8. Ruther to J. H. Clohecy, November 9, 1897, SLP Papers. Debs had, in fact, urged all Socialists to vote for the S.L.P. since the Social Democracy had been unable to get a ticket in the field for the fall elections.

action was anticlimactic, since Gordon had already avowed his intention of joining the Social Democracy. He planned, furthermore, to recommend to others the same course of action. The New York hierarchy also noted suspiciously F. G. R. Gordon's changed address: c/o James F. Carey, Haverhill, Massachusetts.[9]

Gordon moved to Haverhill to work in the municipal campaign, regarding which the *People* was conspicuously silent, though the candidates ran on the S.L.P. ticket. John C. Chase replaced Carey at the head of the slate; Carey ran for the Common Council from the fifth ward, where Socialist support had steadily grown. The platform included democratic reforms such as the initiative and referendum; municipal ownership of some public utilities; public works projects for the unemployed. Other planks were of local importance: abolition of unguarded railway crossings, a longtime concern of reform groups in the city; free clothing for children who would otherwise be unable to attend school.

The *People* might pay no attention to Haverhill, but in the city itself the Socialist upsurge was big news. The Haverhill *Gazette,* a staunchly Republican daily, reported the Socialist campaign fully and fairly. It thought the entire Socialist ticket "a good one," and singled out Carey as a particularly attractive candidate. "On the whole, the Gazette is convinced that the election of a man of Mr. James F. Carey's strong individuality . . . would be a good thing." Why not elect "a few brainy men" to city government "by way of variety?" the *Gazette* asked. Socialism, wrote editor John B. Wright, would "be a benefit and not a curse . . ."; the doctrine promised to harm only "those whose highest ambition is to live on the earnings of others." [10]

9. Gordon to Henry O'Neil, enclosed in Whitehouse to Kuhn, November 5, 1897; Gordon to Whitehouse, October 20, 1897, SLP Papers.
10. *Gazette,* November 12, 15, 26, 27, 1897.

The Socialist campaign went well. A week before the election, Carey was reported "developing great strength in totally unexpected quarters." On election day, the *Gazette* observed that workingmen of the city found John Chase's opponents unappealing; he might, indeed, get 1,000 votes.

The estimate was not far off. Chase received 950 votes, about one in every seven cast. But James F. Carey, running in only one ward, received more than 900 votes, led in every precinct, and was elected to the city's Common Council. Socialists predicted that Carey would soon go to Congress and the editor of the *Gazette* too had kind words to bestow. The Socialists, John B. Wright predicted, would become an even more important factor in future municipal campaigns. He was sure Carey would keep his colleagues "on their toes" and enliven the proceedings of the Common Council.[11]

The very first sessions of the newly-elected Council justified Wright's prediction. As a result of a deadlock between the major parties, the Council elected Carey its president, a turn of events that elated the editor of the *Gazette* and roused his local pride: "Verily this was the case where an individual in no sense a self-seeker was exalted. Mr. Carey may be depended upon to wield the gavel gracefully and with conspicuous impartiality. . . . But think of it! One of the most conspicuous Socialists of New England chosen to a position of great importance in one of the most thriving cities of New England." And Carey's initial actions were not disappointing. His committee appointments were splendid; his open administration of the business of the city merited "the thanks of the voters." If this was Socialism, said the editor, "the study of that much derided system . . . will at once be stimulated

11. *Ibid.*, November 23, 1897; December 6, 7, 9, 1897; *Bulletin,* December 14, 1897.

in this vicinity." To the extent that Carey was an example of socialistic principles, they were "worthy of praise, not censure." [12]

The Socialist Labor party's directorate in New York was not at all sure Carey's principles were in fact socialistic. Martha Avery, a rabid DeLeonite, cautiously notified New York of Carey's victory: "If Haverhill is still in the S.L.P.," she wrote, "we have Cary [sic] as a Common Councilman in that city." The People, after a confused early account of Carey's election, ran a corrected story the following week under the headline "Bravo Haverhill!" [13] But it did not find Carey's presidency of the Council worth mentioning. He received much more support from the local Republican press than from the official journal of his own party.

For the Socialist Labor party was beginning to suspect its successful local in Haverhill. Bits and pieces of evidence seemed to add up to ideological treason. For instance, a letter from John Chase in 1896 had reported Haverhill's displeasure with the People's constant criticism of trade union officials. Later in the same year came a veiled warning from Michael Berry, one of DeLeon's sturdiest supporters in Haverhill. Berry viewed the growth of his party in Haverhill with misgivings. While the movement was small, it had been ideologically sound. As it expanded, trade union leaders began to maintain a Socialist facade, proclaiming their doctrine to be "a broader type" than that of the S.L.P. Finally, Carey had a long record of independence from the national S.L.P. He had once refused to endorse part of the state ticket and always rejected the party's model platforms in favor of those he himself wrote. Under his influence, the Haverhill

12. *Gazette,* January 4, 5, 1898.
13. Avery to Kuhn, December 9, 1897, SLP Papers; *People,* December 12, 19, 1897.

movement gave propaganda and speakers sent by the national office a reception that varied from chilly to frigid. Yet Eugene Debs drew a large, cheering crowd in spite of a heavy rain.[14]

After the municipal election, the case against Carey no longer rested on inference. When Thomas Brophy requested biographical data, Carey replied curtly that he did not wish to be mentioned in anything Brophy might write. Brophy looked at Carey's closing "Yours for Democratic Socialism," and forwarded the letter to New York. And in Holyoke, Moritz Ruther received two letters that were frank and specific. "I am seriously thinking of getting out of the S.L.P.," Carey wrote the state secretary, "for I have no hope, absolutely none[,] of bringing about the changes so necessary to reasonable progress." The tactics of the S.L.P., he continued, "have discouraged and disheartened me." Carey assured Ruther that he had never said he was going to join the Social Democracy; all he would promise was that "in the future, as . . . in the past," he would follow his convictions. The personal cost of these convictions had already been immense, Carey concluded in a passage that may have led to the nickname "Weeping James," one of several that the S.L.P. later derisively bestowed on him.

. . . I have suffered want and hunger. I have seen the faces of those dear to me grow hard and set at my approach. I have seen the companions of my boyhood turn against me. I have seen the hope of a home, of a wife, of children, weaken and die. I have endured the condemnation of my mother, my father, my brother, my sisters. I have been ostracized, maligned, misunderstood, hated, blacklisted, and persecuted, and now after all this, after all the years of soul-hunger which I have endured, with the best years of my life gone forever,

14. Chase to Kuhn, September 13, 1896; Berry to Kuhn, October 11, 1896, SLP Papers; *People*, March 27, 1898; August 7, 1898; *Bulletin*, November 11, 1897; *Gazette*, November 11, 1897.

with my health shattered, you tell me should I do a certain thing, some will call me "traitor." Think you I fear? . . . No . . . I follow my convictions though they lead to death.[15]

Moritz Ruther discreetly decided to keep his heresies at home, and for the time being said nothing to New York about Carey's outbursts. But a few days after Carey became president of the Common Council, apparently in spite of specific instructions from the party to refuse the post, Ruther decided to alert headquarters of potential trouble. "We have reason to believe," he reported, "that James F. Carey is going Debsward." Ruther explained that his Haverhill comrade was "in the last stages of consumption," which presumably explained his erratic conduct. The state committee, according to its secretary, would counter any attempt to spread rebellion beyond Haverhill. Two days later, Ruther was not sure he had a rebellion after all. Although he had had letters indicating that Carey was leaning toward the Social Democracy, Ruther said he had no "positive proof" that the Haverhill leader would desert. The secretary was even hopeful that Carey had changed his mind.[16]

Arthur Keep, a vigilant DeLeonite who could spot a deviation in Haverhill from his vantage-point in Washington, D.C., prodded Henry Kuhn. "Mr. Carey," Keep wrote, "has about as much class consciousness as an oyster. . . ." He was very dubious about Carey's "ability to steer a straight course," for the Haverhill councilman was by nature too "meek," too "forgiving," too "liable to be

15. Carey to Brophy, December 15, 1897, copy in SLP Papers. Carey to Comrade [Ruther], SLP Papers. Neither of the two letters from Carey to Ruther is dated. Both are copies, which Harry Carless, an organizer for the national party, made and mailed to New York (Carless to Kuhn, January 15, 1898). There seems no reason to doubt the authenticity of the copies, although the few other extant Carey letters are much less emotional. Ruther later acknowledged that he had had letters from Carey expressing dissatisfaction (Ruther to Kuhn, January 11, 1898).

16. Ruther to Kuhn, January 9, 11, 1898, SLP Papers.

manipulated by smooth politicians," too "thick" with F. G. R. Gordon, and "too namby pamby." Carey was, Keep concluded, "not the right sort to begin or continue a fight." [17]

Keep underestimated Carey's ability and misjudged his determination. Michael T. Berry, who labored diligently to keep the Haverhill sections in the S.L.P., respected Carey as "one of the most eloquent speakers in the Bay State." The editor of the Knights of Labor *Yearbook* for 1898 was more expansive: Carey was "the best Socialist speaker in New England." Moritz Ruther noted sourly that Socialists in Haverhill thought Carey a "tin god." And the testimony of his friends was glowing. He was a brilliant debater, who made his points with a ready smile and without a trace of triumph or bitterness. His warm personality, sparkling wit, and obvious sincerity won the friendship even of those who did not share his political creed. His most casual remarks on industrial and social questions drew an audience; if he strolled through the Haverhill shoe district during lunch hour, he had a hundred people talking and joking with him within a few minutes. James F. Carey, one of his admirers recalled, was "among the best loved fellows in the city." [18]

Secure in the support of a loyal local following, Carey did not shy from a conflict with the national Socialist Labor party. On February 17, 1898, when John C. Chase mailed the charter of the American section to New York, the Haverhill group officially withdrew from the party. Henry Kuhn immediately asked Moritz Ruther what was happening in Haverhill. Ruther replied that his information was not very current; he had tried to contact people in Haverhill, but they seemed under Carey's spell. Haver-

17. Keep to Kuhn, January 8, 1898, DeLeon Papers.
18. Berry to Kuhn, February 22, 1898; Ruther to Kuhn, February 20, 1898, SLP Papers; Knights of Labor, *Yearbook for 1898* (Jersey City, 1898); interview with Ralph Gardner, August 19, 1960.

hill for some time "seemed to have little love for the S.L.P.," Ruther added. The state committee would ask the comrades in Lawrence to undertake a reorganization of the section in Haverhill.[19]

Michael T. Berry, outraged at the action of his own section, volunteered to undertake the reorganization himself. The decision to withdraw, he claimed, had been taken at a hastily called meeting at which only about a third of the membership had been present. The vote on the question was 13–3, an inconclusive margin, since the section had about seventy members. He believed twenty or thirty would keep the faith in Haverhill.

The National Executive Committee had one more card to play. After his nomination to the Common Council, Carey had followed standard party procedure by giving the secretary of his local a signed, undated letter of resignation from his office. Presumably the letter insured that the office-holder would submit to the party's direction and remain steadfast in his advocacy of Socialist principles. The N.E.C. wanted that resignation submitted forthwith, a notion that the Haverhill *Gazette* branded a "huge joke." Carey, said the *Gazette*, owed his election to a constituency, not to a party, and these constituents alone could effect his retirement. Carey himself doubted that Haverhill's fifth ward would take dictation from party functionaries in New York. And the letter of resignation itself proved elusive. The National Executive Committee finally sent Carey a registered letter demanding once more that he resign an office that was "party property." The letter came back unopened.[20]

While national headquarters played out this farce,

19. Chase to Kuhn, February 17, 1898; Ruther to Kuhn, February 20, 1898, SLP Papers.
20. Berry to Kuhn, February 22, 1898, SLP Papers; *Gazette*, March 7, 10, 1898; *People*, March 6, 20, 27, 1898; March 21, 1903; *Bulletin*, March 7, 1898.

Thomas Hickey, a national organizer, arrived to help Berry's salvage operation in Haverhill. Carey explained to Hickey that his followers objected to the expulsion and vilification of F. G. R. Gordon, found the party's policy of antagonizing trade unions unacceptable, and resented the *People*'s unfair treatment of honest differences of opinion in the party. Hickey dismissed Carey's answers contemptuously and challenged the councilman to defend himself in a public debate.

Hickey warmed up for the occasion with a rather conventional speech denouncing the A.F. of L. and praising the militantly class-conscious S.T. & L.A. The Haverhill *Bulletin* thought about twenty people listened. The following evening, he broadened his attack to include Debs, the Social Democracy, and James F. Carey as well. His speech, Hickey wrote the *People* proudly, "really finished the job." Haverhill had been informed that "we have washed our hands of" Carey. His future misbehavior would not reflect on the party. The S.L.P.'s champion did not report that his rally drew "just 41 people, including two speakers and two reporters." Later in the same month, by contrast, when Herbert Casson joined Carey to address another rally, an estimated eight hundred listened to the two expelled Socialist Laborites.[21]

The S.L.P. was more interested in doctrinal purity than in numerical support. The *People* found the split profoundly satisfying: Carey, who was guilty of "premeditated and deliberate . . . moral turpitude," no longer infested the ranks. As the *People* followed Carey's political career, it discovered other reasons for the expulsion. In June, 1898, as a part of local participation in the Spanish-American War, the city government, with Carey's support, appropriated money to refurbish an armory. DeLeon

21. *People*, March 27, 1898; *Gazette*, March 11, 1898; *Bulletin*, March 10, 11, 26, 1898.

subsequently used the incident to demonstrate Carey's political opportunism and the insincerity of his devotion to the working class. The armory issue became an *ex post facto* justification for Carey's excommunication, and it was almost forgotten that the result preceded the official cause.[22] Yet Socialist doctrine was not the primary reason for the split. Chase stated simply that there was a difference of "tactics and methods." The root of the disagreement was the desire of the Haverhill Socialists to manage their own movement in their own way. In demanding local autonomy, they were instinctively following the pattern of successful American political parties. But DeLeon's concept of regimented party unity never permitted permanent home rule.[23]

It was no coincidence that Eugene V. Debs again visited Haverhill just as the dispute between Carey and DeLeon boiled into open recrimination. Following a noisy welcome at the crowded lecture hall, Debs called for unity among groups that sought to educate the working population. The rally, he noted, was sponsored jointly by the Socialist Labor party and the Social Democracy. Labor unions and Socialists, twin remedies for contemporary industrial problems, must cooperate. Debs included no denunciation of labor fakirs, no insistence that trade unions were betraying the workers to their employers. Representatives of local unions, seated with honor on the platform, took note.[24]

Within a few days James Carey was describing the So-

22. *People*, March 27, 1898; August 7, 1898; October 6, 1900; March 23, 1901; April 6, 1901; August 17, 1901.

23. *Gazette*, March 7, 1898. David Shannon has observed that local authority in matters of doctrine and political tactics was an important element in early Socialist success. *The Socialist Party of America* (New York, 1955), 6–7, 258–259. See also Daniel Bell, "Marxian Socialism in the United States," in Donald D. Egbert and Stow Persons, ed., *Socialism and American Life* (Princeton, 1952), I, 293.

24. *Gazette*, March 3, 1898; *Bulletin*, March 3, 1898.

cial Democracy as the American version of international Socialism, an organization that employed "methods and tactics consistent with the American character and American institutions." He formally announced that he and his fellow dissidents in the Haverhill S.L.P. had been converted from DeLeon to Debs. The *Gazette* began to refer to Carey and his supporters as "Debsites." John C. Chase became the local organizer for the Social Democracy and promptly received more than sixty applications for membership. Meanwhile, Michael Berry started a new section of the S.L.P. with twelve charter members. Even the *People* reluctantly acknowledged that Haverhill's Socialist movement was "exclusively . . . the personal following of Carey." [25]

Not content with expelling one of the few locals with a chance of political success, the Socialist Labor party simultaneously picked a fight with John F. Tobin and the Boot and Shoe Workers' Union. Tobin was even more hostile than Carey to the Socialist Trade and Labor Alliance. The issue had arisen at the union's convention in 1897, when a Philadelphia local suggested that the union withdraw from the A.F. of L. and affiliate with the S.T. & L.A. Tobin beat back this challenge without the formality of a roll call, but Socialist Laborites were difficult to discourage.[26]

In December, 1897, as Carey was winning his race in Haverhill, Tobin took the offensive against the S.T. & L.A. While DeLeon journeyed from New York to Boston to liven up the municipal campaign, Tobin went from Boston to New York to steal DeLeon's shoe workers. The S.T. & L.A. had organized a few shoe workers around New

25. *Gazette,* March 7, 1898; *Bulletin,* March 10, 1898; *People,* March 13, 1898.
26. Boot and Shoe Workers' Union, *Report of Proceedings of the . . . Convention . . . 1897* (Lynn, Mass., 1897), 98–100; Augusta E. Galster, *The Labor Movement in the Shoe Industry* (New York, 1924), 192–193.

York, and Tobin had previously agreed with DeLeon to avoid conflict in the latter's back yard. Tobin's decision to break the truce soon led to a formal debate that completed the estrangement between the two old allies. Tobin said DeLeon's "sorry effort" gave evidence of "a most pronounced . . . senility." Finally, in June, Tobin avowed his complete break with the S.L.P. He confessed that he had "for years" admired DeLeon as "an able exponent of . . . Socialism." He had always had "unbounded faith," Tobin continued, in his sincerity and integrity. No longer. Daniel DeLeon had become "an unscrupulous falsifier." When the fall campaigns rolled around, John F. Tobin joined Eugene Debs and James F. Carey on lecture platforms in Massachusetts.[27]

Although Haverhill's Socialist Laborites chafed in the national party's disciplinary harness, and although the latent conflict between the Socialist Trade and Labor Alliance and the trade unions would soon explode, the S.L.P. avoided an open crisis during the campaign of 1897. In its annual summary of the political gains during the year, the *People* emphasized the promising returns from municipal elections in Massachusetts.

Opportunity seemed also to knock for the Socialist Trade and Labor Alliance in Massachusetts. On January 17, 1898, the perennially depressed textile workers of New Bedford went on strike rather than accept a wage reduction. Their timing could hardly have been worse. January in New Bedford was no time to throw up a job that meant coal and bread. Textile workers were predominantly unorganized; previous attempts to establish unions had foundered. Four unions, each containing only a small por-

27. Transcript of Debate between DeLeon, Tobin and others, Archives of the Boot and Shoe Workers' Union, Boston; Boot and Shoe Workers' Union, *Monthly Report*, May, 1898, 10; June, 1898, 20.

tion of the strikers, competed to provide leadership once the strike had begun. Former mill workers, displaced by labor-saving machinery, formed a pool of potential strike-breakers. Most of the corporations were financially able to withstand a strike; many had a consistent dividend rate of ten per cent or better.

To the S.L.P., however, the strike seemed a splendid chance to advance Socialist unionism and make Socialist votes in New Bedford. For years a small section of the party had been telling textile workers of the class struggle. Daniel DeLeon himself had once come to the city to expound Socialist principles during an earlier unsuccessful strike. Now Harry Carless, a national organizer, attracted a capacity audience to New Bedford's City Hall. Local Socialists distributed more than a thousand tracts before the treasury was exhausted. A letter to the *People* asked the National Executive Committee to raise funds for more speakers and more literature. Those on the scene reported an unsurpassed occasion for great gains. Daniel DeLeon went to New Bedford to consolidate them.[28]

DeLeon's speech was one of his best efforts. He promised not to amuse the audience "with promises . . . funny anecdotes, bombastic recitations . . . and wind." [29] Some strikers, "accustomed to a different diet," might find his offering dull. For he had come, said DeLeon, not to entertain, but to enlighten, to explain "a few elemental principles of political economy and sociology" which the strikers needed "more than bread." In point of fact, DeLeon did explain Socialist economics. His outline was familiar: labor produced all value and the capitalist took most of labor's product as profit; the result was a struggle between capital and labor; given the present economic

28. *People*, December 26, 1897; February 6, 13, 1898; March 27, 1898; April 3, 1898.
29. Daniel DeLeon, *What Means This Strike?* (New York, 1960), 3. Subsequent quotations are also drawn from this pamphlet.

situation, with the rapid introduction of machinery and consequent unemployment, strikes were usually futile, even if the strikers won; trade unions, whose aim was to secure immediate concessions through strikes or the threat of strikes, were therefore useless; the one permanent answer was socialism, which could be achieved only through the Socialist Trade and Labor Alliance and the Socialist Labor party.

Though apologetic for not entertaining, DeLeon revealed an unaccustomed light touch. At the beginning, he was the patronizing professor trying once more to instruct dull pupils in spite of "persistent errors," and "illusions." But before he had finished, DeLeon laid aside the bludgeon of logic and began to appeal to his crowd by using the needle of wit and ridicule.

He posed as an employing capitalist and brushed aside rhetorical inquiries about the origin of his wealth as "un-American." Enjoying his performance as a leisured stockholder, he continued the caricature: "If it is too cold in the north I go down to Florida; if it is too hot there I go to the Adirondack mountains; occasionally I take a spin across the Atlantic and run the gauntlet of all the gambling dens . . . ; I spend my time with fast horses and faster women." But surely the capitalist supplied management which deserved some return? DeLeon was scornful: the "work" of the capitalist class was "no more . . . productive" than the "intense mental strain . . . of the 'work' done by the pickpocket. . . ." Capital was only "the child of fraudulent failures and fires, of high-handed crime . . . or of . . . sneaking crime. . . ." No capitalist would dream of actually working for a living. The employer "will tell you, and pay his politicians, professors and political parsons, to tell you, that 'labor is honorable.' He is willing to let you have that undivided honor, and will do all he can that you may not be deprived of any part of it; but, as to himself, he has for work a constitutional aversion. . . ."

Nor could workers seek protection in the trade unions when machinery and a surplus of labor robbed them of bargaining power. Such outmoded organizations were not only useless under existing conditions; so depraved, so corrupt, so ignorant was their leadership that no capitalist and no worker could respect them. Then DeLeon sank the hook: "I shall not consider my time well spent with you if I . . . leave not behind me . . . local Alliances of . . . the Socialist Trade and Labor Alliance."

It was a virtuoso performance. Yet for all he accomplished, DeLeon might as well have addressed his usual crowd of dedicated Socialists. Like many of his speeches, "What Means This Strike?" was remarkable for what he left unsaid. The striker who looked under the oratorical gloss found no specific advice on conducting strikes, no assurances of financial support, no coal, no bread. Nothing, in fact, but the prospect that the cooperative commonwealth would some day extinguish want. Such was DeLeon's "answer to hunger here-and-now." [30]

The party tried to take advantage of the great effort of its chief. Eventually Thomas Hickey organized a local Alliance with twenty-one charter members. Before he could enlarge the nucleus, he was sent to combat Carey in Haverhill. Socialists in New York raised $50 for relief of the strikers, but total contributions from all sources amounted to less than twenty-five cents per striker per week at a time when 2,000 were trying to sustain themselves in hastily established soup kitchens. By the end of

30. The phrase is Howard Gitelman's; see his unpublished Ph.D. dissertation, "Attempts to Unify the Labor Movement, 1865–1900" (University of Wisconsin, 1960), Chapter 9, page 24. Gitelman points out that DeLeon "and his family lived on the border line of penury for the 'cause,' and it must never have occurred to him that the workers might not be willing to do the same" (p. 24).

March, the New Bedford Socialists were discouraged. The local organizer wrote Henry Kuhn that the strikers were badly divided; "a considerable number," he estimated, would return when the manufacturers opened the gates.[31] The *People*, absorbed in the threat of war with Spain, let the strike dribble away unnoticed to its inevitable conclusion.

While prospects for the Alliance dimmed in New Bedford, they brightened in Lynn, where persistent agitation among shoe workers seemed about to pay off. The Lynn Lasters, an affiliate of John F. Tobin's Boot and Shoe Workers, elected two Socialist Laborites to positions in the local organization. The Lynn union again pleased the S.L.P. when it sent a small contribution to a group of strikers in Lowell. Enclosed with the money was a letter from Fred S. Carter, secretary of the lasters, explaining that collective ownership was a more effective solution for labor's problems than a triumphant strike.[32] Under Carter's influence, the Lynn Lasters withdrew from the Boot and Shoe Workers' Union in mid-summer. The jubilant *People* predicted that affiliation with the S.T. & L.A. was only a matter of time.

But the shoe workers never fulfilled the party's hopes. The revolt against Tobin did spread among lasters in Essex County during the summer of 1898. Groups in Beverly, Danvers, Salem, Marblehead, Stoneham and Haverhill seceded from the Boot and Shoe Workers. But disaffection sprang less from Socialist ideology than from conditions in the shoe factories. Threatened with the loss of livelihood and skill, the lasters wanted Tobin to oppose the introduction of machinery, a policy which the latter thought futile. Though disgusted with Tobin's leadership,

31. *People*, February 27, 1898; March 13, 27, 1898; April 3, 1898; Hickey to N. Y. *Volkzeitung*, March 4, 1898, DeLeon Papers; James Hancock to Kuhn, March 31, 1898, SLP Papers.

32. J. H. Clohecy to DeLeon, March 29, 1898, SLP Papers; *People*, April 24, 1898.

the lasters would not substitute DeLeon. They formed an independent organization and repeatedly refused to join the S.T. & L.A.[33]

As the Socialist Trade and Labor Alliance met frustration in Massachusetts, so the Socialist Labor party feared political oblivion. The battle, of course, was not only with Republicans and Democrats; a "flank movement of capitalism, the Debs Democracy" had perversely entered the arena to confuse the voters.[34] For DeLeon no longer conceded the good intent of his Socialist rivals. In the summer of 1898, the Social Democracy had split. One faction, of which Eugene Debs was the spokesman, had formed the Social Democratic party to bring the cooperative commonwealth through political action. James Carey and the Massachusetts Social Democrats belonged to Debs's group. Daniel DeLeon reserved his harshest criticism for those who appealed to his minute political following.

Throughout 1898, the Massachusetts Socialist Laborites told each other how well they were doing. Worcester had a thousand Socialists of whom ten per cent had completed the required reading for membership in the local organization. Ruther boasted that the Debs movement had no prospect of success in Holyoke. Westfield proudly announced that the S.L.P. had polled six per cent of the vote in the town election.[35]

Behind this optimistic pose, however, the party's hierarchy must have been more sober. Michael Berry, for instance, admitted that the Social Democrats in Haverhill had the initiative in the fall campaign, even though he still hoped to defeat Carey. "The bunch of midnight assassins" had made so many slanderous accusations that

33. *Monthly Report,* July, August, 1898; see also the issue dated November, 1898–March, 1899. The Boot and Shoe Workers' Union Scrapbook I, in the union's archives in Boston, contains many clippings from Lynn newspapers on this dispute.
34. *People,* June 19, 1898.
35. L. D. Usher to Kuhn, n.d.; Ruther to Kuhn, February 6, 1898, SLP Papers; *People,* January 23, 1898; April 10, 1898.

the S.L.P. found it almost impossible to correct them in spite of frantic activity. Thomas Hickey wrote of his big audience in Groveland; unfortunately the crowd dwindled before he was able to make a collection so the party's war chest did not benefit by his effort. His rally in Haverhill, he continued, was preceded by a parade complete with a Negro band that had cost the party four dollars. Once again his listeners—Hickey estimated he had had 500—escaped as the hat was passing; total receipts amounted to thirty cents. The Haverhill *Gazette* reported that the S.L.P. did in fact draw attentive and reasonably large crowds in September. But the spectators, probably tired of the message that was the unvarying theme, thinned out as the campaign closed.[36]

While the S.L.P. was at least pretending to cover the state, Social Democrats concentrated their efforts, particularly in Haverhill. Here the Social Democrats hoped to cause a sensation in their initial campaign. In James F. Carey the party had a practiced, popular, and shrewd political strategist. Haverhill's major industry was the manufacture of shoes, and the Boot and Shoe Workers' Union, unafraid of political activity, advocated a socialist program. As early as January, 1898, John F. Tobin and James F. Carey addressed a meeting of local shoe workers. Tobin had urged the audience "to seek deliverance from their industrial bondage through the . . . ballot," while Carey extolled "the beauties and benefits of trade unionism." [37] Haverhill's normally dominant Republican machine was in temporarily bad repair, and the Democrats, after a brief and uninspiring resurgence, were retreating to a more congenial token opposition. Finally, an ugly labor dispute on the city's street railway line threatened the safety of riders and the peace of the community,

36. Berry to Kuhn, October 3, 1898; Hickey to Kuhn, October 25, 1898, SLP Papers; *Gazette*, September 21–November 4, 1898, *passim*.
37. *Gazette*, January 11, 1898.

and offered Socialists a splendid political opportunity. They exploited every advantage.

The *Gazette* warmly praised Carey's work in the Common Council. Though his attempt to legislate a two-dollar minimum wage and an eight-hour day for city employees failed to pass, the *Gazette* thought the reform not too generous for "men with families dependent upon them for support." When Carey refused to accept the customary pass from the local street railway company, the *Gazette* again applauded. Carey had succeeded, the paper said, "by the mere force of his example, in accomplishing much good. . . ." When a councilman tried to block a hearing for a discharged member of the street department, Carey gavelled him to silence. The president's conduct of the meeting, noted an editorial, was impeccable: "only men who have nothing to offer against sober argument . . . resort to filibustering. . . ." When a contractor tried to pass off shoddy work on the city, the *Gazette* noted that Councilman Carey and one other alert official had prevented the fraud. When Carey introduced legislation to require the city to run utility wires underground, the paper thought the project sound, but too expensive. It suggested that perhaps the utility companies should pay the cost. When the president of the Council himself resorted to parliamentary trickery in battling to limit the hours of municipal employees, the *Gazette* thought his performance justified because of the "heavy odds against him. . . ." After Carey succeeded in driving an amended bill on wages and hours through the city government, the superintendent of streets ignored the new regulations. Carey was irate; the *Gazette*, although disagreeing, complimented him for his willingness to fight for his cause "at all times and in all circumstances." [38]

Carey, in short, had a good record. He also had an ad-

38. *Ibid.*, January 8, 21, 22, 1898; March 5, 1898; April 8, 1898; May 28, 1898; July 21, 27, 1898; August 16–September 15, 1898, *passim*.

miring editorial champion, who intimated that he might prefer a larger arena: "President Carey . . . would make a very useful member of the legislature, and the *Gazette* hopes to see him there one of these days." John Wright's suggestion was not motivated solely by admiration. Republican leaders hoped a legislative campaign would eliminate Carey as a possible candidate for mayor. Carey took the bait. A caucus of Social Democrats nominated him for the General Court. Just two weeks before the election, the S.D.P. in another Haverhill district gave him a running mate when Louis M. Scates accepted a similar nomination.[39]

Scates had once been a shoe worker, and would later be a member of the staff of the Boot and Shoe Workers' Union. In the fall of 1898, he was an unemployed street car conductor, who had resigned rather than submit to the demands of his employers. His presence on the ticket was shrewdly calculated. Scates's candidacy not only demonstrated support for the conductors, but also put the Social Democrats squarely on the popular side of the struggle.

The dispute was the result of management's demand that street car conductors be bonded at their own expense, a step that implied that employees were liable in case of accidents. The conductors voted unanimously not to apply for bonds, but the corporation would not compromise. Within the week more than half the conductors resigned rather than apply for the required insurance. Public support for the conductors brought Haverhill to the edge of violence. Stones flew, accidents were narrowly averted, a mob almost derailed a car, and inevitably arrests ensued. James Carey worked within the municipal government to obtain a solution that would satisfy

39. *Ibid.,* August 25, 1898; September 15, 1898; October 27, 1898; *Saturday Evening Criterion* (Haverhill), June 15, 1901.

the conductors. In public appearances he warned against disorder and pointedly reminded his listeners that they could express their resentment at the ballot box.[40]

A few days before the election, the Social Democrats brought the campaign to a peak with a rally so large that hundreds were turned away. James F. Carey, the chairman for the evening, introduced the two principal speakers, John F. Tobin and Eugene V. Debs. Tobin, who, rumor had it, was toying with the idea of seeking Socialist support to try to unseat Samuel Gompers, pleaded for combined economic and political action through the trade union and the Social Democratic party. Debs called up the spirits of New England's abolitionists in denouncing the new wage slavery. The cheers from the campaign lasted through the balloting. No one was particularly surprised when Carey trounced three opponents and polled nearly sixty per cent of the total vote. But Scates also won a slim plurality on the strength of only one issue: the trouble on the street railway line.[41]

Editors in the capital of the Commonwealth faced the prospect of Socialist legislators calmly. The Boston *Herald* thought the two Socialists "intelligent men," who would "do no harm," and might "relieve the monotony of the . . . proceedings." The *Transcript,* guessing Carey's bark was worse than his bite, predicted that he would turn out to be an "inoffensive" and "harmless" legislator. The Haverhill *Gazette,* picking up both remarks, reproved the blasé Bostonians: "Mr. Carey means what he says. He may entertain erroneous views . . . but he will go to the state house with clean hands and return in the same condition. When he speaks to the assembled wisdom of the state his hearers may depend upon it that they are listen-

40. *Gazette,* August 26–October 22, 1898, *passim.*
41. *Ibid.,* November 5, 8, 1898; Berry to DeLeon, November 27, 1898, DeLeon Papers.

ing to a man whose vote is not for sale to the highest bidder, a fact well worth considering." [42]

Socialists reacted along party lines. Social Democrats were ecstatic; Socialist Laborites were irate. In October, the *Social Democratic Herald* had scented success; when the results were in, the headline proclaimed "Our First Campaign A Glorious Victory." "At last, American Socialism, springing naturally from American conditions, is finding expression in the only effective way. . . ." A Socialist Laborite, writing to Henry Kuhn, echoed the *Transcript's* estimate of Carey, who, he thought, would soon become involved with the "boodle machine," and "never pose as a Socialist again." The *People* referred to Scates with some accuracy as Carey's "silent partner," and scorned the "native American movement" that consisted of "ex-Pops, mistaken Democrats, non-union wrecking fakirs, and friends of the capitalists." The S.L.P. could never decide whether to smear Carey's supporters as native American, or, as another correspondent put it, "a corral of blind followers made up of some few New England 'Yanks,' more anarchist Jews, . . . and still more French Canadians." The vision of the Socialist Laborites may have been blurred by the election returns: the De-Leonite who ran against Carey received exactly 49 votes to Carey's 751; Scates mustered 674, while his S.L.P. opponent received 86 ballots. [43]

The Haverhill Social Democrats celebrated at a victory rally that closed one campaign and opened another. With the municipal election only a few weeks away, they decided to present a full ticket, headed by John C. Chase for mayor. The platform began with the usual Socialist preamble. The immediate steps toward socialism were even

42. *Gazette*, November 11, 15, 1898.
43. *SDH*, October 1, 1898; November 12, 1898; *People*, November 27, 1898; *Gazette*, November 10, 1898; Badger to Kuhn, November 8, 1898; Berry to Kuhn, October 3, 1898, SLP Papers.

more familiar, since Massachusetts Socialists had for years talked about public ownership of utilities, the abolition of the contract system of public construction, and public works projects for the unemployed. Other proposals were more local: Carey's demands for the eight-hour day and the two-dollar wage were included, as was his proposal that all sessions of the city government be open to the public. The Social Democrats also declared for abolition of unguarded railway crossings within the city, an issue that would eventually serve them well.[44]

The *Gazette*, still fair in its coverage of the campaign, found "people as a rule in hearty sympathy" with "many things these Socialists ask." John C. Chase was "so good a man" that it would require a major effort to keep him out of City Hall. But Chase's party was "wholly unfitted by reason of inexperience to cope with the issues which press for settlement in Haverhill today." The *Gazette* had another reservation: could the city's treasury stand the expense of the Socialist program?

Prohibitionists, normally Republicans, were dissatisfied with Moses Dow, the regular Republican nominee, and put up Frank Rand, a strong independent candidate, who ultimately polled as many votes as the incumbent Democrat. Socialists grew increasingly optimistic. Two S.D.P. candidates for alderman spurned a proffered endorsement from the Democrats, a gesture that reflected as much confidence as it did ideological orthodoxy. (Michael Berry noted disgustedly that the Social Democrats would get Democratic votes anyway.) Workingmen around the city began to bet on a Socialist victory, forming syndicates when necessary to cover large wagers on other candidates.

Even the Socialist Labor party was dispirited. A few days after the election of Carey and Scates, Michael Berry wrote of elation in the Social Democratic camp and gloom

44. *Gazette*, November 15, 17, 1898.

among the Socialist Laborites. Carey's party, he reported, had over 200 members and was enrolling new ones "by the gross." He feared that the Social Democrats would elect Chase and "several more" in the municipal race. "Every labor fakir [i.e., trade unionist] in town is with them," and "the treasury" of the Central Labor Union was "at their disposal." By contrast, Berry could count eighteen members of the S.L.P., and, of these, only six could contribute toward the campaign. Berry asked the National Committee to ship him free literature, in Hebrew, French, and English. He wanted to challenge Debs to come to Haverhill and debate. He hoped Daniel DeLeon would also visit the city to show the working people that he was a human being, and not, as the "Carey element" had depicted him, the "Spanish Inquisition intensified 100%," who every year spitefully drove the best men from the party in order to slow Socialist growth.

Daniel DeLeon duly arrived in Haverhill to show the face behind the myth. But his speech was no match for his effort in New Bedford. He gave an economic interpretation of American history from the Revolution to the Spanish-American War. He derided political success, an odd note in a campaign speech. The number of ballots, he argued, was not important; only principles had significance. "We can imagine no worse calamity for the Socialist Labor Party than to have a candidate elected by a constituency that did not comprehend what it was supporting."

DeLeon need not have worried. His candidate for mayor obtained sixty-eight class-conscious ballots. John C. Chase received nearly 2,300 votes, 350 more than the Republican nominee, and almost forty per cent of the total. And John C. Chase was mayor-elect of Haverhill.[45]

45. Berry to DeLeon, November 21, 25, 1898; Berry to Kuhn, November 25, 1898, SLP Papers; Berry to DeLeon, November 27, 1898, DeLeon Papers; *Gazette*, November 18–December 10, 1898, *passim*.

The Social Democrats had organized their effort superbly. They had counted with such care that their estimate of Chase's total vote missed by only seven ballots. A week before the election, the Haverhill correspondent of the *Social Democratic Herald* predicted the election of Chase, three of seven aldermen, and an increase to three in the party's representation on the Common Council. The results exactly fulfilled expectations.

With the exception of DeLeon's *People*, the Socialist press was exultant. "Outpost Number One Of The Citadel Of Capitalism" has fallen, headlined the *Social Democratic Herald*, which quoted Eugene Debs's warm remarks about "alert and progressive" trade unionists in Haverhill. There were, said Debs, "none better anywhere." The *Herald* introduced Chase to the nation in two glowing articles. The *Appeal to Reason*, Julius Wayland's widely-read Socialist paper, thought Chase's victory had "done more to direct attention to Socialism than could have been done by any other means.[46]

The Boston press continued to view with detachment the peculiarities of Haverhill's voters. The *Herald* distinguished among the various Socialist parties for its uninformed readers and pointed out that Chase owed his election to the split in Republican ranks, a judgment shared by the New York *Sun* and the *Outlook*. The *Outlook*, accustomed to finding a German base for Socialist agitation, was surprised to discover Socialist strength in "the most American of all the larger places in Massachusetts." The Boston *Transcript* was no more alarmed than it had been over Carey's election. "The Socialist," said the *Transcript* sagely, "is very much like other men."

Give him the opportunity to speak freely . . . and give him responsibility, and it is not long before he begins to weigh his

---

46. *SDH*, December 3, 1898; December 17, 1898; January 7, 1899; *Appeal to Reason* (Girard, Kansas), December 24, 1898.

words and to be careful of his actions. It is not at all unlikely that after a while he will develop into an extreme conservative. His elevation to public service will . . . [make] him a safer citizen, as it has opened his eyes to the fact that it is one thing to criticize and quite another to administer the affairs of government. . . .[47]

The *Gazette,* like the Boston *Herald,* attributed Chase's election partly to divisions among Republicans. But it also stressed the uncompromising honesty and ability of the Socialist candidates, and the skill with which they canvassed the city and exploited the still-simmering street railway dispute. John Wright wondered how their proposals would affect the tax rate, but, on the whole, he too was placid.

. . . it is dollars to doughnuts that, with the exception of a ripple here and there upon the surface of municipal life, things will move along in the same old way. Many of Mayor Chase's recommendations smack too strongly of a tendency to provide for the lame and lazy to find much favor in this thriving New England city.[48]

While they were deservedly overshadowed by the results in Haverhill, the elections in Massachusetts also held one cheery item for Socialist Laborites. Moritz Ruther, whom DeLeon never completely trusted, was elected to the Holyoke Board of Aldermen. In 1898, DeLeon had to look hard for victories, so Ruther's became a triumph for orthodox socialism, though in fact his program differed but little from that of Carey.

For years Ruther had adapted socialism to the taste of a

47. *Outlook,* December 17, 1898, 939; *Literary Digest,* January 14, 1899, 35.
48. *Gazette,* December 10, 1898. The last phrase of this quotation is a clue to the *Gazette's* support of the Socialists. The editor was proud of his city, and if he did not personally endorse socialism or Social Democratic candidates, he would defend them against detractors who suggested that there was something queer about Haverhill. See, e.g., editorial notes in the *Gazette* for December 8, 1898; March 28, 1899; July 17, 1899.

growing following in Holyoke. Once the votes were counted, he sent his excuses to New York. In 1896, for instance, his vote in the municipal election had been greater than the party's total in the November race. Ruther claimed he had made no explicit appeal for the votes of non-Socialists. Rather, a new city charter had made the municipal ballot very confusing. (Only a Socialist Laborite would ever have explained why he got too many votes.) Although the Holyoke S.L.P. had made the party's standard platform "suitable to our local affairs" and although "local conditions" sometimes made "exceptional tactics necessary," the local had hewed to the party line.

Before accepting that party line, Ruther had to check his natural instinct. He protested when the *People* decided that the United States Post Office was no longer an example of the efficiency to be gained under governmental operation. "In my opinion," he wrote, "any argument will do as long as we accomplish results." He appealed to ideological authority: "did not Marx tell us," he asked, to "try and assimulate [*sic*] our agitation in the line of thought of those people whom we want to reach?" Ruther, it will be recalled, had also been blind to deviation. He had hired F. G. R. Gordon and defended him when attacked; he admired Debs long after such admiration was officially disapproved; he had been slow to join the clamor for the head of James F. Carey. Yet Ruther never openly broke with DeLeon. In January, 1898, Harry Carless, a national party functionary, wrote that Ruther still believed Debs "innocent," that a meeting in Holyoke had been unsatisfactory, and that Ruther was making excuses for Carey. If the hierarchy contemplated corrective action, however, an almost simultaneous letter from Ruther forestalled such a decision. The comrades around here, wrote Ruther with his usual enthusiasm, "say Carless beats Debs all to hell and I agree with them." Later

Ruther publicly rejected an invitation to organize for the Social Democrats in his area. After his election in 1899, he once more acknowledged DeLeon's ideological leadership. The Holyoke alderman, in searching his files, had come across some of DeLeon's letters.

. . . I owe it to you to admit what you prophesied has happened. What seemed to me then a harsh and dogmatical letter seems now a bit of mighty good and friendly advice. Events proved your words true. . . . It took me several years to see the truth, but it is all the plainer now. . . . In conclusion, let me say that The People is laying a solid foundation for Socialism and when I now hear people kicking against The People I know that they do not understand Socialism. The work of The People will be appreciated and honored when such things as Gordon, Casson, and Carey lay [sic] rotting in the ground, forgotten.[49]

Perhaps the fact that Ruther so often professed his loyalty enabled DeLeon to forgive his political activity. For Ruther's platform and his record in office were strikingly similar to those of the Social Democrats that DeLeon had scathingly criticized as "reformist." Ruther won on a program that advocated a more democratic and economical city government, better recreational facilities, and more educational opportunity. Like the Social Democrats in Haverhill, the Holyoke S.L.P. demanded that the city itself undertake public works instead of letting contracts to local businessmen. Like the Social Democrats in Haverhill, the Holyoke S.L.P. favored municipal ownership, but its program was more specific: the city should operate the coal yards, an employment bureau, public baths and reading rooms, a pharmacy, liquor stores, and housing devel-

49. Ruther to Kuhn, October 17, 1896; December 13, 1896; December 15, 1898; January 16, 1898; Carless to Kuhn, January 15, 1898, SLP Papers; *People*, June 5, 1898; Ruther to DeLeon, December 13, 1896, DeLeon Papers; Ruther to DeLeon, March 27, 1899, quoted in Kuhn, "Reminiscences of Daniel DeLeon," in *Daniel DeLeon: The Man and His Work* (New York, 1934), 128.

opments, as well as public utilities. In campaign speeches, Ruther also suggested that the Connecticut River be made navigable to Holyoke, that the city erect a new union railway terminal, and that nearby streams be stocked with fish.

The new Holyoke alderman generated a flurry of activity with his first appearance at City Hall. He introduced an order authorizing the city to employ tramps; he wanted a rat-infested building torn down; he asked for new sidewalks and wider streets; he suggested that the city buy some vacant lots and build a skating rink. Before Holyoke had quite recovered from the first onslaught, Ruther was back with more. He wanted a new bridge, some model homes, construction of a municipal electric plant. He asked that poolrooms be padlocked at eleven o'clock. He opposed an appropriation of $500 to be spent to welcome President William McKinley to the city.[50]

Ruther lacked Carey's political skill. When Carey was the only Socialist in Haverhill's administration, he chose his issues wisely, rarely taking a stand just for the record and then only when he thought he had public support. He was less obtrusive, less frenzied than Ruther. And, if Carey did not write his program into law, he did secure a broader following for the reforms he sought. Moritz Ruther could not even close Holyoke's poolrooms.

Although the Social Democrats of Massachusetts were more successful than those of any other state, they nonetheless had to take their encouragement from trifles. Amesbury elected a Social Democratic selectman in 1899 and added a school committeeman in 1900; by 1903 all three selectmen were Socialists. Voters in Georgetown chose a Socialist overseer of the poor. Newburyport Socialists entered municipal politics in 1899, finished second

50. *People,* November 20, 1898; Ruther Scrapbook, SLP Papers.

in the mayoral race, but won one seat on the Common Council and another on the school committee. An alderman in Chicopee, a steadily increasing vote in Worcester, loss by a small margin in Milford or Holbrook, nine hundred votes in Boston for a Populist-turned-Socialist of impeccable New England lineage—such was the evidence of vitality.[51]

James F. Carey's full schedule helped stir enthusiasm. While campaigning in September, 1899, Carey found time to organize and secure charters for four new branches. Sessions of the General Court left evenings free to talk all over the state. Each speech meant a notice in some local paper; though the notice was often small, it was sometimes favorable. In March, 1903, Carey made twenty-six addresses and was only slightly more busy than usual. A "mishap to Carey's throat," a Socialist paper once observed, would have brought serious "misfortune to the party in Massachusetts."[52]

Haverhill provided a platform as well as leadership. Sometimes, as in Everett in 1899, the Haverhill program was simply adopted without change. Occasionally, as in Boston in 1899, a platform publicly acknowledged indebtedness to the Haverhill organization. More often, Haverhill's basic proposals were adapted to another community's situation.[53] The state platform also bore the marks of Haverhill's draftsmen, for Carey, Chase, or William Mailly often introduced or rewrote the resolutions.[54]

51. *SDH,* March 18, 1899; *HSD,* November 25, 1899; December 2, 16, 23, 1899; March 10, 1900; the *Worker* (New York), January 4, 1903; March 15, 1903; Kangaroo *People,* March 24, 1901.

52. *SDH,* October 7, 1899; *Worker,* April 27, 1902; March 12, 1903; Kangaroo *People,* April 14, 1901.

53. *HSD,* December 2, 1899; cf. the platforms of Adams (Kangaroo *People,* March 24, 1901); Chicopee (*Worker,* November 24, 1901); Brockton (Chapter 4 below).

54. See, e.g., *Gazette,* May 29, 1899, for an account of the convention of 1899, or *Worker,* September 14, 1902, for Mailly's proposed new constitution.

While Socialist Laborites continued to insist that these platforms promised a miserable patchwork of reforms when the situation called for sterner measures, the S.L.P. was more an annoyance than a rival. In 1899, for the last time, the S.L.P.'s candidate for governor outpolled his Social Democratic opponent by about 2,500 votes. By 1900, the Social Democrats ran almost 5,000 votes ahead of the S.L.P.

Social Democrats rejoiced when they buried the S.L.P.'s state ticket, for overtaking the major parties seemed temporarily impossible. In Haverhill, however, these opponents were well within reach. In April, 1899, the *Gazette* noted that Socialists were already campaigning for the fall elections, and warned that ignoring them might "prove fatal once more." A few days later, editor John B. Wright lectured the major parties in the city for their corruption, lack of principle, and conspiracy to keep important issues out of elections. These failings, he said, had brought the Socialists their following.

The campaigns of 1899 tested Socialist strength, for Haverhill's Democrats and Republicans frequently combined forces to banish the upstart Socialists. When Democrats were on the ballot, their effort was minimal, while the Republicans mounted an expensive, energetic campaign. William H. Moody, the G.O.P. Congressman from the district, whom Theodore Roosevelt would make successively Secretary of the Navy, Attorney-General and an Associate Justice of the Supreme Court, set the tone for other Republicans. Socialist candidates, he conceded, were honest and even capable men. But they lacked judgment; they rejected individualism; they subjected their office-holders to the party's dictation; they claimed more than they could possibly deliver. Other Republicans elaborated the theme: socialism, from Plato to Brook Farm, had never worked; Carey could not really do anything for his constituents; a Republican administration had purchased the city's water works, which proved the party's acceptance of prudent municipal ownership. Republicans expected to win all but one contest.[55]

The exception was James Carey's seat in the General Court. In September, the G.O.P. had trouble finding a nominee, for Carey's political appeal intimidated prospective aspirants. Socialists used Carey's record, and that of his colleague Louis M. Scates, as the raw material of their campaign. The party's newly-established weekly paper, the *Social Democrat*, held that the party could campaign without apologizing "for the actions of the Social Democrats occupying office during the past year," and that this resource assured a happy outcome. Social Democrats, motivated "solely by love of country and their fellow men," would prevail against "all the corruption and bribery of the capitalists" and "win the final victory against the gold of the world." [56]

While Carey's seat seemed safe—he himself said the odds were 10 to 3—Scates's position was precarious. The street railway dispute had cooled and he had no substitute issue. His district, unlike Carey's, had a high percentage of middle class voters. Scates himself never developed a personal following. Even though a Democrat disregarded the party's intent and secured a place on the ballot, Republicans expected to beat Scates.

The election allowed Republicans to celebrate victories and Social Democrats to salvage self-respect. Scates lost by three hundred votes, but he and every other Social Democrat on the ballot had greater support than ever before. In a city-wide race, Joe Bean, the Socialist nominee for the Massachusetts Senate, was less than two hundred

55. *Gazette*, April 27, 1899; May 3, 1899; October 21, 26, 30, 1899.
56. *HSD*, October 7, 1899; the equation of gold with evil in the final phrase may be an echo of Populism.

votes short of the victorious Republican. James Carey collected more than sixty per cent of the ballots in his district to win a second term.[57]

Other politicians sought a formula that would knit anti-Socialists together for the municipal campaign. In mid-October, Republican and Democratic leaders were reportedly haggling over their respective portions of a non-partisan Citizens' ticket, which was finally announced in November. Headed by Mellen Pingree, a corporation attorney, as the mayoral nominee, the candidates were united only in opposition to Socialism and had to evade substantive questions. The vague platform invited Socialists to take the initiative. Scenting a winning issue, they stressed the hazards of unguarded railway crossings and charged that Republican legislators had thwarted Carey's attempt to shield the city from this danger. A referendum on the matter would be on the ballot, but the Citizens' coalition took no position on elimination of grade crossings. Nor did the Socialists' opponents take a stand on the eight-hour day for municipal employees, which was also to be settled by referendum. Candidates were pledged to administer the city's business as if it were their own, and to use their best judgment on other questions of city government.

Since the platform was unlikely to stir enthusiasm, and since neither party was interested in a non-partisan campaign, Pingree sought to make anti-socialism exciting. News columns in the *Gazette* reflected popular reluctance to swallow the contrived ticket that John B. Wright's editorials supported. The paper also ran a daily unidentified advertisement disguised as a news story. It explained "DANGERS THAT LURK IN THE VAGARIES OF SOCIAL DEMOCRACY," and other such topics. The Citizens' party professed

57. *Gazette*, September 30, 1899; October 27, 30, 1899; *HSD*, November 11, 1899.

respect for individual Socialists but denounced the Socialist "discipline" which could override the judgment of these men. The coalition dropped this issue, however, when Carey responded that the Citizens' ticket was hardly in a position to discuss "bossism." The claim that an impractical Socialist platform would mean higher taxes also failed to generate much response. And so Mellen Pingree began to talk about un-Americanism, free love, the threat to organized religion, and other subversive elements implicit in Socialist doctrine. Socialists held their meetings on Sunday; they set aside "New England traditions . . ."; the doctrine was "imported from foreign countries where monarchies [were] prevalent."

Such charges did not describe Haverhill's Socialists, as most voters were aware. Socialist candidates were well-known in the community; they had occupied municipal office without taxing churches or abolishing marriage. Social Democrats talked not of atheism but of wages, hours, schools, grade crossings, and municipal ownership. They nominated candidates in open caucus, not in a secret committee meeting. They had a platform that was not an obvious attempt to be all things to all men. And they were enthusiastically confident. Just once did they slip into mere opposition, the posture that the coalition had constantly to assume. When the Citizens' ticket was first announced, the *Social Democrat*'s unguarded language betrayed fear: ". . . with the shameless disregard for decency and honor only to be expected from charlatans and demagogues . . . , the republican and democratic leaders of Haverhill have again joined hands . . . to perserve [*sic*] to themselves and their masters perpetuity in public office at the expense of society."

The Socialists soon became more constructive. They had brought the city one step nearer the eight-hour day, the two-dollar daily wage, and the abolition of grade crossings. They were doggedly pursuing the local gas utility and were about to secure cheaper rates for its customers. They had built streets and sewers more cheaply than previous administrations. Eugene Debs was very moderate when he brought the campaign to a climax. Socialists did not oppose private property. They were fighting to preserve small businessmen from predatory capitalists. From the nominations to the final rousing parade, the Socialists made few tactical errors. Chase predicted he would poll 3,500 votes and win by 300.[58]

All sides agreed with the *Gazette*'s description of the campaign as "the most memorable within the recollection of the oldest inhabitant." Chase's estimate proved once more the industry and reliability of the party's canvassers. He received 3,542 votes and a plurality of 223; he gained more than 1,200 votes over his winning effort of 1898, and an absolute majority for the first time. Swept in with Chase were Joe Bean, Parkman B. Flanders, and Louis Scates as alderman, and three councilmen. The Socialists collected election bets—one leading businessman was said to have counted his losses in four figures—and celebrated what one volunteer campaign worker called "the greatest event in the history of Haverhill. . . ."

When political observers outside the city suggested that Socialists flourished where wages were low, the *Social Democrat* set the record straight. Shoe workers in Haverhill and Brockton were better paid than textile workers in Fall River or Lawrence. Indeed, Socialism could only prosper initially among the aristocracy of the labor movement. "The hardest workers in the Socialist movement . . . are the most intelligent, the cream of the working class. . . . The social revolution must come from a proletaire who can think. . . . The cooperative

58. *Gazette*, October–November, 1899, *passim;* HSD, October 28–December 9, 1899, *passim*.

commonwealth cannot be built upon ignorance or despair. In Lowell, Lawrence, and other mill cities, the Social Democratic movement is gaining a foothold . . . among the most intelligent of the working class. . . ." [59]

Michael Berry, who received just sixty votes as the S.L.P. candidate against Chase, was more accurate than usual in explaining the Social Democratic victory. Chase and his party had successfully tied themselves to the abolition of grade crossings, which the voters approved by a handsome margin. Furthermore, Berry continued, "the well-known middle class nature of the S.D.P." had allowed disgusted citizens safely to demonstrate unhappiness with the dictated coalition ticket. He disapproved of the S.D.P.'s use of a band, of Carey's humor, and of pseudo-Socialist doctrine that contained just enough radicalism to catch the unwary worker, while never passing "the bounds of a 'middle-of-the-road' populist." But Berry correctly judged that such tactics had attracted votes.

Much of what Berry wrote merely gave a different emphasis to John B. Wright's interpretation. The *Gazette's* editor knew that ambitious politicians in both parties resented the coalition ticket. "The number of those disaffected" in this way, Wright thought, "was sufficiently large" to account for the result. Socialism had not really blossomed in Haverhill, nor was private property in danger. Rather the voters of the city had demonstrated a vague desire for reform and an unmistakable disgust with political leadership that had too long served itself better than the community. The Social Democrats, in fact, had won in spite of socialism, not because of it. [60]

As office-holders, Social Democrats were unable to enact dramatic reform, let alone deliver the cooperative

59. *HSD,* November 18, 1899; December 9, 16, 1899; *Gazette,* December 6, 1899.
60. *People,* January 7, 1900; *Gazette,* December 6, 7, 11, 1899.

commonwealth. Chase himself knew the folly of high expectations and warned his supporters not to hope for too
much. In assessing his first term for a national magazine,
he admitted that his achievements were "confined mainly
to minor reforms in municipal government." The Socialists had a ready alibi; political opposition in City Hall, in
the State House, or in the courts, combined with restrictions in the municipal charter and the state constitution,
stymied their efforts.[61] The explanation was no substitute
for results. And results the Socialists could not produce.

Early in Chase's first administration the Socialists tried
to force the local gas company, which had just paid a fifty
per cent dividend, to reduce rates. The utility announced
a token reduction, which Socialists sought to increase by
appeal to the state regulatory commission. The utility ob-
structed the investigation. When the commission ordered
lower charges, the company took the issue to court and
maintained its former rate structure pending a decision.
Before the courts could rule, Chase was out of office. The
maddening retreat from the local level to other echelons
of government was a pattern Socialists recognized. James
Carey vented his exasperation after a similar experience:
"When I was in the city council of Haverhill fighting for a
shorter work day, [my opponents] told me to go to the
legislature; now [they] tell me to go to Congress for a national law. When I get there and demand it, they will tell
me to go to hell." [62]

Most of Chase's proposals were blocked without re-
course to other governmental levels. His appointments
were systematically tabled. Aldermen stripped him of his
power to appoint them to committees. When the referen-

61. John C. Chase, "Municipal Socialism in America," *Independent*,
January 25, 1899, 250; *SDH,* December 31, 1898.
62. *Gazette,* April 13, 25, 1899; May 2, 1899; November 21–December
15, 1899, *passim; HSD,* January 27, 1900; Kangaroo *People,* June 17,
1900.

dum bound the city to an eight-hour day, the Common Council voted to reduce wages in proportion, and a seemingly endless discussion ensued before the two-dollar wage was restored. An attempt to review the franchise of the local street railway in order to force better service failed to get enough support in the city's legislative bodies, as did a motion to require the telephone company to use union labor on work permitted by a city franchise. An attempt to build a school with city-employed union labor was blocked by an injunction. During the campaign of 1899, the anti-Socialist city treasurer warned that Chase's expenditure would necessitate a bond issue to keep the city solvent. Street maintenance stopped. The treasurer announced that he was making ingenious transfers of funds to enable the city to meet immediate obligations. After the election, when it was time to pay salaries, he suddenly had plenty of resources and said the city's financial plight had been exaggerated.[63]

Carey was doomed to similar frustration in Boston. He and other Socialist legislators regularly introduced several bills that were just as regularly interred in committee. Their record was progressive and fulfilled the pledges of the party's platform. But it was a record of almost unrelieved defeat. Socialists asked the legislature to require school attendance to age 16, two years beyond the statutory minimum. The first time the measure lost, Carey was eloquently enraged. Opponents had not produced "a single rational argument" against his bill. He dismissed the assertion that Massachusetts mills would be unable to compete if forced to give up cheap child labor. This statement, he thought, deserved a wide audience, for certainly a society that relied on child labor was seriously sick. Massachusetts had long enjoyed a tradition of leadership

63. Based on nearly weekly accounts in *HSD*, 1899–1900 and even more frequent accounts in the *Gazette*.

of righteous causes; Carey mentioned Bunker Hill and William Lloyd Garrison. Now, he suggested, legislators should restore a healthy flush to the cheeks of children and a sparkle to their eyes. The bill got scant support. Carey soon learned to take defeat in stride.

For losses were constant. When a bill to require railroads to compensate employees for injuries sustained in accidents could not pass, a bill for public ownership of transportation plainly stood little chance. The attempt to curb corporate power by forcing lobbyists to register was as futile as the attempt to curb a judge's power to interfere in labor disputes. Socialists could not protect the public from allegedly exorbitant interest rates on installment sales nor withhold the first ten dollars of a worker's wages from attachment to satisfy debts. They could not secure home rule for cities, nor even municipal use of initiative and referendum without legislative consent. The eight-hour day remained a local option, but the authority to own and operate a gas company or an ice house was not.[64]

While the Socialist representatives often annoyed fellow legislators, they were admired by the reform-minded Springfield *Republican.* Its review of the 1900 session found the two Socialists more deserving of public attention than any other two men in the General Court. They were "fearless fighters"; they had a "mission to perform," and "political principles on which to act. . . ." They seemed "to have a closer touch with the . . . progress of the times and with the uplift of humanity" than other members. They were sometimes extravagant, sometimes unwise, sometimes unfair. But their presence in the legislature had been good for the state. The Boston *Traveller,*

64. James F. Carey, *Child Labor* (leaflet in "Social Democratic Series," Vol. I, #2); see *HSD*, October 28, 1899 and October 27, 1900, for reviews of two legislative sessions.

more succinct, wished only that Carey were "a republican in good standing" so that some of his legislation, which deserved to pass, would do so.[65] The suggestion, made in jest, could have been seriously advanced a decade later. For much of James F. Carey's socialistic program would then be sound progressive Republican doctrine.

65. Quoted in *HSD*, July 21, 1900; January 26, 1901.

CHAPTER IV

Brockton: Socialism in One City

In Brockton, as in Haverhill, political reformers periodically tempted voters to slough off traditional partisan loyalties. In Brockton, as in Haverhill, the majority of these voters were shoe workers; in greater numbers than in Haverhill, they were members of the Boot and Shoe Workers' Union. The union backed political action to obtain government ownership of the means of production. As the nineteenth century closed, Brockton joined Haverhill in the vanguard of American Socialism.

The Socialist movements of Haverhill and Brockton shared more than the overriding importance of the shoe industry in each community. Both cities had relatively small numbers of foreign-born citizens.[1] Both had usually been found in the Republican column on election day. Many Socialist leaders in both cities had served an apprenticeship in labor's earlier political efforts; almost all had been Populists. In each case, they knew which issues would interest local voters. Connection with local unions kept Socialists aware of the immediate concerns of the workers in their neighborhood; the problems of the international working class did not obscure those of the shoe

1. The *Outlook* (New York), twice remarked that the Massachusetts Socialist movement did not have the conventional immigrant base (December 17, 1898, 939; December 16, 1899, 904).

worker next door. In neither city was a grasp of orthodox socialist doctrine the key to prominence.

The Brockton organization was more parochial than that of Haverhill, and sometimes did not give even lip service to the Socialist faith. Haverhill was more interested in national party affairs and achieved more national recognition. Brockton Socialists were rarely concerned with matters beyond the city limits, and almost never beyond the Commonwealth of Massachusetts. They learned to cope with the common problems of Socialists—capitalism, Catholicism, conservative craft unions, Republicans, Democrats. They had more difficulty enforcing prohibition, disciplining personal ambition, and finding fresh issues to inspire a sated electorate. These problems were unusual partly because they were so completely local; they were also unusual because they stemmed from success.

In 1885, Carlton Beals, a young shoe cutter, won election to the Brockton Common Council on the People's ticket, the local manifestation of the Greenback party. So satisfactory was his record that he was re-elected with Democratic support in 1886. When Beals moved to another ward the following year, he missed re-election by eleven votes on an independent Workingman's slate. Democrats again endorsed him when he carried Populist hopes in a campaign for the state Senate, but he fell about a hundred votes short. He opposed adoption of the silver panacea as a delegate to the Populist convention of 1896. Two years later, Carlton Beals was a charter member of the Brockton branch of the Social Democracy of America. At the end of 1899, a Social Democratic mayor-elect announced that Beals would be the first city marshal in the new century.

Carlton Beals was also a union man. He helped to organize his fellow cutters and was the first president of their local union. At the first convention of the Boot and Shoe Workers' Union, he worked to bring together rival shoe unions. He had served several terms as president of the Brockton Central Labor Union before becoming a municipal official.

The career of the mayor who appointed Beals was similar. A plumber by occupation, Charles H. Coulter too organized his craft in the city and was once president of his local union. Initially a Democrat, he switched to Populism and ran unsuccessfully for the state legislature in 1896 and 1897 with combined Democrat-Populist backing. Like Beals, he was an early member of the Brockton Social Democracy, and in 1898, he received 626 votes in his first bid for mayor. In 1899, Coulter received nearly 3,400 votes, and won by more than 1,500. Not quite thirty when inaugurated, Coulter was serving his fourth term as Beals' successor in the presidency of the Central Labor Union.[2]

Elected with Coulter were two Socialist aldermen, Elihu R. Perry and Reverend S. L. Beal. Perry, once a Democratic member of the Common Council, was a shoe cutter who had been an official of his branch of the Knights of Labor. Beal was a Universalist minister from the Campello district of the city, an area inhabited largely by shoe workers.

The Social Democratic movement in Brockton was rooted in the trade unions and under leadership whose socialism was not doctrinaire. Only dimly aware of Marxist theory, few Brockton Socialists had joined the Socialist Labor party. If they had heard of the Socialist Trade and Labor Alliance, what they had heard was probably uncomplimentary. The S.L.P. was never even an annoyance to the Social Democrats of Brockton. They did not have to live down its unsavory reputation, explain away its revo-

2. Brockton *Times*, December 6, 8, 1899; *Gazette*, December 8, 1899.

lutionary rhetoric, or apologize for its dual unionism. Nor did they ever feel obliged to measure their actions by a Marxist yardstick. If they knew it existed, they also knew it was irrelevant to their situation.

The Socialist Labor party did not fail for want of trying. In 1896, two Swedish fraternal organizations voted the S.L.P. an unsolicited endorsement; a year later Jeremiah O'Fihelly of North Abington, Daniel DeLeon's lieutenant in the area, hoped to put an organizer to work among Brockton's Swedes. "Poor fellows," wrote O'Fihelly patronizingly, "they meant well, but unfortunately they did not know anything about Socialism, the class struggle, or class consciousness."

Like the rest of Brockton, the Swedes remained unenlightened. In 1897, O'Fihelly enrolled seven men from the city in his North Abington local. Other recruits, he reported, had succumbed to the lure of "the Debs movement." He requested two thousand copies of the *People* to demonstrate the ideological shortcomings of the Social Democracy. He tried to book S.L.P. candidates for lectures among the Brockton unions. Preliminary negotiations seemed hopeful; then suddenly communication ceased. O'Fihelly later learned that the Central Labor Union, of which Charles Coulter was president, had quietly informed its affiliates that trade unions usually found contact with the S.L.P. to be harmful. Union leaders in Brockton, as O'Fihelly noted, were Social Democrats, an affiliation which colored their advice.[3]

J. F. Malloney, another S.L.P. organizer, took his turn in 1899. He chartered a section of fourteen members, and claimed a hundred readers for the *People*. When he re-

3. *People*, October 27, 1900; O'Fihelly to Kuhn, November 12, 1897; November 13, 1898; December 2, 1898, SLP Papers.

turned to check on the organization a few months later, his address attracted a dozen listeners. In November, when Malloney was the S.L.P.'s candidate for President, he got exactly fourteen votes in Brockton; 1,246 voters marked ballots for Eugene V. Debs. The Socialist Labor party did not bother to find a candidate to oppose Coulter in the municipal election, and washed its hands of the city. "Never in the history of the world," ran O'Fihelly's hyperbole, had "the higher set" been so favored and "the lower set" so persecuted as in Brockton. When DeLeon set O'Fihelly's article in type, the lead read "SOCIAL DEMO-CRATIC PARTY—THE LAST DESPERATE STAND OF THE BEATEN MIDDLE CLASS." The substance of the account suggested another loser.[4]

The Social Democratic party at its first formal meeting in Brockton hardly resembled a bulwark of any sort. Margaret Haile, a founder of the national organization, talked with a small group of Brockton Populists in August, 1898. Miss Haile was officially the secretary of the Massachusetts Social Democratic organization, and unofficially campaign manager, tour coordinator, reporter for the Socialist press, and chief recruiter. She left in Brockton a newly-established branch that at once began political activity.

For unlike Socialist Laborites, Brockton Social Democrats counted numbers as the measure of their movement. Coulter's first campaign more than tripled previous totals. The branch claimed an average attendance of four hundred at regular Sunday lectures during the winter of 1899. In the spring it hired a salesman to promote Socialism and Socialist literature in the area. When Mary Elizabeth Lease stopped in Brockton, she had an audience of eight hundred. When the state convention assembled in June,

4. *Times*, March 4, 1900; *People*, October 27, 1900.

Brockton had more paid-up members than any other local in the state; it was reportedly the largest Socialist local in the nation.[5]

Political agitation did not absorb all the energy. A Social Democratic Bicycle Club went on frequent outings. Athletic contests preceded James Carey's speech at the Labor Day celebration which the Socialists sponsored with the Central Labor Union. A Social Democratic band drew crowds to political rallies and also played on nonpartisan occasions. A women's auxiliary held social meetings. In Brockton, bands and bicycles substituted for the study clubs that Socialist organizations elsewhere often established to lighten the workers' leisure hours.[6]

But Brockton Socialists took campaigning seriously. As the election of 1899 approached, their strategists and those of other parties tried to estimate the political impact of an upheaval in the shoe unions. The Boot and Shoe Workers' Union, at its convention in 1899, had made constitutional changes requiring sharply increased dues to finance higher benefits and welfare funds. Outspokenly critical of these changes, Brockton locals accused John F. Tobin and his staff of ramming the program through a packed convention and then refusing to hold the referendum which members felt it was their right to demand. When Tobin remained adamant, the dispute was still bubbling as the fall political campaigns ran their course. Tobin shrewdly selected the case to prove his determination. After employees of the People's Cooperative Shoe

5. John B. Nutter, "The Social Democratic Party and the Brockton Municipal Election of 1899," Typescript in author's possession, 2–3; Roland D. Sawyer, *A Personal Narrative* (Farmington, Me., 1930), 73–74; Frederic Heath, ed., *Social Democracy Red Book* (Terre Haute, Ind., 1900), 112–113; *SDH*, February 11, 1899, April, 1899, *passim;* Sawyer Scrapbook 11.

6. *Times,* September 5, 14, 18, 1899; October 4, 11, 1899; see also Boot and Shoe Workers' Union Scrapbook 1, Archives of the Boot and Shoe Workers' Union, Boston, Mass.

Company refused to pay the higher dues, Tobin demanded the return of the union stamp. The company, in which the employees were financially interested, had a backlog of orders requiring the union label, which could be affixed only when Tobin's union organized the shop. Within a week the employees were again members in good standing.

Victory in one relatively small shop did not end resistance among the city's workers. Again threatening to recall the union stamp, Tobin secured the cooperation of William L. Douglas, who owned the largest of Brockton's shoe factories. Douglas's employees sullenly paid their dues rather than lose their jobs with a firm known as a fair and generous employer. Cutters at the R. B. Grover Company, on the other hand, refused to apply for the new Boot and Shoe Workers charter. Management honored the union stamp contract by firing the stubborn cutters; the union fulfilled its obligation by recruiting replacements to maintain uninterrupted production. In effect, the union had imported strike-breakers, an action that often thrust communities into labor violence. The displaced cutters blamed Tobin for bringing in scabs, but since work was plentiful, they took other jobs instead of battling at the picket lines. Unconvinced and often resentful, Brockton shoe workers remained in Tobin's union. A potentially explosive situation simply disappeared under the prosperity of high production and Brockton's relatively high wages.[7]

The labor dispute never ruffled the simultaneous political campaigns. Irritation with Tobin did not inhibit the growth of the Social Democratic party he was known to favor. Neither major party raised economic issues that might endanger local prosperity. Unions did not force candidates to take a stand on a matter of concern only to

7. *Times*, September 6, 1899–December 30, 1899, *passim;* see also Boot and Shoe Workers' Union Scrapbook 1.

labor. So the politicians talked about trusts or imperialism in the Philippines; when they turned to local issues, they stressed prohibition, taxes, and the climbing municipal budget.

The Social Democrats nominated candidates for the state legislature in August and campaigned until the municipal election was won in December. The typical Socialist rally began with a few selections by the Social Democratic band to attract a crowd. An earnest speaker— James Carey, or Fred G. R. Gordon, or a local candidate —gave an address about the maldistribution of wealth, or the inhumanity of the factory system, or the virtues of economic cooperation. Part of the crowd wandered off when the band stopped, but to groups ranging from fifty to a thousand or more, the Socialists delivered their plea. They also went to the crowds. The party hired a large wagon late in the campaign, loaded the band and F. G. R. Gordon into it, and stopped at several important intersections every evening, where the band played and Gordon spoke briefly. The show then moved on. When colder weather drove the rallies indoors, the band played part of its program outside and lured the crowd into the hall with the promise of more music, which was followed by the Socialist message.[8]

The major parties were unimpressed with both the message and the quality of the S.L.P. candidates. The Brockton *Democrat* snorted that Elihu Perry, a nominee for the General Court, was so devoid of conviction that he had been a member of every political party that offered him a nomination. Other candidates included a tinsmith, a newsdealer, and several shoe workers. Crowds, however, impress politicians, and those at Social Democratic rallies were noticeable. The local boasted four hundred dues-

8. *SDH*, July 15, 1899; Times, September 5, 23, 1899; October, 1899, *passim*.

paying members. Membership took a sudden spurt late in the campaign when the Democratic club in the fifth ward renounced its affiliation and joined the Social Democrats, who promptly sent the band to the celebration.

The major parties eventually decided to stamp out the Social Democrats. E. Gerry Brown, a Populist-turned-Bryan-Democrat, agreed to meet Gordon for nearly two and a half hours of debate. A member of the typographical union, Brown was a prominent labor leader and would be an important figure in the Democratic party. In 1899 he expounded the party's hostility to trusts, to expansion in the Philippines, and to the dream of the cooperative commonwealth. He also stressed Democratic planks on municipal ownership in an attempt to counter the Socialist appeal. Socialism, Brown asserted, was no novelty: ". . . Jefferson and Jackson fought . . . great battles along these lines. Those men were exponents of good everyday socialism, and I find enough of it in the Democratic party for me."

Republicans went out of town for a champion. Congressman William Moody of Haverhill had dealt with Socialists in his district for some time. But Moody's crowd was dismayingly small, perhaps, one politician thought, because Saturday night was a bad time for political rallies. Social Democrats in the audience heard Moody out and then trooped off to their own rally, which the *Times* described as "well-attended." Socialists did not take Saturday night off, nor any other time. Even as E. Gerry Brown debated with Fred Gordon, Socialist orators elsewhere in the city were championing the cause.

The Social Democrats did not win anything in November, but, as the *Times* said, they were "MUCH IN EVIDENCE." Republicans won all but one contest, which went to a Democrat. The Socialist choice for governor, however, ran only thirty-five votes behind the Democrat, and the nominee for the state Senate finished well ahead of his Democratic rival. If Republicans still held the offices, Social Democrats were becoming the second party in the city. In the offing was the municipal election, where party lines were traditionally loose. The *Times* predicted that the "exceedingly rapid development of voting strength" of the S.D.P. would "surprise . . . very many people." [9]

Early in October, Mayor Emery M. Low announced that he could no longer do justice to the city and his own business. Although Low's ineffective enforcement of the city's prohibition code might have embarrassed his party, his retirement left the Republicans in a quandary. The city committee openly opposed the candidacy of E. B. Estes, the front-running aspirant. Trial balloons of other hopefuls ascended and popped almost daily as party leaders sought an ultra-respectable businessman to head the ticket. On November 1, they found their man, when Baalis Sanford, "a sterling business man of well-known ability," entered the lists. Commercial leaders of the city appointed committees to get out the vote in each ward, and attended a banquet where the speeches sounded curiously like inverted Marx. The chairman of the evening appealed to businessmen of Brockton to "unite" behind "a businessman" who would manage the city "in a business-like manner."

Baalis Sanford did not remain long in the race. After the results of the state election had been tabulated, he abruptly discovered that his health would not permit a campaign. Sanford's withdrawal cheered the Social Democrats, for it was widely attributed to his realization that a campaign against them would have to be strenuously waged.

Repairs to the Republican machine were not entirely

9. *Times*, October 3–November 14, 1899, *passim;* Boot and Shoe Workers' Union Scrapbook 1.

effective. The caucus selected unpledged delegates who eventually agreed on Arthur E. Kendrick, a shoe manufacturer and member of the Common Council. Kendrick was not much of a Republican; he had in fact been a Democrat until 1892. But the G.O.P. nominated him and denied Estes's backers even the crumb of a school committee nomination.

Conservative Democrats had their businessman even before Sanford retired. Henry E. Garfield, mayor of the city in 1898, gratified a delegation of Main Street merchants who wanted him to give the city another year of financially sound administration. Yet Bryan Democrats, led by E. Gerry Brown, thought Garfield too conservative. They considered, and abandoned, an independent campaign. Lack of a formal break, however, did not indicate Democratic unity.

Social Democrats wasted no energy looking for a respectable businessman when a respectable union man like Charles Coulter was available. The platform was also safely respectable. The enduring legacy of past administrations, it said, was an inflated tax rate. Social Democrats defined their national program as "equal opportunities for all, special privileges for none." They proposed to implement the slogan in Brockton with a series of specific proposals. Public works were to be constructed by public employees, all of whom should work an eight-hour day. Sanitary regulations would be enforced, and public comfort stations erected. Highways and street lighting would be improved with due consideration of cyclists. Public utilities should become publicly owned. Massachusetts Nationalists and Populists would have recognized the platform; even the Democrats had used part of it earlier in the year. Social Democrats did not venture far beyond earlier reform movements.

Although the Brockton *Times* found "Coulter clubs"

117

mushrooming in the factories and heard "more Coulter talk" as the election neared, both major parties mounted lackluster campaigns stressing honest, economical administration. The Social Democrats brought on Eugene Debs to close their effort with a flourish. Debs had been in Brockton before, and, as a local editor noted, many who were not Socialists would listen to him any time he spoke. Though the hall was jammed, the band played anyhow. Debs spoke for two hours about the maldistribution of wealth, the injustice of high profits, the ruthlessness of competitive enterprise and the price it exacted from humanity. Rewards must follow toil; workers must have leisure; chain stores must not send corner grocers to the wall. When in Brockton, Debs too was safe.

A week before the election, both Republicans and Democrats guessed Coulter would finish second. Reverend S. L. Beal, the Socialist candidate for alderman from Campello, was regarded as the only certain winner on the ballot. On election day, Beal, in fact, received nearly sixty per cent of the vote in his three-cornered contest. Elihu Perry joined Beal on the Board of Aldermen after a much tighter race. And Charles Coulter, with nearly 3,400 votes, had 1,523 more than Garfield and 1,544 more than Kendrick. The *Times* used phrases like "political marvel" and "social democratic lightning." [10]

Even Socialists were stunned at the size of Coulter's victory. True, other candidates who ran at-large were beaten, polling about half Coulter's vote. Still, whether the result was due to Coulter's popularity, divisions in the major parties, the aggressive campaign, or the hope of reform, it was worth celebrating. Social Democrats gave their band leader a new horn and heard Coulter's explana-

10. The campaign of 1899 can be traced in the *Times*, October 2–December 6, 1899; see also Nutter, ". . . the Brockton Municipal Election of 1899," *loc. cit.*, 22–23.

tion of his success. The "workingmen went to the polls as a unit," and that, said Coulter, was that. Of course, those same workingmen now stretched out "the hand of friendship to the businessmen, with the aim of obtaining the best results in municipal government." What would the new mayor propose? He could not really accomplish much, said Coulter, preparing an alibi in advance, until the state legislature amended the city charter. He hoped not to raise the tax rate, but he would like to build some public comfort stations.[11] At least the city might own the toilets.

An editorial writer in Philadelphia watched reports come in from Massachusetts during the fall of 1899. When the last returns from the last election of the nineteenth century were in, the Philadelphia *Press* explained the peculiar habits of a growing number of voters in the Bay State.

The expansion and growth of so-called Socialism in Massachusetts can probably be found in an increasing dissatisfaction with the abuses which have grown up under the present system of municipal government. . . . There is no sign that social order and the sacredness of private property are threatened in Massachusetts, but there is evidence of discontent with the wasteful expenditure of money, the ease with which favored rings obtain municipal contracts and the voting away of franchises without adequate return to the public. If these abuses are not corrected by existing parties, the people will probably take matters into their own hands and under the name of Socialists compel a change for the better.[12]

The Brockton *Times* printed the editorial without comment. The local editor knew when enough had been said.

Blocked by Republican majorities in both deliberative branches of city government, by restrictions in the city

11. *Times,* December 6, 1899; *HSD,* December 9, 1899.
12. *Times,* December 14, 1899.

charter, and by disagreements among Socialists, Mayor Coulter's administration was barren. After several weeks of discussion, the city government, at the urging of the new mayor, resolved to insist on the union label on all city printing. When Coulter came to sum up his accomplishments in the campaign for re-election, he was proud of that resolution. He also noted that city employees were receiving two dollars for an eight-hour day, but since this reform had been passed by referendum when Coulter was elected, it was hardly an exclusively Socialist measure. He took credit for the city's decision to maintain its own streets, claiming that the job had been well done without corrupting contracts with private firms.[13]

The Socialists also had apologies and excuses. A spokesman said he could prove that it was not the fault of Socialists "that the committee on public comfort stations did not report. . . ." Coulter argued that he should not be blamed for renewal of a telephone franchise that contained anti-union provisions. Undeniably some of Coulter's proposals disappeared in unsympathetic committees, but there were not many proposals to bury. The platform for 1900 was an implicit confession of failure, for it was virtually a carbon copy of that of the previous year. The Socialists pointed with pleasure to a reduced tax rate, and nailed the same planks back to the platform.[14]

Brockton Social Democrats were busy in 1900, even if their activity did not make an impressive record. Like other parties in the city, they indulged in intramural bickering; unlike others, they resolved most of their disagreements in time for elections. They also strengthened their identification with a stronger Boot and Shoe Workers' Union, and picked up important help from the leaders of

13. *Ibid.*, January, 1900, *passim;* October 27, 1900.
14. *HSD,* November 17, 1900; *Times,* October 27, 1900; November 23, 1900.

the temperance movement, which had for years commanded a majority of the city's voters. While the Socialist vote declined in 1900, the party avoided disaster and renewed its lease on City Hall.

In March, the Brockton local formally instructed Elihu Perry and Charles Coulter to oppose extension of a telephone franchise unless the company would agree to pay union wages. When the question came before the aldermen, both Perry and Reverend S. L. Beal, a member of the Campello branch and thus not bound by instructions from Brockton, voted for the unrestricted extension of the franchise. The Brockton organization expelled Perry, but a movement to censure Beal temporarily lapsed. In July, the state convention sustained a Brockton delegate's protest against the seating of Beal. Other Campello delegates withdrew with their excluded leader. When a segment of the Campello organization subsequently voted to split from the Brockton movement, Coulter effectively soothed the ruffled feelings. In the fall, Beal meekly submitted to party discipline, but his defeat made the question less pressing.[15]

The refusal to seat Beal was the least of the problems confronting that Social Democratic convention in July. The question that preoccupied most delegates was of minor concern to Brockton. The convention hoped to effect unity with the so-called "Kangaroos," a group of bolting Socialist Laborites led nationally by Morris Hillquit, Max Hayes and Job Harriman. Socialists in Haverhill were particularly anxious to bring about a Socialist juncture, and for months they had written letters, attended meetings, and planned strategy toward this end.

Brockton Socialists did not share Haverhill's sense of urgency. They had never been Socialist Laborites and had

15. *Times*, March 17–April 3, 1900, *passim;* July 9, 18–21, 1900; September 21, 1900.

no ties with former comrades. Nor had they ever faced strong S.L.P. opposition, which might have stirred resentment. Brockton had no Kangaroos to swell the Socialist vote. Having had almost no direct contact with the S.L.P., Brockton's Socialists feared vaguely that it was too revolutionary, too opposed to trade unions. Yet no matter of exclusively national or state importance interested Brockton Socialists long. In 1901, when a second convention at Indianapolis amalgamated Kangaroos and Social Democrats into the Socialist Party of America, Charles H. Coulter was in Brockton attending to the routine business of the city. The Brockton city committee was meeting to plan campaigns that were still months away. With one of the largest Socialist organizations in the nation, the city was only indirectly represented at Indianapolis. Brockton's Socialists always put first things first.[16]

Brockton's attitude toward Socialist unity—indifference tinged with hostility—brought the city one bonus. In the fall, when Eugene Debs made his swing through Massachusetts, he shunned Socialists who had promoted the merger. A week before the national election, Debs and Job Harriman, his running mate, spoke to 2,000 people in Brockton.

Brockton needed Debs to invigorate a sagging campaign. The Social Democratic band balked; it demanded a bigger share of the receipts from a fund-raising effort. Coulter forgot to prepare one of the few political speeches he was asked to give, and had to fall back on what the papers called "his characteristic speech" on Socialism as the remedy for the world's ills. Candidates for the General Court gave up public meetings and began campaigning door to door.

Democrats held no meetings, spent no money, and did

16. *Ibid.*, July 30, 1901. See Chapter 5 for a detailed discussion of the role of the Massachusetts movement in promoting Socialist unity.

little to rouse the electorate. Nor did the Republicans make any effort until mid-October, when they decided to combat the Socialist "menace." A speaker told county Republicans that Socialism was "more insidious and infinitely more dangerous than the wildest vagaries of Bryanism." The Brockton G.O.P. began to distribute an anti-Socialist tract by Arthur Washburn; Carey thought it so bad he asked for copies to distribute in Haverhill. Washburn retorted that Carey's wit hardly matched the logic of "economists and publicists of world-wide reputation, including Herbert Spencer." He added that his mission was to combat "un-American" Socialists by raising the "stars and stripes" wherever "they hoist the red flag of socialism. . . ."

Charles Laird, chairman of the Socialist city committee, wanted Washburn's documentation. Surely, he wrote, Washburn had not read the party's platform nor listened to its fine speakers. Laird provided a dubious bibliography: "If Mr. W. . . . will consult such men as William Dean Howells or John Brisbee Walker, editor of the Cosmopolitan, he may perhaps get a better understanding of the aims, objects and principles of socialism." [17]

The minimal Republican effort was enough to win all the offices. Debs received nearly 1,250 votes—about a third of McKinley's total and eight hundred votes less than Bryan's. Debs gloomily predicted that four more years of McKinley would mean panic, strikes, and bloodshed. The Brockton *Times*, which knew the town's Socialists, wondered whether Debs was safe after all. "Mr. Debs has a strong . . . following in this city; but we greatly mistake the men here . . . if they have any sympathy or tolerance for such an insane utterance as that with which

17. *SDH*, November 10, 1900; William Butscher to G. B. Leonard, October 11, 1900, Butscher Letterbook 2, SP Papers; *Times*, May 26, 1900; September 13, 15, 1900; October 13–30, 1900; November 1, 3, 1900; *People*, October 27, 1900.

he is credited." In Haverhill, the official newspaper of Massachusetts Socialists scrambled to correct the erring leader. Debs had probably been misquoted, said the *Social Democrat*. Of course the United States was moving toward revolution. But the revolution would "bring . . . the peace that knoweth life everlasting," and would not be a "revolution of blood, for this Comrade Debs or the Social Democrats never predicted or desired." [18]

Perpetual peace escaped the Brockton electorate. The empty Democratic treasury was suddenly full from the bounty, it was rumored, of Republicans who wanted a strong nominee to siphon off Coulter's support. Neither major party was united. E. B. Estes once more sought the G.O.P. nomination, which was once more denied him when the machine awarded it to David Battles, a former legislator and chairman of the party's city committee. E. Gerry Brown offered reform Democrats his independent candidacy when regular Democrats nominated Alderman Edward Gilmore. Both Gilmore and Battles attempted to keep their parties from splitting by saying nothing controversial. When Coulter proposed a bond issue for a new source of municipal water, Battles observed that the question was complex and if elected he would consider it carefully. While Gilmore opposed the bond issue, he admitted that the improvement had to be made. He thought other alternatives ought to be examined before spending so much money.

Coulter hoped to gain support not only with his solution to the problem of the city's water supply, but also with his advocacy of a new high school. Neither proposal, however, was so important as the endorsement of Reverend Alan Hudson, a Brockton temperance leader. Brockton annually voted local prohibition by margins of at least five hundred votes. In 1900, when Coulter stressed his

18. *HSD*, November 17, 1900; *Times*, November 10, 1900.

accomplishments, his vigorous and impartial enforcement of the city's liquor ordinance was as vital as the claim that he had achieved a slightly lower tax rate. And the word that the temperance forces were "thoroughly satisfied with his administration," pulled Charles Coulter through. The margin was slim. He won by a scant thirty-three votes over Battles and about a thousand over Gilmore. E. Gerry Brown found only fifty reform Democrats.

But the election was no triumph for the Social Democrats. They had nominated twenty-eight other candidates, including three officials of the Boot and Shoe Workers' Union and eighteen additional shoe workers. While identification with the union was intentional and clear, the base was not broad enough. The Socialists lost every other race on the ballot, and even Coulter's tally of nearly three thousand votes was considerably below his total of 1899. Republicans made no secret of their resentment of the last-minute endorsement by the temperance committee. The *Times*, congratulating Coulter on his popularity, pointed out that his party was obviously slipping. Though Coulter replied that his re-election was a victory for the working-man and for Socialism, the paper was closer to the mark.[19]

Nothing in 1901 roused Brockton's indifferent electorate. To a bored audience, politicians played the tune of 1900 through to a different ending. Republicans knew a humdrum campaign was in their interest, since a majority of the city's voters were traditionally Republican. Even the assassination of President William McKinley, which set off anti-radical agitation elsewhere in the country, caused only grief in Brockton. Democrats again tried to be more friendly to labor, more reform-oriented, and safer than Socialists. Josiah Quincy, the Democratic nominee for governor, suggested to a Brockton audience that So-

19. *Times*, November 22, 28, 1900; December 1, 3, 5, 6, 10, 1900.

125

cialists and Democrats cooperate to advance reform: "It is not necessary to be a political socialist," he asserted, "to be in spirit with the socialistic spirit of the age."

After years of hustling for objectives that even political success could not bring, Socialists slowed their pace. Their experience with Gaylord Wilshire, the "millionaire Socialist" publisher of the *Challenge*, was symptomatic. In July, before the local political season opened, Wilshire spoke to an estimated 2,000 people, and reported that Brockton had perhaps "the liveliest Socialist movement" he had ever seen. Coulter was a "rattling good man"; the local contained "the very cream of the proletariat." In November, Wilshire left an embarrassing gap in the Socialist campaign when he failed to appear at a rally where he had been scheduled to speak.[20]

Socialists tried to catch the coat tails of a bustling labor movement. As delegates left for the state convention of the A.F. of L., the *Times* suggested that the Federation gather another year in Brockton, "the most perfect union city in the Commonwealth." When the A.F. of L. selected Brockton, the *Times* thought the most deserving city had been chosen. The paper also noted the Federation's refusal to endorse the Socialist party. At least in Brockton, however, no such endorsement was required; every local Socialist nominee in November was a member of the Boot and Shoe Workers' Union, and every nominee in December carried a union card. Socialists hoped union votes would elect union candidates. They stressed this theme in their campaign.[21]

It was not a winning issue. In November the Republicans carried the city without stirring. They made only a

20. *Ibid.*, October 27, 1901; November 4, 5, 1901; *The Challenge*, August 7, 1901, 8.
21. *Times*, October 5, 11, 1901; November 21, 1901; *The Clarion* (Haverhill), September 21, 1901.

modest effort for the municipal election. The strategy was apparent early, when G.O.P. aldermen attacked Coulter's allegedly shoddy enforcement of prohibition. The sally hurt; within a few days a rash of raids brought in a good deal of illegal liquor. Reverend Alan Hudson said openly that Coulter had lost his zeal. While Hudson did not endorse anyone, his action could only benefit the G.O.P., since local Democrats were known to be moderate wets. Coulter knew the perils of Hudson's disapproval. So the mayor again tried to substitute the municipal water supply as the campaign's central issue. He had recommended the use of a new source at Silver Lake, and had secured the backing of engineers, shoe manufacturers, and twelve hundred petitioning voters. When Coulter's effort seemed to generate a response, David Battles, once more the Republican nominee, let it be known that he too approved the Silver Lake source.

Republican strategy was sound. Battles had a plurality of some three hundred over Coulter and about 1,300 over Edward Gilmore, again the Democratic nominee. Republicans won twenty-one of twenty-eight places in the city government; Socialists were shut out. The municipality remained dry by a margin of a thousand votes, and that issue, the Socialists knew, had ejected them from City Hall. Republicans convinced the electorate, a Socialist weekly explained, that "a rumless millennium" would "at once be set up in Brockton." [22]

The Socialist party faced 1902 without one municipal official to serve as a spokesman. Even the consolation that each campaign spread Socialist doctrine was lacking, for the Brockton movement spread little more socialism than did Democrats. The Socialists in the city resembled noth-

22. *Times,* September 27, 1901; October 25, 30, 1901; November 22, 23, 30, 1901; *The Clarion* (Boston), December 7, 1901; see also the *Worker* (New York), December 15, 1901.

ing so much as a flash in the pan. Early in 1902, they even resorted to Marx for guidance.[23]

Yet when the situation should have become darker, it suddenly grew light. 1902 was the banner year of the Massachusetts Socialists, and Brockton was at the head of the parade with an electoral triumph surpassed only in the best days of the Milwaukee Socialist movement. As usual, the explanation was partly local, though national events increased local opportunity. The coal strike of 1902 raised the price of fuel in Brockton to record levels. George F. Baer, the spokesman for the mine owners and defender of the divine right of property, gave the Socialists an opening which they were quick to exploit to put capitalism and the major parties on the defensive.

William Mailly, the former editor from Haverhill who was in 1902 the salaried secretary of the state organization, keynoted the Brockton campaign with a Labor Day account of his recent visit to the mining area. After describing conditions there, he drew the socialist moral. Labor's problems were not local, nor were socialist solutions. He had heard socialism called "Coulterism" in Brockton, he said, but the party offered a broad program that would help all workers everywhere. Like most campaign speakers, Mailly shaded the truth. Local Socialists were in fact "Coulterists." They were also capable of seizing a good political issue. Mailly quoted George F. Baer's notorious remark that "the rights and interests of the laboring men will be protected and cared for, not by the labor agitators, but by the Christian men to whom God in his infinite wisdom, has given control of the property interests of country." [24] Brockton's labor agitators took to the stump.

As cold weather sent fuel prices up, the Brockton Cen-

23. *Worker,* January 26, 1902.
24. *Times,* September 4, 1902.

Lawrence strikers demonstrate patriotism

JOHN C. CHASE
First Socialist Mayor
in the nation

DAVID GOLDSTEIN
A vigorous opponent
of socialism

JAMES F. CAREY
First Socialist
Public Official
in Massachusetts

Equal Suffrage

Regardless

of Sex

For Governor
ROLAND D. SAWYER

For Lieut-Governor
ROBERT B MARTIN

Initiative

— AND —

Referendum

For Secy. of State
ELLEN HAYES

SOCIALIST PARTY
CANDIDATES
STATE OF MASSACHUSETTS

FOR GOVERNOR

ROLAND D. SAWYER
OF WARE

For Lieut-Governor
ROBERT B. MARTIN
OF BOSTON

For Secy. of State
ELLEN HAYES
OF WELLESLEY

For Treasurer
LOUIS F. WEISS
OF WORCESTER

For Auditor
SYLVESTER J. McBRIDE
OF WATERTOWN

For Attorney General
GEORGE E. ROEWER, Jr.
OF BOSTON

ELECTION TUESDAY, NOV. 5

WE CALL UPON THE WORKERS TO ORGANIZE POLITICALLY AND INDUSTRIALLY, TO SEIZE THE POWERS OF GOVERNMENT THROUGH THE BALLOT, AND GAIN POSSESSION OF ALL INDUSTRY — LAND, RAILROADS, MINES, FACTORIES, ETC.—FOR THE SERVICE OF ALL THE PEOPLE.

Popular

Election

— OF —

Judges

For Treasurer
LOUIS F. WEISS

For Auditor
SYLVESTER J. McBRIDE

Home Rule

— FOR —

Massachusetts

Cities

For Atty. General
GEORGE E. ROEWER, Jr.

Finnish Soc. Pub. Co. Fitchburg. Mass.

Campaign poster, 1912

Haywood addresses Lawrence strikers

tral Labor Union called a presumably nonpartisan meeting to discuss the critical coal shortage. The assembly shouted through a resolution demanding government ownership of mines. The conservative carpenters, unhappy with the apparent encouragement of socialism in the Central Labor Union, withdrew from the body. The city government called another non-partisan meeting to discuss steps to relieve the fuel shortage. Mayor Battles had to gavel down another resolution for government ownership. John C. Chase, the party's nominee for governor, visited Brockton with "Mother" Mary Jones, already a legendary figure in the coal fields. She reported that the oppressed miners looked to Bay State voters for the first long stride toward the cooperative commonwealth.

The Democrats made a last-minute appeal for the labor vote, while Republicans, in another quiet campaign, talked decorously of the tariff, even after Theodore Roosevelt's intervention in the coal strike gave them an opportunity to counter the Socialists. Strategic silence, so right for 1901, was almost disastrous in 1902. Socialists made great gains in Brockton. Many Republicans in the city and across the Commonwealth staggered through to victory, but voters had given the G.O.P. a clear warning.

Brockton's Socialists cheered their first success in a state campaign. Wallace C. Ransden, a modest shoe worker from Campello, was the only non-Republican in the Brockton delegation to the General Court. A Protestant and a prohibitionist, Ransden had become interested in economic issues about 1896; he had become a Socialist after reading Robert Blatchford's *Merrie England*. Ransden doubled the previous Socialist vote in his district, and won with about forty per cent of the total. Chase ran ahead of the Democratic nominee and raised the city's previous Socialist gubernatorial vote by almost one hundred per cent. Jubilant Socialists, positive that the coming municipal election would be won, piled into several special coaches and went off to Boston to celebrate.[25]

Some opponents of Socialism in Brockton hoped to redeem the city by running a single opposition slate, but neither major party warmed to the idea. Both pointed to the failure of a similar scheme in Haverhill in 1899; both feared resulting disorder in their ranks. Mayor Battles, running for re-election, emphasized particularly his ability to carry through the Silver Lake water project. The slogan "Get Together" indicated that the Republicans were divided, a familiar condition that a meeting of three hundred volunteer campaign planners could hardly have solved. Democrats hoped to persuade Emmet Walls to run for mayor. A national officer of the Boot and Shoe Workers' Union and president of the Central Labor Union, Walls would have been a formidable candidate. But he refused to run and the Democrats fell back on E. Gerry Brown, who vainly tried to mount a campaign. No one cooperated: opponents ignored his challenge to debate; his party failed to nominate ward and precinct candidates who might have enticed straight-ticket voters to the polls. Brown's party wasted almost no money on a hopeless campaign and gave him the nomination he had so long sought only because there was no chance he might win.

Socialists, acknowledging that their treasury was low, asked comrades around the nation for contributions. The party hired Dan White, a former iron moulder who would settle in Brockton, to speak from the campaign wagon that had become a local tradition. The Socialists had more volunteer campaign workers than they could use, and so many new members that the party outgrew its quarters.

25. *Ibid.,* September 26, 1902; October 10, 14–16, 23, 30, 1902; November 5–10, 1902; *Worker,* October 12, 1902; November 3, 10, 1902; *Comrade* (New York), February, 1903, 102.

The prohibition question slumbered as if by agreement. With 4,300 votes, Charles Coulter won an absolute majority for the first time. Brown's total of 553 was almost 1,400 less than Democrats had polled in 1901, while Battles actually had a larger vote than he had had in winning the year before. Coulter's victory had been expected. The surprise was in the magnitude of the sweep. Three of seven aldermen, eight of twenty-one councilmen, and two of three members of the school committee were also Socialists. The editor of the *Times* called the victory "a socialistic cyclone," and correctly noted that the result took "first rank among the achievements of this party in the United States."

Republicans were stunned. They had thought a narrow defeat possible; a rout was completely unexpected. Socialists had a more accurate grasp of the situation; their pre-election prediction underestimated Coulter's total by 167 votes. And everyone knew the explanation. Mayor Battles wrote Moritz Ruther, still a functionary of the state S.L.P., that tacit fusion of Socialists and Democrats had brought his defeat. Brown acknowledged that Democrats figured he had no chance to win and consequently had supported one of the other candidates. The *Times* suggested that Coulter appoint Brown city marshal out of gratitude.

Unquestionably Democratic votes helped elect Socialists. Equally important was the fact that Socialists had candidates and a program that Democrats found attractive. Five of the seven nominees for aldermen were sufficiently respected in their unions to be elected delegates to the Central Labor Union. The three elected aldermen were native-born shoe workers and members of the Boot and Shoe Workers' Union. One was the business agent of his local and president of the Joint Shoe Council, a group representing all the crafts in the industry. Of eight elected councilmen, seven were shoe workers, one a carpenter. Of two elected members of the school committee, one was a shoe worker-turned-lawyer; the other was an English-born housewife whose presence on the ballot was enough of a novelty to attract attention, but not so unprecedented that it connoted a radical break.[26]

A unique combination of circumstances produced the Socialist successes in 1902. Part of the formula was old: a slate dramatizing the party's connection with the city's labor organizations and headed by a two-term mayor whose previous administrations had not indulged in economic experimentation. The simultaneous lack of spirit and unity in both major parties was an incalculable asset, particularly since Socialists were unusually spirited and united. Lack of a vital local issue, and especially the silence of the temperance forces, enabled the Socialists to campaign on personalities when their candidates had proven popularity. And the coal strike, distant though it was, gave the Socialist clichés an impact previously lacking. A vote for the Socialist ticket was a pointed, but safe, protest against the high price of fuel, the smugness of the Baers, and the failure of orthodox local politicians to take a stand on the issue. Jubilant Socialists might talk about the inevitable progress of Socialism. The only real inevitability was that circumstances would never again be the same.

In Rockland, a town of about 5,500 not far from Brockton, Reverend Frederic O. MacCartney sat in the Unitarian parsonage and felt the renewed pricking of his social conscience. Thirty-five years old in 1899, MacCartney had

26. *Times*, November 8–30, 1902, *passim;* December 1, 3, 1902; *Worker,* November 10, 1902; December 14, 1902; *People,* December 27, 1902; January 17, 1903.

long since learned that his conscience would not settle for quiet contemplation. In May, 1899, he resigned his pastorate to become secretary of the Industrial Peace Society and to organize for the Social Democratic party.

The decision was not ill-considered. Educated at Grinnell College and Andover Theological Seminary, MacCartney had read *Looking Backward* and followed the Nationalists into the People's party. Upon graduation in 1893, he moved left theologically, dropping Congregationalism to become assistant pastor of the Second Unitarian Church of Boston. In 1894, he took charge of the Unitarian parish in Rockland, where he soon won the friendship and respect of the whole community. He was, a Republican judge said years later, welcome in any house in town, and everyone knew he counted the day lost when he had righted no wrongs before the sun went down.[27]

MacCartney found economic and social wrongs to correct. Disturbed by the gulf between rich and poor, by the long hours and small rewards given labor, and by the apparent acceptance of such evils, the young minister at first turned to cooperatives as the answer. He never lost the ideal of replacing competition with social harmony through cooperation, but he moved beyond establishing cooperative enterprises as the means. In 1896, he worked for the election of William Jennings Bryan and published a piece in the *Christian Register* criticising the unchecked growth "of a mammoth mammon power" that menaced "the continuation of republican institutions."[28] In 1899, after talking with Carey and Chase and studying the Social Democratic movement, he left his parsonage to follow a new vocation. A Social Democratic organizer kept busy; in 1902, when he had been a Socialist member of the legis-

27. George W. Kelley, quoted in New York *Call*, October 20, 1908.
28. Quoted in *American Fabian* (Boston), December 1896, 2.

lature for three years, MacCartney was still trying to find time to begin his study of Marx.[29]

About six months after joining the party, MacCartney was a candidate for the state legislature from the Fourth Plymouth District, comprising Hanover, Hanson, and Rockland. Rockland had perhaps forty Social Democrats. There were fewer in the two smaller towns. Yet eight hundred people listened to MacCartney's final campaign speech. More than seven hundred voted for him, giving him a plurality of more than one hundred. A Worcester paper wondered about the third Socialist ever elected to the state legislature, and from Brockton, where MacCartney was well known, came reassurance. His voice, said the Brockton *Times*, would be "intelligent and conservative"; apprehensions of radicalism were groundless.

Before going to Boston to take his seat, MacCartney spoke to Brockton's Presbyterian Youth on "What Socialism Stands For." His explanation, which would have served for almost any Social Democrat in the Commonwealth, bore out the observation of the *Times*. As trusts developed, MacCartney said, wealth became concentrated in progressively fewer hands. Such an economic condition could no longer be called competitive; monopolistic capitalism had replaced individualism. Further, such concentration of wealth had historically foreshadowed the fall of a culture. Cataclysm was no remedy. Political action could prevent continued monopolistic control of the means of production. Following Edward Bellamy, MacCartney said that the trust was "a part of natural evolution" and could "no more be legislated out of existence than can history be stayed." Socialists planned to guide this evolutionary development "to a safe and

29. This account of MacCartney's career is based on material in the *HSD*, November 18, 1899; *SD Red Book*, 114–115; and MacCartney's article, "How I Became a Socialist," *Comrade*, September, 1902, 266–268.

peaceful fulfillment" in a society where the nation owned the means of production.[30]

In the State House, MacCartney interpreted the needs of the workingman broadly. He sponsored or supported legislation to promote labor unions, education, municipal ownership, more democratic government, and leisure and security for the working population. One of his first bills would have allowed hunting and fishing on Sunday; it was, he explained, the only day factory workers could get to the woods.[31]

Whatever MacCartney did, the people of his district approved. In his successful campaign for re-election in 1900, he ran about six hundred votes ahead of Eugene Debs and Charles Bradley, the S.D.P. nominee for governor. When he spoke around Rockland, which was less and less often as other Bay State Socialists needed him to bolster drooping morale, he drew overflow crowds. In 1902, after MacCartney had won his fourth consecutive term in the General Court, the Brockton *Times* said he seemed "to have a mortgage on the job." [32]

The mortgage expired six months later when he died at thirty-eight. From Socialists all over the country came warm tributes. Eugene Debs acknowledged the loss to the cause and clipped a notice of the funeral for his scrapbook. Margaret Haile said MacCartney had given the Massachusetts party "the standing necessary to win recognition from the conservative and eminently respectable citizens of the Old Bay State." Even DeLeon's *People* knew MacCartney's death was "an irreparable loss," and the phrase echoed through his own party. William Mailly,

30. *Times*, November 7, 10, 1899; December 22, 1899; *SD Red Book*, 124; *HSD*, November 18, 1899.

31. Based on summaries in *HSD*, January 27, 1900; *Gazette*, April 13, 1900; *People*, March 23, 1901.

32. *Times*, October 30, 1901; November 5, 1902; *HSD*, November 10, 1900.

the party's national secretary, who happened to be in Massachusetts when MacCartney died, was the spokesman for the state's Socialists when he wrote: ". . . no man in Massachusetts was more deeply loved and highly respected by his co-workers. . . ."[33]

The Socialist movement in Brockton, as the election of 1905 would show, was not one man's to command. The trade unions furnished a stable base; the constant round of elections afforded political experience; an occasional victory encouraged responsibility. There was no comparable Socialist movement in MacCartney's district. Socialists there were only Socialists when voting for MacCartney; he was the campaigner; his the responsibility. The magic could not be transferred, even when Franklin Wentworth, a leading Bay State Socialist of the MacCartney stripe, moved into Hanson to try to take MacCartney's place in the General Court.

Socialist victories by Coulter or MacCartney or candidates for the Brockton Common Council did not really portend a flooding Socialist tide. Nor did losses indicate that the tide was ebbing. No candidate of the Socialist party in Massachusetts ever gave a voter a real chance to express a firm opinion about orthodox Socialism, as the outrage of the purist S.L.P. attests. The Brockton Socialist movement was the product of local conditions; the movement in the Fourth Plymouth District was the product of one man. Conditions change; men die. The inexorable march to Socialism soon stumbled to a halt.

33. MacCartney's death was widely noticed in the Socialist press: see, e.g., *SDH,* June 6, 1903; *Wilshire's Magazine,* July, 1903, 30; Chicago *Socialist,* May 30, 1903; June 6, 13, 1903; Seattle *Socialist,* June 21, 1903; New York *Call,* October 20, 1908; *People,* June 20, 1903; Mailly to C. P. Gildea, June 18, 1903, Mailly Letterbook 6, SP Papers; Debs Scrapbook 3, Debs Papers, Tamiment Library of New York University.

CHAPTER V

The View at the Top

Political success gave the Massachusetts Socialists great prestige in the national movement. Victory in Haverhill automatically made John Chase and James Carey party leaders, and both turned early triumphs into careers in the party. John Chase left Haverhill in 1903 to work as a speaker, party functionary, and sometime candidate in New York, West Virginia, Nebraska and elsewhere. With the exception of national lecture tours and brief retirements to Maine, Carey remained in the Bay State, where he ran for governor about every other year and filled various posts in the party's hierarchy. Carey had the respect and friendship of Socialists all over the nation and retained a wide influence in the party.

Early political success also placed the Massachusetts movement on one side of the delicately balanced Social Democracy of America. Those Social Democrats who believed political action more persuasive than any experimental colony thought the returns from Massachusetts strengthened their case. The dispute within the organization developed into a formal split at the Chicago convention in June, 1898. When the colonizers seemed to have packed the meeting, Margaret Haile, the secretary of the Massachusetts state committee, threatened to lead her delegation out of the hall and out of the organization. A compromise brought comparative tranquility until a final confrontation over the platform. Miss Haile joined Victor Berger in a majority report limiting the Social Democracy to political action. A minority report gave equal emphasis to colonization. In the tumult that followed the convention's adoption of the minority version, supporters of political action walked out. Among the bolters were both delegates from Massachusetts, Margaret Haile and James F. Carey.

Carey, Miss Haile, and thirty-one other dissidents immediately established the Social Democratic party (S.D.P.) to propagate socialism through politics. The founders included Theodore Debs, whose presence symbolized the support of his ailing brother; Victor Berger, who ruled the Wisconsin movement; and Jesse Cox and Seymour Stedman of Illinois. Fred G. R. Gordon, with Carey the veteran of an earlier Socialist division, joined him in another. Other former Socialist Laborites included William Butscher, a New Yorker who in 1900 would be the spokesman for one wing of the party against Debs and Berger; and William Mailly, a young organizer among coal miners.[1]

The S.D.P. in Massachusetts added the leverage of numbers to the prestige of political success and national leadership. Before the end of the party's first year, half the total membership lived in Massachusetts. Haverhill alone added fifty new members in a fortnight, thereby providing a quarter of the total national growth in the period. The bustling Massachusetts movement began to resent direction from a National Executive Board entirely made up of midwesterners. Bay State Social Democrats wanted the party to drop that part of the platform designed to catch the votes of farmers, which, they maintained, cluttered up an otherwise sound appeal to the working class. When the N.E.B. sought a party conference in the summer of 1899,

1. Howard H. Quint, *The Forging of American Socialism* (Columbia, S.C., 1953) 310–321; Frederic Heath, ed., *Social Democracy Red Book* (Terre Haute, 1900), Chapter 7; *SDH*, July 9, 1898.

John Chase expressed the state's disapproval. When the conference bent to its task of promoting harmony, Massachusetts was unrepresented. When decisions were taken, Massachusetts was critical, suggesting that the proposed scheme for representation at a forthcoming national convention would not give eastern states their full weight. The bickering saddened Eugene Debs, who lectured the Bay Staters:

> Massachusetts comes to the front promptly with a big "kick" at the slightest provocation. . . . But Massachusetts should also be in when the coin is needed. If other states had done as little as Massachusetts for the national party since it was organized a year ago, we would not now have a sign of a national party in existence. I admire Massachusetts, glory in her progress, and rejoice in the victory of her comrades, but she and they are all wrapped up in Massachusetts. . . . They have met every appeal for finance . . . with a deaf ear. . . .

With what must have been intentional irony, the editor of the *Social Democratic Herald* printed Debs's outburst next to a letter from Margaret Haile, who hoped the party's constitution would soon find the waste basket it merited. The Massachusetts organization, she boasted, made no pretense of living within restrictions on state autonomy, because "we have not tried to trim our movement to any written constitution. . . ." She hinted that Massachusetts might find other, more congenial Socialist companions. A month later Carey and Chase addressed an Independent Labor party gathering in New York City, at which miscellaneous Socialists and members of trade unions groped toward another radical political alliance.[2] The Social Democrats eventually withdrew, but the appearance of Carey and Chase suggested that their allegiance to the S.D.P. was tentative. Most Socialists in

2. *SDH,* January 28, 1899; July 29, 1899; August 5, 1899; *Gazette,* September 1, 1899.

Massachusetts insisted, under Debs as under DeLeon, that decisions be made at home. While Social Democrats had one split and toyed with a second, Socialist Laborites had a grand schism. In February, 1899, Michael Berry wrote DeLeon that the Bay State S.L.P. was "seething instead of settled."[3] In July, the entire party came apart in a forthright family scrap that included a pitched battle for national headquarters in New York. Two editions of the *People,* two parties claiming the S.L.P. label, two party hierarchies resulted. DeLeon consolidated his hold on one remnant; the other faction, which he dubbed the "Kangaroos," included Morris Hillquit, Henry Slobodin, A. M. Simons, Max Hayes, Job Harriman, J. Mahlon Barnes, and a flock of others whose loss the S.L.P. would never replace.

Every local in the nation felt the aftershock of the upheaval in New York. The Boston organization, never more than precariously united, promptly burst into several fragments. A group of DeLeonites in Lawrence referred to the rebels as "Tammany's catspaw," while rivals in the city observed that DeLeon would soon obtain harmony by becoming a party of one. The Springfield *Proletarian,* the Bay State's official S.L.P. newspaper, fell to the Kangaroos. But important party figures like David Goldstein, Martha Avery, and Michael Berry remained with DeLeon for the moment. Berry scurried for his pen when an issue of the wrong *People* arrived on his Haverhill doorstep. The paper contained Horace Eaton's congratulatory note and his order for one hundred copies of the Kangaroo sheet for distribution to locals of the Boot and Shoe Workers' Union. Berry lumped Eaton and Carey together, denounced them both, and announced defiantly that "that kind of Socialism don't go here. . . ."[4]

3. Berry to DeLeon, February 5, 1899, DeLeon Papers.
4. J. J. Duffy to Henry Slobodin, August 28, 1899; F. Tepper to Slobodin, October 11, 1899; Avery to Slobodin, July 17, 1899; Berry to Slobodin, July 21, 1899, Socialist Labor Party Papers, Tamiment Institute

Berry's claim to define Haverhill's Socialism had had no validity for years; by his own admission he spoke for precisely six fellows.[5] DeLeonites elsewhere in Massachusetts had key organizational positions. Using only a little chicanery, DeLeon retained what was left of the Socialist Labor party at the state convention in Worcester. Both DeLeon and Hillquit came to the meeting to corral wavering delegates. The Worcester press, amused at the energy expended for control of an insignificant organization, reported the tempest with tolerant and detached good humor: it was a "faction fight betwixt tweedledum and tweedledee . . ."; only a "poor specimen . . . could not get in half a dozen speeches . . ."; "the Chairman didn't seem to know the difference between a point of order and a pint of ale. . . ." The whole raucous, ridiculous affair was over as soon as the DeLeonites elected the committee on credentials, which could be trusted to handle contested seats in the same arbitrarily partisan way the DeLeonite chairman ran the meeting. Kangaroo delegates from Clinton, Springfield, Holyoke, Worcester, and Westfield walked out and nominated their own slate for the state election.

Social Democrats carefully observed the proceedings in Worcester. When, in mid-October, the Kangaroos withdrew their ticket from the ballot, Social Democratic interest mounted. Margaret Haile suggested that dissident Socialist Laborites might agree with Social Democrats on a common slate, while otherwise maintaining separate organizations. The offer was rudely rebuffed. In November, Morris Kaplan, an S.L.P. rebel from Boston, again raised the subject. He thought "more practical methods" impera-

Division of New York University Libraries. This collection will be referred to hereafter as Slobodin Papers. Berry may have misdated his letter, for the issue of the Kangaroo *People* to which he took exception was July 23, 1899. See also Kangaroo *People*, July 30, 1899; August 6, 1899; November 12, 1899.
5. Berry to Slobodin, July 16, 1899, Slobodin Papers.

tive; "further dilly dallying" would only increase the discouragement that already pervaded the whole Socialist movement. Socialism could be rescued and enthusiasm would return, Kaplan said, only if Social Democrats and his Kangaroos could hold simultaneous conventions and work out a plan of union.[6]

Kaplan's comrades saw barriers. Having shed DeLeon, they were in no mood to be bossed by Victor Berger. The Springfield *Proletarian* wanted nothing to do with the S.D.P.

> The Social-Democratic party has too much of the Jesuitical, compromising spirit in its propaganda, and too many ex-ministers and Y.M.C.A. workers (we never knew anything good to come from them) in its leadership. We want to see the leaders spring from the industrial proletaire. . . . The Socialist movement is a movement of the unwashed working class. . . .

The *Proletarian* preferred to eliminate DeLeon and then rejoin the S.L.P. "Comrade DeLeon," admonished the paper, "you are standing in the way of a reuniting of our forces. . . ."

Morris Kaplan was not ready to discard his idea. With unblushing exaggeration, he argued that all Social Democratic leaders were fine proletarians and former members of the S.L.P. He pointed out that prospects for growth would be severely limited if Socialists rejected everyone who had once belonged to some church. Kaplan finally got some high-level help. The Kangaroo editor of the *People* rebuked the *Proletarian*'s reference to "the unwashed working class. . . ." Non-proletarians, said the *People*, could make a constructive contribution, and were welcome in the Socialist movement.[7]

6. Kangaroo *People*, October 1, 1899; November 12, 1899. Tamiment Library holds a scrapbook of clippings about the Worcester convention. This account is based largely on those clippings.

7. The *Proletarian* (Springfield), December 24, 1899; Kangaroo *People*, November 26, 1899; December 17, 31, 1899.

Benjamin Feigenbaum, a New York Kangaroo, decided to clear up some misconceptions. He wrote to James Carey suggesting that the Haverhill politician make a formal statement answering charges that appeared almost weekly in the DeLeonite press. Carey's soft answer was obviously designed to turn away wrath. His vote for the notorious armory appropriation, he wrote, had not indicated support for a fortress for strike breakers, but was only an attempt to secure adequate sanitary facilities. He had not resigned from the Common Council as the national office had demanded because his local had not recognized the jurisdiction of the national party. The Haverhill movement had emphatically not combined with the Democrats, as rejection of proffered endorsements demonstrated. Finally, Feigenbaum was authorized to assure his colleagues that Carey was "unqualifiedly for union" on any honorable basis and that he would "retire from the movement" if his presence was a barrier to Socialist unity.

The major obstacle to a union of Bay State Socialists was indeed people, not ideas. Except for a few DeLeonites, no Massachusetts Socialist objected to James F. Carey; but almost without exception, no Socialist wanted anything to do with David Goldstein and Martha Moore Avery, two Bostonians who had aided DeLeon at Worcester. By mid-November a DeLeonite found the pair so despicable that he would not even wish them on the Kangaroos. Martha Avery, wrote Frank MacDonald, "would, for her own mean, petty, personal ends" make an alliance with anybody. She recently had decided the Kangaroos were more likely to succeed and was shifting her allegiance. The Worcester Kangaroos, perhaps partly in response to this warning, but on another pretext, adopted a resolution explicitly condemning Mrs. Avery.[8]

8. *SDH*, December 2, 1899; Frank MacDonald to C. E. Spelman, November 20, 1899, in Kangaroo *People*, December 10, 1899; see also November 12, 1899; December 3, 1899.

But David Goldstein outmaneuvered everyone. With the connivance of L. D. Usher, the DeLeonite state secretary, Goldstein in January reported the defection of the entire official hierarchy. Noting the absence of a rival, he boldly claimed to speak for all Massachusetts Kangaroos. Morris Kaplan protested that Goldstein was "endeavoring to build up a machine of his own." Mrs. Avery, Kaplan noted, was a cynical opportunist. Both had deserted the S.L.P. one jump ahead of the auditors, and neither should be admitted to the new party without a referendum of the state's members. L. S. Oliver, an officer of the Westfield branch, asked the national officers not to recognize Goldstein's committee and advanced a scheme to rid the party of its unwanted, self-proclaimed directorate. "Above all," wrote Oliver, "we don't want Avery state organizer."

We recognize her knowledge, ability, etc, as to the principles of socialism and the tactics of the Socialist Party, . . . but we know also, that wherever Avery is there also is strife among the comrades, for she is productive of discord wherever she goes.[9]

While Goldstein and Mrs. Avery did not inspire confidence in Massachusetts, they won recognition from national headquarters. The Kangaroo *People* deplored Mrs. Avery's intellectual arrogance but published her explanation for her tardy decision to bolt. Only at the Worcester convention, she said, did she realize that Daniel DeLeon would ruin the S.L.P. if he could not rule it. She too wished to break with such tyranny. This unconvincing statement failed to disclose why Mrs. Avery's discovery had come some months after the Worcester convention adjourned or to excuse her own role there in abetting De-Leon. DeLeonites had another explanation. The financial records of the Goldstein-Usher state committee baffled the

9. Kaplan to Slobodin, January 14, 1900; Oliver to Slobodin, January 9, 1899 [*sic*], Slobodin Papers.

S.L.P.'s auditors. The dubious items were payments to Usher and Mrs. Avery. Morris Kaplan later remembered that Goldstein had once before been accused of channelling party funds to Mrs. Avery without authorization; Kaplan had himself seen Goldstein's juggled ledgers. L. S. Oliver suggested that the pair had deserted DeLeon only because there was no treasury left to loot.[10]

If Kangaroos mistrusted Goldstein and Mrs. Avery, Social Democrats found them even less attractive. Those who had once been their comrades in the S.L.P., like Carey and Squire Putney, disliked them personally and found their brand of Socialism irrelevant. Social Democrats who lacked this previous association knew that Mrs. Avery babbled about Marxism and had been jeered by labor audiences. Shoe workers in Brockton, never interested in Socialist ideology, had read Horace Eaton's derisive account of her appearance before striking shoe workers in Marlboro. She had denounced the Boot and Shoe Workers' Union for its lack of class consciousness, and had generated so much public disapproval that State Police had to escort her to her hotel.[11] Staid Brockton shoe workers, the core of one of the state's most important and strongest locals, had little use for such a harpy.

With unity becoming a topic of general interest among Bay State Socialists, Squire Putney, who had himself left the S.L.P. only a year before, decided to apply a brake.[12]

10. Kangaroo *People*, January 14, 21, 28, 1900; Oliver to Slobodin, January 12, 1900, Slobodin Papers; Undated Memorandum of Kaplan, SP Papers.

11. Boot and Shoe Workers' Union, *Monthly Report*, November–December, 1898, January–February–March, 1899, 14–15. (The Union's *Monthly Report* did not appear so often as the title promised.)

12. In view of Victor Berger's later stand, it seems reasonable to suppose that he urged friends in Massachusetts to check the spontaneous demand for unity. Berger was in the state in mid-January on an unspecified mission connected with a forthcoming convention. The substance of his discussion with Haverhill leaders, for instance, was not disclosed. (*HSD*, January 20, 1900; *Gazette*, January 18, 1900.)

In January, he acknowledged reservations about unity because of the emerging leadership of the Bay State Kangaroos. Later, while Putney cheered the union of Socialists in Massachusetts, he confessed grave misgivings about a few DeLeonites who, he believed, would sneak into the Social Democratic party and bring discord. While Putney was not specific, his reference to Goldstein and Mrs. Avery was unmistakable. Fred Gordon remarked that the better one knew "these S.L.P. people of both sexes," the less one wanted to be associated with them. Michael Berry knew that Carey shared these sentiments completely. Carey himself later seemed at a loss to explain just how Goldstein and Avery had become Social Democrats; somehow, he wrote, "Davy and Mrs. A. *Appeared* in our organization." [13]

Nonetheless, the drive toward unity gathered momentum. In December, 1899 the *Haverhill Social Democrat,* while advocating unity in principle, doubted that the two factions could ever work in harmony. In January, Chase asked the Haverhill local to consider the matter. It voted to postpone consideration until after the Kangaroo convention that was to meet in Rochester, New York, at the end of the month. But from Clinton and Chelsea came resolutions for unity from joint meetings of Social Democrats and Socialist Laborites. Then, from the Rochester convention, came words of conciliation and news of a Permanent Committee of Socialist Union that would seek an honorable merger with Social Democrats at that party's March convention in Indianapolis. [14]

The political situation in Massachusetts was much on the minds of the delegates in Rochester. Morris Hillquit

13. Kangaroo *People,* March 25, 1900; *SDH,* January 27, 1900; May 5, 1900; *People,* June 6, 1903; Carey to C. D. Thompson, January 12, 1914, SP Papers.

14. Kangaroo *People,* January 7, 28, 1900; *HSD,* December 30, 1899; January 13, 1900.

noted that the S.D.P. and the Kangaroo organization there were of about equal size, and that strife between them would inevitably be fierce. The Kangaroo newspaper, reviewing the convention, noted that the S.D.P. had recently had great success in Massachusetts,—Chase's re-election, Carey's re-election, and the initial victories in Brockton,—and that these accomplishments had mellowed previous hostility in the S.D.P. hierarchy. The *People* added a threat: "any attempt on the part of the leading element of the S.D.P. to frustrate unity . . . would cause the membership . . . practically to bring it about over the heads of the leaders.[15] A few leaders from Haverhill, working with Morris Hillquit, Job Harriman, and other Kangaroos, and relying on the emotional desire for union that had grown up among Socialists everywhere, ultimately did in fact bring union over the bitter protest of the national leaders of the S.D.P.

The *Proletarian*, opposed to union before the Rochester meeting, surrendered. The *Haverhill Social Democrat*, which had been reserving judgment, also declared for union. For the moment, Massachusetts Socialists were unreservedly in favor of a joyous official wedding. The *Proletarian* welcomed the end of fraternal quarrels: "The Socialist movement in America has entered a new era. . . . A common cause, a common enemy must produce unity of action. In a movement . . . of the working class, differences of method . . . must occur, but all that is necessary for comradeship among Socialists is the agreement on fundamental questions." [16]

Unity meant taking the bitter with the sweet, and the Massachusetts Socialists eventually had to swallow both Mrs. Avery and David Goldstein. Not even Eugene Debs's

15. "Proceedings of the Tenth Annual Convention of the Socialist Labor Party" (Reproduction of typescript, Tamiment Institute Library), Second Session, 14; Kangaroo *People*, February 11, 1900.
16. Quoted in Kangaroo *People*, February 25, 1900.

warning that the Kangaroos had not fully purged the taint of DeLeonism deterred those in Massachusetts who wanted unity. As Social Democrats assembled in Indianapolis to discuss the problem, Addison Barr, a Worcester Social Democrat, said Debs's remark had done "more to obstruct Socialist organization" than DeLeon had accomplished in a decade. The need to combine, Barr held, was "undeniable"; only petty matters of place and individual prestige held Socialists apart; continued division would only "disgust our friends and amuse our enemies. . . ." [17]

Agreement at Indianapolis proved difficult. Midwestern Social Democrats, in full control of party machinery, did not welcome growth if it meant a change in management. For some time Massachusetts had objected to direction from Wisconsin and Illinois. The National Executive Board had no interest in adding either to the friction or to the strength of those who objected.

But the hierarchy could not master the fractious convention. Massachusetts delegates were constantly in the spotlight. John C. Chase and William Mailly, the editor of the Haverhill paper, were among the party leaders elected to preside. James Carey helped to smash the attempt to put the discarded program for the farmer back into the platform. He also offered a resolution defining the party's relation to organized labor that enraged Victor Berger. The resolution, which proclaimed the party's disapproval of any effort to divert trade unions from economic to political ends, seemed to Berger "a slap in the face of the Milwaukee comrades," because of their close tie with the local Federated Trade Council. He shouted Milwaukee's resentment of "instructions from the little city of Haverhill. . . ." The motion was recommitted, but Carey salvaged the substance of the resolution by a few tactful changes in wording.

17. Kangaroo *People,* March 4, 1900; *SDH,* January 20, 1900.

Union with the Kangaroos, represented at Indianapolis by Hillquit, Harriman, and Hayes, among others, could not be effected with semantic compromises. Frederic O. MacCartney, Carey's newly elected comrade in the Massachusetts General Court, brought in the majority report on the problem. MacCartney's document indicated how far the party's directors had been pushed toward union. It proposed a joint committee to work out unresolved details, but insisted that the new party bear the Social Democratic name. A minority report recommended retention of the name, but did not make it a condition of union.

The squabble over the party's name was symbolic. Since the convention obviously favored union, the question was whether it would be proposed with conditions that might alienate Kangaroos. On this issue the Massachusetts delegates divided, with Margaret Haile supporting MacCartney's resolution, while Squire Putney, Carey, and Chase argued for the minority report. The convention was in no mood to quibble. When the roll was called, the minority report had the backing of the majority of delegates, including, quite unexpectedly, Seymour Stedman, a member of the National Executive Board, Eugene Debs, and even Frederic MacCartney, who had been won over during the debate. The nine-member committee to negotiate final terms with the S.L.P. included Carey, Chase, and Margaret Haile.

Only selection of the party's nominees for President and vice-president remained. Here too differences between midwestern leaders and the Haverhill politicians obtruded. The Kangaroos had already nominated Harriman and Max Hayes for these offices, but they expected the convention to agree on a unified slate of Debs and Harriman. Frederic MacCartney nominated Debs, but to the consternation of all, Debs said his health prevented his candidacy. The S.D.P. leadership may have expected to

trade a suddenly healthy Debs for concessions from the
S.L.P., particularly the assurance that the Social Democratic name would be unchanged. For a moment, the
convention lacked direction. MacCartney declined the
presidential nomination, as did Theodore Debs. Berger
and his followers would let the pressure build before beginning discussion with the Kangaroos. But the party
leaders had calculated without the Haverhill contingent,
which moved to take charge. While confused delegates
pondered three refusals of the honor, James Carey, with
superb timing, nominated Job Harriman. Meyer London,
a New Yorker who was suspicious of Socialist Laborites,
objected that Harriman was not a member of the party
and therefore could not be nominated. From the chair,
John Chase ruled the point of order not well taken. William Mailly rose to second Harriman's nomination, and
then nominated Max Hayes for vice-president. Only a
motion to adjourn stopped a stampede. Haverhill had
served its ultimatum; Carey's action, according to Berger's
lieutenant Fred Heath, confirmed the open secret that
Haverhill might establish a new party.

Leaders of both groups thereupon shut themselves in a
hotel room to hammer out details of union. The precise
terms of the bargain were almost immediately a matter of
dispute. The concrete result was a ticket of Debs and Harriman. The delegates ratified the nominees by acclama-
tion, and believing that unity was secure, went home.[18]

Two weeks later the joint committee on unity met in
New York and harmony vanished in a matter of hours.
The exact nature of the agreement at Indianapolis was the
ostensible cause of the argument; the precise form of the
referendum on the party's name furnished an opportunity

18. This account of the convention is based on material in the Kangaroo *People*, March 18, 1900; *HSD*, March 10–March 24, 1900; *SDH*,
May 12, 1900; *People*, March 18, 25, 1900; Quint, *Forging*, 344–349.

for disgruntled Social Democrats to cry "bad faith." The pretext was trivial. The fundamental issue was control of the party organization, and eastern determination to take over could hardly have been more obvious. The committee considered the location of party headquarters, a crucial decision, since the controlling executive board of the party would be selected from nearby states to save transportation expense. Stedman and Haile, speaking for the S.D.P. leadership, preferred Chicago; eventually the rest of the group settled on Springfield, Massachusetts. Carey and Chase helped put through a motion that the executive committee consist of four members each from New York and Massachusetts and two from Connecticut. The coup was complete.

The National Executive Board of the Social Democratic party scanned reports of the conference in New York and disavowed everything. The Chicago group had no intention of passively dissolving and announced its own referendum to discover whether union was desirable, a question about which there had previously been little doubt. Phrases in the N.E.B.'s manifesto about the deceit of Kangaroo leaders and treachery in the ranks were pointed hints to the appropriate vote.[19]

Haverhill's Social Democrats had made their decision: unity of all Socialists if possible, but unity only on terms that guaranteed Haverhill's autonomy. The group had enormous prestige among Socialists; a choice of Hillquit and the Kangaroos over Berger and the Social Democrats might bring two regional parties. The Haverhill leaders used the threat of such a choice—and the knowledge that resulting divisions would shake American Socialism for years—to promote a union of the two groups. Their influence, tactical skill, and continuing political importance

19. *SDH*, April 7, 1900; *HSD*, April 7, 1900.

helped pave the way back to Indianapolis, a second convention, and unity.

William Mailly read the N.E.B.'s manifesto and decided to preserve official silence in the *Haverhill Social Democrat*. Silence did not connote hesitation. The Kangaroos learned immediately that the manifesto enraged Carey. Mailly sent a reassuring letter telling Morris Hillquit of the "universal condemnation" the manifesto had roused in Haverhill. Mailly hoped that the Kangaroos would not indiscriminately blame all Social Democrats for the precipitate action of a few muddled individuals. Haverhill would "continue to agitate for the name social democratic party," but this position was meant to reduce barriers to union, and "at the same time remove the conduct of the movement" from the N.E.B. In reply, Hillquit agreed to support the Social Democratic label in order to forestall the formation of a rump S.D.P. that might steal a ready-made following, particularly in Massachusetts.[20]

John Chase thought the joint committee on unity might appeal to the membership around the stubborn Chicago officials. The operation would require care and should be tried only after the referendum was completed. Chase also reported that emissaries from Haverhill were "working night and day to secure a favorable vote." Along with their "encouraging reports" came word that "the enemy" was "doing an awful hustle to carry it their [*sic*] way." Chase still thought the rank and file in Massachusetts was safely for union, but he was not sure which way the state committee would jump.[21]

The fight looked too close to forego any weapons. Mailly committed the *Social Democrat* in a two-column editorial. He deplored the N.E.B.'s action, and predicted

20. F. Tepper to Slobodin, April 8, 1900, Slobodin Papers; Mailly to Hillquit, April 8, 1900; April 10, 1900, Hillquit Papers.
21. Chase to Hillquit, April 12, 1900; April 13, 1900, Hillquit Papers.

that "the few who promulgated it" would be rebuked by "the disapproval of the great majority of party members." Dissatisfaction "because things [were] not going their way" was no excuse for Social Democrats to emulate DeLeon.[22] From that moment on, the *Social Democrat* was a foremost champion of Socialist unity.

While appealing to Socialists all over the state, the *Social Democrat* spoke only for Haverhill. While some Socialists decided for unity, others were in opposition. The Brockton local, never very concerned about the question, had sent no delegates to Indianapolis; it voted 58 to 2 to sustain the N.E.B. Frederic MacCartney and Margaret Haile recorded their approval of the manifesto. The state committee, as Chase had predicted, was so divided it could come to no decision after five hours of debate. And Eugene Debs published a letter in the *Social Democratic Herald* that Mailly feared would have great influence in the Bay State. Debs supposed time would mellow the Kangaroos but thought it better to preserve separate identities until after the national election. Mailly wrote a worried and confidential report to Hillquit.

Here in Mass. those branches whom we have reached are all right, though . . . we have little time for visiting. . . . Haile and MacCartney are running around to all the branches they can get into. . . . [W]e think it well . . . to prepare for the worst, so that in case union be voted down we can take steps immediately *to have union anyhow.* It will be impossible for us to work in the same party with those who have engineered the fight against Socialist unity. . . . I speak for Comrades Chase, Carey, Hayman, besides myself. . . . Now, we suggest . . . a private conference be held. . . . We can discuss the situation and arrive at a plan . . . in the event that union is voted down.[23]

22. *HSD,* April 21, 1900.
23. *SDH,* April 7, 14, 21, 28, 1900; *HSD,* April 28, 1900; May 12, 1900; Mailly to Hillquit, April 24, 1900, Hillquit Papers. The emphasis is Mailly's.

Through April and early May, the *Social Democrat* plumped for union until the *Social Democratic Herald* observed irritably that "the constitution and not the Haverhill Social Democrat" was "the law of the . . . party." The N.E.B.'s position seemed sustained when its referendum revealed 1,213 votes against union and 930 in favor. Massachusetts sent exactly one-third of the votes for union; of these 310, 174 were from Haverhill. Massachusetts also had 251 members who opposed union; of those, two were from Haverhill. The total vote, in the nation as in Massachusetts, was manifestly no more than a fraction of the membership. The N.E.B. threw out the votes of twelve locals in Massachusetts alone on the grounds that their dues were not current. These ballots would not have altered the result, but the unionists could plausibly argue that a fair vote of the entire S.D.P. had yet to be taken.

While the Socialist press kept up the propaganda battle through the early summer, Haverhill politicians schemed with Job Harriman to bring union in Massachusetts. Harriman approved the S.L.P.'s participation in a joint convention and reported to Hillquit that Massachusetts Socialists would come out of the meeting united. "The Haverhill boys are firm, and will stand with us to the end," he noted. The proposed joint convention pleased William Mailly. The united Socialists would retain the party machinery and the right to be "Social Democrats" on the ballot in November. "We have something to lose in Haverhill and Mass.," Mailly wrote Morris Hillquit. Haverhill did not intend to lose.[24]

Margaret Haile knew something was afoot but lacked the votes on the state committee to block motions of the unity forces. She estimated that Brockton and twenty-five

<hr>

24. *SDH*, May 5, 12, 19, 1900; *HSD*, May 12, 1900; June 16, 1900; Harriman to Hillquit, June 13, 1900; Mailly to Hillquit, June 15, 1900, Hillquit Papers.

other branches were "loyal to principle," while perhaps
fifteen branches followed Haverhill's "unworthy lead."
Two weeks later, she thought thirty branches would stay
with the Chicago board: "The old Bay State is all right
Comrades. She stands pat!"

But the Haverhill steamroller flattened the opposition.
After Margaret Haile, as state secretary, broke an initial
tie, her opponents had everything their own way. "We
started out," she recalled, "exactly even in numbers, but
very uneven in equipment."

One man made all the motions and all the others had to do
was holler for them and to remember their slates for the . . .
committees. . . . The loyal comrades . . . came into the convention expecting it would be carried on with a semblance of
fairness. It did not take them long to realize they were up
against a labor-saving machine, and they did not know how to
deal with it.[25]

The convention invited waiting S.L.P. delegates to join. In
an emotional moment, they marched in under a huge red
banner to a warm demonstration. The combined parties
promptly voted to run one Social Democratic ticket. The
two state committees were instructed to work jointly in
managing the campaign. The important Brockton local,
which had been suspicious of Kangaroos, accepted the
convention's decision, and the possibility of a split in the
state disappeared.[26] Haverhill's bosses could give even
Victor Berger a lesson in party control.

With a national campaign also in the offing, Socialists
opposed to the N.E.B. established headquarters at Springfield under the newly-elected national secretary, William
Butscher. The Springfield faction was initially too proud
to invite Debs to campaign in the eastern states, and Har-

25. *SDH*, June 23, 1900, July 7, 28, 1900.
26. *HSD*, July 14, 1900; Brockton *Times*, July 9, 1900. A split in Brockton did occur as a result of action at the convention, but the quarrel was
unrelated to the unity problem and is treated in Chapter 4.

riman, for one, was in private sarcastically critical of his running mate, though he knew Debs would attract votes that would otherwise be lost. John Chase too was "utterly disgusted" with the Chicago Socialists "from top to bottom." But his better judgment told him that provoking an open fight was bad politics. Butscher's pique would never let him admit that he needed the presidential candidate, even when he finally encouraged the unified state committee to invite Debs to Massachusetts. "In some places in the east," noted the secretary ungraciously, ". . . we have forced [Debs] to speak under our auspices, as his following is so small that the meeting would be a fizzle without our aid." When Debs toured Massachusetts, he visited only communities that had opposed unity. Haverhill was conspicuously not on his itinerary.[27]

After the election, Massachusetts Socialists renewed their pressure for union. In mid-November, Socialists of all factions, meeting in Boston, resolved that immediate unity was desirable. The *Haverhill Social Democrat* urged the Chicago leadership to drop its "narrow and intolerant, DeLeonite (we hope Comrade Daniel will pardon the comparison) tactics." Haverhill even had a hymn that minimized internal quarrels:

> Like a mighty army
> Moves the S.D.P.
> Fighting, ever fighting
> Slaves of toil to free;
> Splits are only seeming,
> All one body we.
> One in hope and goal and
> Solidarity.[28]

27. Harriman to Hillquit, August 18, 1900; Chase to Hillquit, July 24, 1900, Hillquit Papers; William Butscher to H. D. Thomas (August 28, 1900), A. M. Simons (August 13, 1900), T. Morgan (September 17, 1900), and G. B. Leonard (October 11, 1900), Butscher Letterbooks in SP Papers. See also *SDH,* November 10, 1900.

28. Kangaroo *People,* November 26, 1900; *HSD,* December 22, 1900; January 19, 1901.

The Chicago N.E.B. soon called a convention restricted to its own following, an action that Butscher publicly deplored. MacCartney and Margaret Haile, still opposed to union, attended and the latter was elected to the new governing committee. Clearly the committee would have progressively less members to direct unless somehow union were achieved. The assembly proposed that another convention assemble at Indianapolis.[29]

Frederic MacCartney returned to his duties at the Massachusetts House of Representatives. Though he and James Carey were at odds on the unity question, they worked in harness in the legislature. As they talked over the divisions in the national movement, the two Massachusetts legislators evolved the strategy that would lead to the formation of the Socialist Party of America. For when Carey and MacCartney agreed, the Massachusetts Socialists were in a position to throw the state's weight, in delegates and prestige, on one side of the balance. Carey urged his Springfield colleagues to be tolerant, to accept the call for the unity convention, and to work for maximum representation. The party had to operate in complete good faith; it must be willing to settle for less than perfect unity, and it should "make *no play for position.*" Discretion was of the essence. Carey shared the plan with Hillquit, who was to inform Harriman and the Springfield governing committee. Nothing must get into print to alarm the N.E.B. "I do not write unadvisedly," he concluded cryptically; "I have faith in the outcome of the con[vention] at Ind[ianapolis] if we pursue this course." Carey even endorsed a plan of union opposed by the *Haverhill Social Democrat.* Nor did he change his mind when Harriman suggested another that the *Social Democrat* preferred. Harriman was quietly annoyed, but Carey

29. *HSD,* December 22, 1900; January 26, 1901; *SDH,* January 26, 1901.

liked the state autonomy Massachusetts had had in the Springfield organization, and he thought Harriman's proposal more centralized than the alternative.[30]

Carey also realized that state autonomy was the key to national unity. Politicians in command of state organizations would not concede direction to national headquarters but might accept union if their local control were not disturbed. The Indianapolis convention accepted a constitution which, according to Frederic MacCartney, had state autonomy as its purpose. Conceivably, Carey and MacCartney had worked out this provision in conversations in Boston. Carey's letter to Hillquit did not disclose the details of these conversations; it only suggested what Hillquit should do. Perhaps Carey feared Hillquit or other Kangaroos would oppose state autonomy and therefore bought delay with a vague letter. At the same time, Carey encouraged Kangaroos to accept any proposal tending toward union as preferable to the current factional strife. James Carey and Frederic MacCartney may have known almost exactly what these proposals would be.

The two legislators continued to play an important part once the convention had assembled in July. MacCartney found the healing compromise on an early procedural question; Carey was a judicious chairman of the second session. They joined members of both factions in opposition to A. M. Simons' attempt to write a platform consisting only of Socialist principles and lacking demands for immediate reform. MacCartney thought the notion as fatuous as the expectation of an immediate second coming of Christ.

. . . let us be the party of the ideal, but let us also be the party of the actual. . . . Imagine Comrade Carey and myself

30. Carey to Hillquit, February 12, 1901, Hillquit Papers; *HSD*, June 8, 15, 1901; July 6, 1901; August 4, 1901; Harriman to Carey, July 9, 1901, copy in William Edlin Papers, Yivo Institute for Jewish Research, New York City.

. . . putting but one bill in during an entire session, and that a bill for the establishment of a Cooperative Commonwealth! We would be the laughing stock of Massachusetts. . . . If you are going to . . . dwell solely upon the social revolution, then I say . . . give up . . . this theatrical proceeding of forming a political party. . . . [B]e nothing but a band of prophets clad in hair cloth and living on locusts. . . .

Reform demands, committing the party to collective ownership, higher wages, shorter hours, national insurance and various proposals for more democratic government, were retained.

Though he favored concrete proposals for immediate reform, Carey would make no concession to midwestern hankering for the farm vote. Farmers were owners of the means of agricultural production, and Carey knew enough about Socialism to appreciate what that meant. Still he was not entirely orthodox. When a delegate moved to include the word "revolutionary" in the preamble of the platform, Carey moved that "scientific, class-conscious, militant, clean-cut" be added as well. Max Hayes, the chairman, aware of Carey's reputation for wit, suspected that the convention was being treated to some. Was the amendment made in good faith? It was, Carey snapped, "no more ridiculous than the other amendment."

The problem of a name for the uniting party was quickly resolved by agreement on the Socialist Party of America, a solution that Carey erroneously recalled having favored the year before. Location of party headquarters proved less easy. Berger advocated Chicago, a proposal to which Carey took immediate exception. He would be happy with any location but New York or Chicago, both of which were too closely associated with intra-party strife. Perhaps Cleveland, he suggested, might be a suitable compromise.

. . . I am unalterably opposed to either New York or Chicago until the formative processes that are going on . . . have evolved a body of men, that are not only agitators, that are not only able to read Marx in the original, that are not only able to write platforms in the wink of an eye, but are able to . . . cooperate with each other for the good of the whole.

St. Louis was the eventual compromise, and Carey supported it.[31]

The Indianapolis convention, indeed, did very little that James Carey could not support. Others compromised, but Carey gave up nothing that he was determined to have. His voting pattern shifted, now with Berger, now with the Kangaroos; he was an orthodox Socialist on the plank for farmers, but scoffed at intellectuals in opposing New York and Chicago as unsuitable headquarters. Unfailingly good natured and never stuffy, he brought union back to Massachusetts on Massachusetts' terms.

Carey and his Massachusetts friends had worked for unity from the time of the Rochester convention. They thought they had won at the first Indianapolis convention but had overplayed their hand when they deprived the Social Democracy's midwestern faction of any role in the party's direction. Yet they would not surrender to the N.E.B., and skillfully threatened to make a strong party without the Chicago group. The probability that the Springfield party would outlive Berger's following was enough to force the N.E.B. to reopen negotiation. This time, James Carey, working with Frederic MacCartney, coaxed the two proud, sensitive, balky rivals to become partners. The condition of the deal was local autonomy, which, by no coincidence, was the one principle on which James Carey had always insisted.

Controversy over Socialist unity meant that the Massachusetts Socialists, for all their protestations to the con-

31. "Proceedings of the Socialist Unity Convention," 296, 45, 60, 138–139, 204–205, 245, 220, 277–278, 380–381. A transcript of the Indianapolis proceedings is in the SP Papers.

trary, were divided during the campaign of 1900. The Kangaroo edition of *People* gave extensive coverage to a losing fight in Haverhill, while only one insignificant item indicated the success of the Brockton group that had opposed unity. Similarly, the *Social Democratic Herald*, which spoke for the N.E.B., seemed almost pleased when John Chase lost his bid for a third term. Elizabeth Thomas, Berger's associate, who had worked in Haverhill during Chase's campaign in 1899, contrasted the moral fervor of that victory with the drab defeat of 1900. Haverhill's decision to break with the Social Democratic leadership, she explained, had deprived the local of both "moral and material aid." The tale had a moral: "The most flourishing branch, if it is cut from the parent tree, withers in a few hours." [32]

Elizabeth Thomas's partisan explanation was not entirely persuasive. Carey, in fact, narrowly won re-election to the legislature and the *Social Democratic Herald* was willing to acknowledge a winner. The N.E.B.'s refusal to aid Chase hardly figured in his losing attempt to defy an unwritten ban on third mayoral terms. Following a brief exile from City Hall, the Republicans in Haverhill swore off intra-party quarrels. The Democrats withdrew their nominee against Chase, an action that created a more harmonious coalition than the formal effort to fuse the two parties in 1899. Everyone in the city grew more cautious because orders at local shoe factories were down from the high level of 1899. Socialists discovered that the electorate thought two years long enough to deliver on old promises, and could not find new ones to enliven a listless campaign.

The Socialists worked to send Chase back to City Hall. They addressed a manifesto to the public denouncing the partisan obstruction of their coalition opponents in the

32. Kangaroo *People*, January 20, 1901; *SDH*, December 15, 1900.

city government. They attacked their opponents' record on street railway and telephone franchises, and the coalition's failure to support school construction and the two-dollar wage for city employees. The attack was blunted by the fact that the Citizens' coalition, as a coalition, had vanished. Chase's opponent was a Republican named Isaac Poor, and the record of the Citizens' organization of the year previous had little relevance. Socialists did not have to write a new program, since their old one was still not enacted. They revived proposals for municipal ownership, political democracy, better streets, and even the abolition of grade crossings.[33]

The G.O.P. ignored the Socialists' choice of issues to campaign on the need for restored business confidence. The *Criterion* sounded the theme as early as July: "Haverhill's reputation abroad is anything but an enviable one. As far west as Denver . . . newspaper readers know this as the home of 'Socialism' . . . ." Residents of Haverhill realized that the local movement was Socialist in name only. Still the notoriety discouraged businessmen from buying Haverhill's products. "Social Democracy," warned the *Criterion*, "has Haverhill in a grip which foretells nothing but ruin." The need, clearly, was an honest, businesslike administration.

Republicans shrewdly nominated a shoe worker to attract the labor vote, and promised efficiency and economy to restore confidence and prosperity and to remove the Socialist blot from the city's reputation. Though Socialists at first blustered that "class conscious workers" would "not be deceived by such a palpable subterfuge . . . ," the Republicans succeeded in making an economic recession the major campaign issue. In vain did the Socialists insist that the entire shoe industry was depressed and that the local situation was hardly their fault. Afraid that Republi-

33. *HSD*, November 17, 24, 1900.

cans were chipping away the middle class support that had carried Chase to victory, Social Democrats reassured the public that Socialists did not advocate confiscation of property or division of the national wealth into equal shares. The *Social Democrat* claimed that home-owning workers and independent small businessmen had more reason to oppose capitalism than to fear socialism. Such soft words, however, were all beside the point. Republicans were not talking about the dangers of Socialist doctrine. Times were hard, they noted, and the incumbent administration was responsible.[34]

Algernon Lee, the editor of the Kangaroo *People*, went to Haverhill for a first-hand look. His "Impressions of Haverhill" stressed the inspiring class solidarity of the movement there, a description romantically unrelated to the facts. Lee, who favored union, probably saw what he thought his readers would like to discover in their allies, for many New York Socialists retained too much of DeLeon's teaching to unite happily with a group that courted the bourgeoisie. Haverhill, the editor wrote, was ideologically sound.

Nowhere, I am sure, is there a more class-conscious movement. It is a class-consciousness that was not learned out of books but has grown up out of the lives of the people. There are some small businessmen among the comrades there . . . , but there is not a trace of middle-class feeling, of compromise, or utopianism. . . . I don't claim that Haverhill is a miniature New Jerusalem. But it may claim to be, in a historic sense, the gateway to the future earthly paradise.[35]

Lee proved as bad a prophet as he was a reporter. The voters of Haverhill decisively retired Chase; all the candidates for alderman were equally convincingly defeated.

34. *Saturday Evening Criterion* (Haverhill), July 29, 1900; *HSD*, November 17, 24, 1900; December 1, 1900; Kangaroo *People*, November 18, 1900.
35. Kangaroo *People*, December 9, 1900.

SOCIALISM AND THE WORKERS

Two members of the Council survived. The Socialist press, including Lee's *People*, insisted that the temporary setback was not indicative of a weakening organization; indeed the Haverhill local was stronger in defeat than it had been in victory. The *Social Democrat* discovered "more class conscious Socialists in Haverhill than ever before." The campaign, conducted against "gigantic odds," was unmatched in the nation "for strict adherence to the letter and spirit of Socialism. . . ." The opposition—"republican and democratic machines, prohibitionists, rum sellers, churches, the daily press," and all other groups that fought progress—had advanced "puerile arguments" and "makeshift issues"; no tactic had been "too mean, low, and despicable" if it served the G.O.P. cause. Haverhill had been exposed to "more solid agitation for Socialism" than any other American city, and the discouraging result limned the "herculean task" the Socialists faced nationally.[36]

Amid the many excuses and accusations was the explanation of Chase's defeat: many non-Socialist voters, who had supported Chase in 1899, were frightened by economic conditions and consequently had returned to the Republican fold. Some were disappointed at Chase's failure to accomplish very much in two years; some rebelled against a third term. More importantly, economic dislocation enabled Republicans to recapture what Chase called the "timid voter and the small property holder." Chase later remembered that the party had come to power partly because the voters blamed the incumbent for economic hardship; the same disillusionment, he thought, was the major cause of his defeat.[37]

36. *Ibid.*, December 9, 16, 1900; *HSD*, December 8, 15, 1900.
37. *Criterion*, December 8, 1900; *Literary Digest*, December 15, 1900, 724; *Independent*, December 13, 1900, 3004; Brockton *Times*, December 6, 1900; *People*, December 29, 1900; *HSD*, May 1, 1901; see also Kangaroo *People*, January 27, 1901, for a discussion of the importance of the prosperity issue.

The usual Socialist response to defeat was a renewed effort to organize more sections and to propagandize more widely. Yet the Haverhill campaign of 1900 had cost more than $700, of which less than $70 had been contributed locally. In spite of support from Socialists elsewhere, therefore, the local entered 1901 with a substantial debt that hampered its educational effort. The party was determined to keep the *Social Democrat* afloat and hired William Edlin after Mailly's resignation left the paper without an editor. A former lecturer and writer for the S.L.P., Edlin was more interested in socialist theory than was his predecessor. Mailly was an able administrator and a talented political organizer; at least in Haverhill, he had not been concerned about his readers' grasp of abstractions. His valedictory scorned those Socialists who took "fond delight in splitting hairs" or who mumbled "over paltry technicalities" of ideology while displaying "no real conception of the monumental task confronting the Socialists of the world." Edlin, by contrast, marvelled that the "untrained, uneducated proletarians" he met could ever have governed the city. He announced that henceforth the paper would publish ideological features to correct those intellectual deficiencies.[38]

Socialists of one precinct in Carey's district had another answer to declining interest. They formed a Socialist club, which bought chairs, games, a news stand, and a pool table for the club rooms. Membership soon climbed and talk of educational meetings was dropped in favor of a steamed clam social. A Fitchburg Socialist reached a similar solution. Socialists there had once rented churches and engaged "high class lecturers"; while this program attracted members, they were not "every day people." Socialists simply could not expect "tired workingmen in

38. Kangaroo *People*, January 27, 1901; *HSD*, December 8, 1900; January 12, 1901; Edlin to Sarah Boudin, December 27, 1900, Edlin Papers.

search of an evening's change and recreation . . . [to] come often to a cheerless hall and listen to even the best of speakers. . . ."[39]

Regardless of pool tables, editorials, and visiting lecturers, enthusiasm seeped out of the Massachusetts Socialist movement during 1901. During the summer, three out-of-town speakers visited Haverhill and local leaders could not be bothered to drum up an audience. Edlin chided his readers about their neglect without noticeably disturbing their apathy. The state convention, moreover, dusted off the standard platform and nominated little-known candidates who were incapable of mounting an exciting campaign in November. A correspondent in Adams noted "the laxity" of the party's effort. A rally in Haverhill attracted less than two hundred people. Leaving the "deadly tame" meeting, one Socialist sighed that things were not as they used to be. Massachusetts voters returned Carey and Mac-Cartney to the General Court. Other candidates for state office fared poorly, and Carey frankly confessed that those dismal results, combined with an unexpected, crushing defeat in Haverhill, would seem a "dull thud" to Socialists outside the state. The *Social Democrat,* rechristened the *Clarion,* moved to Boston where it would soon expire without notice. The *Gazette* clipped an item from the dying weekly to serve as the party's obituary:

The Socialists in Haverhill for a time got partial control of the city government, owing to peculiar local conditions, which enabled them to sweep in a large sympathetic vote of dissatisfied workingmen, whose votes went back to the Republican . . . or . . . Democratic party as soon as the semblance of good times struck them.[40]

39. *HSD,* December 15, 1900; January 5, 19, 1901; the *Clarion* (Haverhill), October 19, 1901. This paper was the successor to the *Haverhill Social Democrat.*
40. *HSD,* July 13, 1901; *Clarion,* September 14, 1901; the *Worker* (New York), September 22, 1901; November 10, 1901; December 29, 1901; *Criterion,* November 30, 1901; *Gazette,* December 15, 1901. The *Worker* succeeded the Kangaroo *People* in April, 1901.

THE VIEW AT THE TOP

William Mailly arrived in Boston during the post-election doldrums of January. With a mixture of cheer-leading, goading, and guidance, he coaxed the party back to life. Since Massachusetts no longer boasted a single Socialist paper, Mailly sent a weekly column to other party papers that circulated in the state. This device allowed locals to share their needs, hopes, and accomplishments with the rest of the movement and gave Mailly a pulpit from which to publicize the party's legislative record or to point to political opportunities.[41] He could not work miracles. Some of his letters went unanswered; some opportunities passed ungrasped. But gradually signs of life began to appear.

From Holyoke came a small money order and a proposed assessment to pay off the debt that had too long hampered the Massachusetts party. From Springfield came a report of new members and record crowds for a lecture by Father Thomas McGrady, a touring priest who had previously helped the state's Socialists. From Lynn came word of a growing interest in socialism among the city's Polish population. From Lawrence came an order for more literature. Sunday speakers reappeared on the Boston Common. Worcester Socialists began to proselyte during lunch hour at the factories. An autumn rally in Haverhill attracted about a thousand people instead of the few hundred of the year before. Weavers in Adams voted to endorse Socialist candidates, as did the Central Labor Union in Springfield. The state committee offered labor organizations throughout the Commonwealth speakers who would inform the membership about socialism; Mailly later thought resulting discussions had been the party's "most effective work. . . ."[42]

41. Mailly's column appeared in the *Worker* regularly after January 26, 1902.
42. Mailly to J. S. Smith, March 12, 1903, Mailly Letterbook II, SP Papers. The rest of the paragraph is based on items in the *Worker* as fol-

With MacCartney's timely help at the state convention, Mailly even resolved a controversy over atheism, which was the year's most worrisome development.[43] The party came out of the convention with a familiar platform, to some of which the national coal strike gave a new relevance. The party emphasized its support for those miners who were "compelled to suffer hunger and privation . . . while the mine and railroad owners" were allowed to manage "their organizations at the expense of the social welfare." To the annoyance of national headquarters, John C. Chase, the choice for governor, was called home from his lecture tour. The state organization demanded an active campaign by a well-known candidate.[44] Atheism was momentarily forgotten in anticipation of a great campaign; when the matter was reopened, neither Mailly nor any other Socialist would submerge it again.

Carey and MacCartney remained in Boston after the convention to address a nonpartisan meeting called to protest the arrogance of mine owners. Carey's opening plea for government ownership met a sympathetic response. From the floor came an unexpected resolution proposing nationalization. The audience roared approval. The party had found the exciting issue previously missing. John Chase got off the train in Boston and told reporters the coal strike was showing people all over the nation the truth of Socialist contentions. During the campaign, when Chase spoke under union sponsorship, he combined politics with an appeal for relief funds for the mine workers. Dr. George Galvin, the Boston Socialist physician, reportedly would not dismiss his patients without a short lecture proving that only public ownership could solve the fuel problem. Mailly, once an organizer among miners, revis-

lows: March 2, May 11 and 25, June 1, September 7, 14, and October 5, 12, and 19, 1902.

43. This problem is treated at length in Chapter 6.

44. *Worker*, September 14, 1902; a copy of the platform is also preserved in the broadside collection of the Tamiment Institute.

ited the coal area and then shared his experiences with audiences all over Massachusetts. "Mother" Jones, whose reputation as a friend of oppressed miners reached into New England, gave nine moving speeches in the Bay State.[45]

As November approached, the demand for Socialist speakers mounted. And the results of the election of 1902, said the Brockton *Times,* "staggered the older parties. . . ." The three hundred per cent Socialist increase in the state, continued the paper, "was nothing short of remarkable" and had "few parallels in political history." Chase polled nearly 34,000 votes; every town and city in the state registered a larger Socialist vote. Wallace Ransden of Brockton joined Carey and MacCartney in the General Court. The S.L.P., whose total dropped to 6,000, attributed the Socialists' showing to the votes of disgruntled Bryan Democrats who voted for Chase rather than William Gaston, the conservative Democratic nominee. Yet Gaston ran considerably ahead of previous Democratic totals, and the explanation was not convincing. The *Times* guessed the Socialists would hold their gains, and wondered whether the curve would continue to rise.[46]

Certainly the municipal contests a month later indicated no dip in Socialist support. Brockton voters gave the party an impressive victory. In Haverhill the Socialists went to court to gain the mayor's chair for Parkman Flanders. The Socialists were in a position to challenge Henri R. Watson, the apparent Republican victor, not because of their own ineffective campaign, but because Democrats nominated a strong candidate who made the race close. On first count, Flanders was fourteen votes short of victory. A recount cut the margin to twelve, and

45. *Worker,* September 21, 1902; October 5, 19, 1902; *Gazette,* October 6, 21, 1902; Boston *Sunday Herald,* January 4, 1903.
46. *Worker,* November 2, 1902; *People,* November 29, 1902; *Gazette,* November 10, 11, 1902; Brockton *Times,* November 5, 1902.

turned up eighteen questionable ballots that had been counted for Watson. These ballots had been marked in the box opposite the blank space for write-in candidates. Since Watson's name was in the space above, election officials reasoned that the voter intended to vote for the Republican candidate. Without these dubious votes, Flanders would be the next mayor of Haverhill. The Socialists hired George Fred Williams, a prominent Bryan Democrat, to take the case to court. The judges threw out the disputed votes, and Parkman B. Flanders was sworn in as mayor of Haverhill in a delayed ceremony in January.[47]

Socialists thought they knew where they had secured their new support in the state. As John Chase observed in a Socialist magazine: "The greater part of the gain . . . came from the ranks of labor, . . . especially from the forces of organized labor." The party, Chase said, had made the workers feel that Socialism was "their movement," and that the party was "their party." Another article in the same periodical emphasized the state's "exceptionally intelligent and well-educated" working class. A. M. Simons suggested that Massachusetts enjoyed the highest Socialist vote in the nation because it also had the lowest rate of illiteracy. "When we combine highly developed capitalism with an intelligent proletariat the result is Socialism. . . ."[48]

No Socialist proposed to let the pace slacken in 1903. The local in Whitman offered a prize for the best essay on Socialism by a high school student. Candidates in March elections in Amesbury, Bridgewater, Hyde Park, Leominster, Norwood, and Wakefield more than doubled the party's vote of 1902, and Stoughton elected an alderman

47. *Gazette*, December, 1902, *passim* and January 14–24, 1903; *Worker*, December 14, 1902.
48. John C. Chase, "Millennium Dawn in Massachusetts," in *Wilshire's Magazine*, January, 1903, 63; M. S. Johnson, "The Rise of Socialism in America," *ibid.*, July, 1903, 9; *ISR*, February, 1903, 361.

and half a dozen lesser officials. Boston Socialists called a mass meeting that declared the high price and limited supply of fuel to be "a result of private ownership of the means of fuel production, distribution, and supply. . . ." Resolutions demanded government ownership to remedy the problem. The state executive committee urged that all locals press town officials to lobby in Boston for a law authorizing municipal fuel yards. This solution harked back to the Bellamy Nationalists, and Henry R. Legate, once a Nationalist, then a Populist, and in 1903 a Socialist, was again travelling through the state for the cause. Carey and MacCartney introduced a bill which was only one of several dealing with the subject. But the Massachusetts Supreme Court, as it had a decade earlier, gave an advisory opinion that municipal fuel yards would violate the state's constitution. And the Socialist party lost a most effective issue.[49]

At the same time, the Massachusetts Socialists lost William Mailly, who was elected the party's national secretary and moved to Omaha to take up larger responsibilities. Within a few months, Mailly was caught in the old rivalry between Socialists from the eastern industrial states and those of the agrarian midwest; he was not at all sure he had made the right decision. Even Carey, of all people, was being stubborn.[50] But Mailly persisted in Omaha, and the national party thus deprived its most thriving state organization of the director of its recent imposing growth.

Massachusetts could furnish national political guidance and leadership. Bay State Socialists understood campaigns and votes. In general, they were less interested in

49. *Wilshire's Magazine*, March, 1903, 29; *Worker*, January 4, 11, 18; February 1, 8; March 15, 1903; *Gazette*, January 3, 1903.

50. Mailly to C. A. Perry, April 27, 1903, Mailly Letterbook IV; Mailly to Carey, March 19, 1903, Mailly Letterbook II, SP Papers.

the refinements of Socialist theory. Their modest intellectual contribution did not constitute a coherent ideology. They rarely published; those who did were often clergymen with no claim as Socialist theoreticians. James Carey, for instance, disliked even to write letters; the few pamphlets that bore his name were transcripts of his speeches.[51] Significantly, the most important publication of the Massachusetts Socialists was the *Haverhill Social Democrat,* a newspaper primarily devoted to politics.[52]

Launched in the middle of the campaign of 1899, the *Social Democrat* was to be more than a temporary campaign broadside. Designed to exhort and inform, the paper proclaimed itself "a permanent fixture, and one of the . . . most useful advocates of Socialism published in the United States." While William Mailly directed editorial policy, socialist theory was subordinated to politics, Socialist unity, and news of interest to labor. William Edlin, Mailly's successor, attempted to balance abstract theory and other coverage. A native of San Francisco whose eastern friends were New Yorkers, Edlin proposed to enlighten the provinces. After a few months on the job, he wrote his fiancée proudly that the paper was "no longer the rag (or country sheet) it used to be under Mailly." Louis Boudin, a New York lawyer, author, and Edlin's future brother-in-law, approved the editor's notion of "informing our comrades of what is going on in the literary world. . . ." Such material, Boudin thought, would "certainly have a salutary influence, broaden their sphere of interest, and soften their coarseness which the fight of

51. Carey's publications include the following pamphlets: *Child Labor* (a speech in the Massachusetts House, March 26, 1899); *The Menace of Socialism* (a debate with Thomas I. Gasson, S.J., 1911); *Socialism, the Creed of Despair* (a debate with George B. Hugo, 1909); *Debate on Socialism* (with Frederick J. Stimson, 1903).

52. This generalization could probably be extended to cover the *Leader,* the official weekly of the party in 1912 and after. Extensive correspondence, however, has turned up only one issue of this paper.

the proletariat for a new humanity necessarily breeds." [53]
Some, however, resisted instruction. After a particularly
fuzzy piece by Martha Avery had appeared in the *Social
Democrat*, an indignant reader protested. Mrs.
Avery's article, wrote the correspondent, was "a hazy effusion of
philosophic and economic ideas," and her language "a
gorgeous display of millinery intended to dazzle the uninitiated." The mission of a Socialist paper, he continued, was "to clarify" Socialism, not to mystify readers;
"to present economic truths" with clarity, "not to furnish a
medium for the display of learning."

Edlin was out of step with his readers. The *Social
Democrat* might defend intellectuals as the "absolutely
indispensible" theoreticians who must supply the party
with the "scientific foundation for the ideals to which the
workingmen aspire. . . ." But James Carey, for one,
could be impatient with the self-importance of intellectuals and residents of big cities, as his remarks at the second
Indianapolis convention demonstrated. He could scorn
"the sophistry of the colleges" or refer sarcastically and
without embarrassment to "the learned ones of the
world." [54] He knew that the intellectual establishment
was on the other side, and while he was no breast-beating
proletarian, he was always proud to call himself a shoe
worker. Edlin edited thirty issues and moved on to New
York.

John Eills, the Harvard-educated Universalist minister
who replaced Edlin, promised major changes. "We shall
have to leave in other hands," he wrote, "abstract essays

53. *HSD*, November 4, 1899; Thomas Beresford to Edlin, February 18,
1901; Edlin to Sarah Boudin, December 30, 1900, April 28, 1901; Louis
Boudin to Edlin, February 27, 1901, Edlin Papers. For an extended dis-
cussion of this paper, see Henry F. Bedford, "The 'Haverhill Social
Democrat': Spokesman for Socialism," in *Labor History* (New York)
Winter, 1961, 82–89.
54. *HSD*, May 11, 25, 1901; Carey and Stimson, *Debate on Socialism*
. . . (Boston, 1903), 11, 62.

and technical discussions. . . ." Eills knew the priority his audience demanded. The campaign of 1901 was about to begin, and the paper ought to be in the battle. In an obvious attempt to break with the recent past, the paper was soon renamed the *Clarion*. Renewed emphasis on politics brought prompt approval from the paper's readers, and the policy was continued until the *Clarion's* demise in December, 1901.[55]

Political discussion was simpler and more interesting than theoretical discussion and was also less likely to cause trouble inside the party. For the Socialists of Massachusetts had a diverse and contradictory intellectual heritage. With no apparent concern for consistency, they used whatever ideas and arguments seemed appropriate at the moment. Their mentors included Edward Bellamy, the utopian Nationalist, Robert Blatchford, the least intellectually respectable English Fabian, Daniel DeLeon, which was as close as most of them ever came to Marx, and Samuel Gompers or John F. Tobin, from whom they learned conservative trade union principles. They inherited a spiritual fervor from the Populists and the Christian Socialists. They agreed on a few broad principles: public ownership of at least some of the means of production; the importance of political action and a more responsive, democratic government; the injustice of contemporary standards of wages and hours; the social evil inherent in the existence of vast fortunes and abysmal poverty; the value of labor unions; the right of the workingman to a larger share of his product. The Massachusetts Socialists did not always agree on interpretations of these principles nor on other matters they considered theoretical detail. Partly to maintain organizational tranquility, and partly because few apparently cared, such problems were seldom raised.

Some ideological conflicts were resolved by ignoring

55. *HSD*, August 24, 31, 1901; September 7, 1901.

them. William Mailly, for instance, found no discrepancy between scientific, materialistic, Marxian socialism, and the Christian, spiritual variety. Party spokesmen had three contradictory answers when asked if the coming socialist state would compensate for pre-empted industry. John Chase, in 1902, saw no reason to compensate mine owners and suggested that the property simply be confiscated. James Carey, in 1909, talked boldly of confiscation and described how the Pilgrims had snatched the land of the Indians and the Union had taken the slaves of the South. But, said Carey anticlimactically, he personally would favor compensation for nationalized property. The third alternative was to dodge the problem: some form of eminent domain could be used and thus the courts would decide; a method would be discovered that was "fully sanctioned by the prevailing public sentiment as just and equitable." [56]

The party's platform typically coupled a declaration that only the cooperative commonwealth would correct capitalistic injustice with a batch of proposed reforms. Logically such reforms were at best unnecessary since only a Socialist republic would bring redress. But the Massachusetts movement included more politicians than logicians. The reform-minded voter, of any class, was the target. A pamphlet issued for the Saugus municipal campaign in 1904 illustrates the dilemma of the revolutionary who would also seek reform through political action.

While the ultimate result of Socialism is a condition of Society that will give to the worker the full product of his toil, which can be obtained only through a class conscious political party, [Socialists] have also immediate demands, among which is honest and faithful administration in office.

56. *Ibid.*, February 10, 1900; December 22, 1900; *Gazette*, October 6, 1902; Carey and Hugo, *Socialism, the Creed of Despair*, 43; *Clarion*, December 7, 1901; Charles C. Hitchcock, *The Socialist Argument* (Chicago, n.d.,), 47.

Last year a Socialist was elected to the Board of Health, and this year, instead of asking for an increased appropriation, the Board will turn back to the town several hundred dollars.[57]

During campaigns, the class struggle was rarely mentioned. But, the campaigns over, Carey discovered in society "the possessing . . . capitalist class, and the dispossessed . . . working class"; between the two, he asserted, there could be "no peace." Subsequently, it developed that Carey's working class included "any man or woman" who performed "useful service to society," from house painter to fine artist, from ditch digger to doctor. The *Social Democrat,* in May, 1900, printed an article that declared: "To assert that there is no class struggle is to show utter ignorance . . . or gross indifference to the truth." Six months later, at election time, the same paper said soothingly that Socialists were "not the enemies of private property. On the contrary, they believe[d] in private property."[58]

Adept use of definitions was another key to avoiding ideological problems. Socialists would not destroy individual initiative, but would substitute a social initiative. In fact they valued individualism more highly than did the industrialist. The Socialist creed, said the party's spokesman, was revolutionary. But the revolution was coming a step at a time and would not be bloody. Socialism, Charles Hitchcock wrote in 1911, was already far advanced in American industry. Political change would soon "be so radical" that the term "revolutionary" was applicable. Socialists were to be distinguished from anarchists and others who espoused "creeds of violence and despair." Anarchists proposed to abolish governments, while Socialists wished to employ the powers of the state, to use, as

57. Quoted in *People,* April 2, 1904.
58. Carey and Stimson, *Debate on Socialism* . . . , 14; Carey and Hugo, *Socialism, the Creed of Despair,* 31; *HSD,* May 19, 1900; November 24, 1900.

the cliché had it, "the ballot, not the bullet." [59] Thus did
a peaceful, evolutionary, political process become revolutionary in the party's rhetoric. Socialists clung to the word
because it distinguished them from mere bourgeois reformers.

Socialists did, in fact, differ from their reforming con-
temporaries. While others talked about smashing trusts,
Socialists argued that monopolies were the inevitable result of competitive capitalism. To break these enterprises
would be foolish; rather businesses should be nationalized. Socialists thought monetary reform a delusion. Perhaps labor certificates would eventually replace gold, silver, or greenbacks; in any case, manipulation of currency
was no substitute for overturning the entire economic system. Women must seek not only political equality but
social and intellectual equality as well. While many reformers were suspicious of labor unions, Massachusetts
Socialists cooperated with unions as closely as possible. In
1900, for instance, when the Haverhill Central Labor
Union dedicated a new headquarters, no less than eight
Socialist politicians spoke, and the *Social Democrat*
moved into offices on the second floor. As William Mailly
wrote, there was "little difference between a Socialist and
a trade unionist in this part of the country." [60]

A few Socialists in the state had some knowledge of
Marxism. For a while, Martha Avery and David Goldstein
conducted a "Karl Marx School" in Boston at which Mrs.
Avery tried to explain scientific socialism. Marx himself
would have been more comprehensible. Mrs. Avery's introduction to a piece called "Labor, the Basis of Value,"
was characteristic:

59. *HSD*, February 24, 1900; September 29, 1900; November 17, 1900;
December 1, 1900; September 14, 1901; C. C. Hitchcock, *The Socialist
Argument*, 15, 42–43.
60. *HSD*, October 14, 1899; February 17, 1900; March 24, 1900;
April 21, 1900; May 26, 1900; October 6, 20, 1900; August 3, 1901; see
also Marion Craig Wentworth's play, *The Flower Shop* (Boston, 1911),
which is a soap-opera plea for emancipated women.

The fleeting character of the special equivalent value form, alone, if there were no other limitations, would prevent pure barter from forcing its way up into the next stage of exchange relations, not to speak of modern industry, where the universal equivalent form, value itself, is necessary to production dominantly based upon exchange. At the conclusion of a bargain struck between A and B, each having owned a non-use-value for which each has obtained the, for him, use-value of the other, there are no traces left of the transaction, nor is there evidence of the intellectual process by which the equation of value took place.

The *Social Democrat* gave Marx intellectual stature by associating him with Charles Darwin. It acknowledged the movement's slight acquaintance with the canon in the injunction not to claim to have read Marx "when you have never seen his books, or . . . when you have never been able to understand a single paragraph of his 'Capital.' " [61]

Occasionally socialist thinking in the state did coincide with Marxian views. The race problem was merely a specialized form of the class struggle. Negroes ought to unite with the rest of the working class to secure redress. Imperialism was the necessary and final expression of capitalism. The Open Door policy in China was designed to ease the "profitable task of fleecing Chinese labor." Yet, while the *Social Democrat* welcomed imperialism as a step toward world socialism, it regretted the development as immoral and unjust.[62]

Concern with morality and justice came in part from the Protestant clergymen of whom Frederic MacCartney was the most prominent. Herbert Casson and W. D. P. Bliss, Christian Socialist stalwarts before the turn of the century, had many successors. John Eills edited the *Social Democrat* briefly and was active afterwards in the Boston

61. *HSD*, May 18, 1901; January 5, 12, 1901.
62. *HSD*, March 31, 1900; December 23, 1899; August 25, 1900; September 1, 1900; October 13, 1900; August 17, 1901; *Gazette*, November 1, 2, 1899.

local. George Elmer Littlefield published the *Ariel*, his own reform periodical, and ran for Congress while pastor of a Unitarian church in Haverhill. Littlefield resigned when his congregation disapproved his proposal to convert the parish into a "cooperative church" that would operate a cooperative store. Some years later, he had established a cooperative farming community in Westwood and projected a second for northern New Jersey.[63] Eliot White, an Episcopal rector from Worcester, was an unsuccessful candidate for Congress and a delegate to the national convention of 1908. Roland Sawyer, a minister from Ware, was the party's nominee for governor in 1912 and one of two Massachusetts members of the national committee.

Littlefield's periodical expounded Socialism as the practical American application of the Golden Rule. Socialism, read one of the few articles that Littlefield did not write, was "the soul of America." It was "opposed only by thieves, politicians, gentry, old ladies of both sexes," and too many preachers. The principles of the party, Littlefield asserted, were "in line with the Eternal Purpose for the welfare of humanity," and coincided with " 'whatsoever things are true, whatsoever things are honest. . . .' " Socialism, indeed, was the spirit of Christmas: "Nearly two thousand years ago a Saviour was born; today millions of His comrades incarnate His social ideal, all faithful, hopeful, and enthusiastic to establish His kingdom of heaven, the Cooperative Commonwealth." (After such a statement, the claim of a Haverhill politician to have learned his Socialism from the Lord's Prayer seems less farfetched.) Littlefield's economic radicalism never extended beyond advocating cooperatives and sometimes seemed not to go that far. He wrote in 1901 that any industrious

63. *Gazette*, September–October, 1902; New York *Call*, October 13, 1912.

individual could find employment: "There is not only room at the top, but plenty of opportunities. . . . To be sure you may go from shop to shop and find no one to employ you; but any hundred persons who have skill and common sense enough to organize . . . can get capital at 3 per cent . . . to start any business." [64]

The *Social Democrat* poked fun at the landlord who refused to rent to a Socialist because he would not promise to exclude Carey from the house. Had not the paper itself warned its readers to mind their conduct? "Don't disgrace Socialism . . . by getting drunk, by gambling, cheating, fighting, swearing . . . or in any way behaving indecently." Carey's Socialism, indeed, endangered neither the landlord's reputation nor his real estate. Socialism, said Carey in 1903, was "not a dream that men dream o' nights, . . . not a scheme evolved from the brains of clever men." Socialism was instead "the expression of the industrial development of the ages." He and his friends had a simple faith in progress, and believed that industrial change required social adaptation. The adaptation they favored was the social ownership of the means of production.[65] Orthodox Marxists might contend that, whatever Carey believed, it was not socialism. But no one in the Bay State had a more convincing grip on the label.

64. The *Ariel* (Haverhill), August 14, 1901; December, 1902; January 16, 1901; see also Julian Hawthorne, *The Soul of America* (Haverhill, 1902), 9; this pamphlet is a reprint of an article that appeared in the *Ariel* for September, 1902; *Gazette,* November 4, 1899.

65. *HSD,* January 5, 1901; May 25, 1901; Carey and Stimson, *Debate on Socialism* . . . , 5–6.

1903: Counterattack

The spectacular Socialist advance in 1902 provoked interest and opposition. Politicians who had regarded the
movement as a noisy nuisance gave more consideration to
silencing the upstart and winning its following. The Boot
and Shoe Workers' Union, becoming more conservative as
its treasury swelled, reconsidered its Socialist alliance.
Disgruntled party members used their familiarity with
Socialist practice and ideology to embarrass the Socialist
cause. And the Roman Catholic Church, whose attitude
before 1903 had ranged from quiet disapproval to complete unconcern, became actively, officially, and effectively hostile.

The Socialist on his soap box has much in common with
the pastor in his pulpit. Both seek converts through an active faith that explains history and human behavior. Both
have sacred writings, saints, and demons. The two creeds
may be mutually exclusive, but the incidence of Christian
Socialism indicates that conflict is not inevitable. An ac-
commodation of religion and socialism depends upon
which aspects of which creed one is willing to subordinate. The socialist who thinks economic determinism too
mechanistic may make a place in his universe for a deity.
The Christian, deciding that economic and social conditions are as responsible as sin in accounting for evil, may
join a Socialist party. But the doctrinaire socialist and the
devout Christian may find that their dogmas clash.

Socialists in Massachusetts hoped not to antagonize the

churches. Although socialism encountered scattered opposition from Protestant ministers, the Protestant clergy
generally ignored it, perhaps because it seemed too inconsequential to ruffle parishes that were predominantly
middle class. Other Protestant pastors, sometimes influenced by the Social Gospel and sometimes as a conse-
quence of independent thinking, aided the Socialist cause;
the ministry furnished several important party leaders.

The Catholic clergy, less tolerant of socialist growth, in
1903 launched a sharp assault on the doctrine and its ad-
herents. Relying on the encyclicals of Pope Leo XIII,
Catholics usually did not oppose progressive change.
While many priests assailed socialism, they would in the
next breath assail existing social and economic conditions.
Their attack was directed neither at the political moderation of the Massachusetts movement nor at its rather
vaguely defined idealistic ends; Catholicism, rather, attacked the philosophy of socialism, its ethic and morality.
Opposition to Marx and Engels necessarily meant opposition to James F. Carey and Charles H. Coulter, though
both hastened to assure everyone that they opposed sin as
vigorously as did the Church. Some Catholic spokesmen
knew orthodox socialist literature far better than did the
Bay State Socialists themselves. Socialists could not disavow their intellectual heritage, and consequently were
condemned to implacable, powerful opposition for beliefs
most of them did not hold.

A mixture of Christianity and social reform was traditional in Massachusetts long before Socialists began to
seek votes. An active Christian Socialist movement ante-
dated the Nationalist clubs. William D. P. Bliss tried to
take Fabian Socialism from Boston to the rest of the nation. Catholic liberals too criticized the social order,
though without adopting socialism; a few had to hedge

radicalism that they had espoused before *Rerum No-varum* appeared in 1891.[1]

The Protestant clergy in Haverhill was not outwardly disturbed when the Socialist Labor party began bringing a tougher, more Marxist variety of socialism to town. A Methodist preacher, Reverend John Bowler, in 1894 deplored the Socialists' overemphasis on material things. But Socialists and Christians, he said, shared a dedication to important ideals and a common hostility to the exploitation of the working population. Both Christian and Socialist, for instance, sought to keep women and children out of the mills, thus preserving a united family. Subsequently, opponents of socialism were to charge that the doctrine was a threat to the sanctity of home and family, an accusation Socialists would meet by pointing, as Bowler had, to the common bonds between Socialists and churches.

In 1898, while Socialists struggled to make a permanent mark in Haverhill, and when the anti-Christian label might have been crippling, the local Republican daily refused to apply it. Editor John B. Wright was surprised at the ignorance of an inquirer who asked whether Socialists were immoral and outside the Christian church. Some Socialists, Wright supposed, were not formal members of churches, but their integrity was unquestionable; others, and the editor reeled off an impressive list, were identifiably Christians. And all, he concluded, were morally capable of leading a reform effort.[2]

Haverhill Socialists were careful not to lose that image, partly as a matter of political tact, partly because, in fact, they were moral and, in some cases, religious men. The *Haverhill Social Democrat* patiently dealt with the reap-

1. Arthur Mann, *Yankee Reformers in the Urban Age* (Cambridge, 1954), Chapters 2, 4; Howard H. Quint, *The Forging of American Socialism* (Columbia, S.C., 1953), Chapter 2.
2. *Gazette*, September 10, 1894; November 25, 1898.

pearing notion that socialism and Christianity were anti-
thetical. Socialism was "neither for nor against religion."
The "profoundly moral element" upon which socialism
rested was "the essence of true religion." Winfield Porter,
a YMCA secretary and an early candidate for governor,
asserted that "all true Christians not only should be,
but . . . must be, and are Socialists. . . ." John Eills, the
Universalist minister who briefly edited the *Social Democrat,* dismissed the charge of "unreligiousness" as "not
very serious." Some day, Eills hoped, churches would realize that "Socialism has never been . . . a materialistic
philosophy at all, but . . . in standing for economic justice and worldwide brotherhood, it has really been apply-
ing ethics and religion to the social life of the world." For
many Christian laymen, as one of them recalled, the "political aspect of the movement was less important than its
religious content." They found in Socialism the fellowship, the concern for humanity, and the moral standard
that they associated with a primitive Christianity. They
believed the "cant and mysticism of the orthodox sects"
had spoiled the faith. Socialism was a way of doing good.[3]

The very fact, however, that a secular doctrine could
become a substitute religion was enough to alienate clergymen of all denominations. Catholics presented special
barriers to the socialist propagandist. Although Leo XIII
endorsed progressive social reform in his encyclical
Rerum Novarum, he condemned socialism. The class
struggle, wrote the Pope, was an "irrational and . . .
false . . . view"; capital and labor were mutually dependent. Divine law protected private property: "the main
tenet of Socialism, the community of goods, must be utterly rejected. . . ." The Church must help improve "the
condition of the masses," but the first principle of such

3. *HSD,* December 23, 1899; May 1, 1901; the *Clarion* (Haverhill),
September 21, 1901. Interview with Ralph Gardner, August 19, 1960.

improvement must be "the inviolability of private property." [4]

The presence of Protestant clergymen in the socialist movement also roused Catholic suspicion. William Stang, the Bishop of Fall River, called Socialism "the natural outgrowth of Protestantism." Protestantism, he held, prepared "the way for Socialism and Anarchism." Socialism, indeed, "with its atheistic tendencies," was "the last and saddest chapter in the history of Protestantism." Bishop Stang's logic may have been askew, but his devils were clear. Radicalism and Protestantism were false dogmas. The Catholic meddled with either at the peril of his soul. The "social evils of modern times" could not be solved without the spiritual resources of Roman Catholicism. [5]

While Bishop Stang was writing his book, which appeared in 1905, the Socialist cause seemed likely to prosper. But even before, when Socialists seemed doomed to sectarian futility, they encountered Catholic hostility. In 1895, for instance, a Haverhill Catholic bulletin lumped socialists with anarchists and drunks.

Would to God that these hardy, honest, sons of toil, the pride and hope of our country, were made to realize that intemperance is a greater enemy than capital! There would be less discontent among workingmen, and the agents of socialism and anarchy, who hatch their schemes in saloons, could no longer get the clear-headed, sober workingman to disgrace . . . labor. . . . Every sensible man admits that the blatherskate anarchist and socialist is an enemy of society. [6]

So long as Socialism remained relatively inconspicuous, the *Pilot*, the semi-official Catholic weekly published in Boston, refrained from polemics. In 1896, the paper endorsed Bryan in an editorial so cordial that there was no

4. *Rerum Novarum* (New York, 1939), 12, 10.
5. William Stang, *Socialism and Christianity* (New York, 1905), 48, 152, 104, 74, and chapter 5, *passim*.
6. *The Index* (Haverhill), December, 1895, 4.

need to condemn the nominee of the tiny Socialist Labor party. Nor, in September, 1897, did it occur to the *Pilot* to include any Socialist in its discussion of the gubernatorial contest. The same issue contained an article by Grant Allen, a regular contributor, that presented socialism as respectable. True, the lead implied that respectable socialism was a variant, but the author did suggest that it would replace squalor with abundance. Furthermore, he wrote, the movement had attracted fine people, including intellectuals, artists, and "the cream and pick of intelligent artisans. . . ."[7]

The Boston *Sunday Herald*, reviewing the state's Socialist movement in 1903, found no pattern in the attitude of Catholic clergymen. In a few towns the priest "openly and actively" opposed the party; "in a majority of cases," the resident priest had "refrained entirely from expressing himself on the point" and had "done nothing to restrain his parishioners from allying themselves with the movement." French Canadian and Italian Catholics were rarely interested in Socialism, even when their priest did not take a stand. The pastor of the Irish congregation in Haverhill was known to oppose Socialism; his counterpart in Brockton showed a benign neutrality. The attitude of the Church in early 1903, summed up the *Herald*, was "certainly not one of systematic ostracism of the Socialist movement. . . ."[8]

Hoping to forestall that systematic ostracism, the Massachusetts Socialists contacted Father Thomas McGrady, a priest of Bellevue, Kentucky, who announced his conversion to Socialism about the turn of the century. Bay State Socialists were soon paying McGrady's rail fare to Massachusetts. He had a crowd-pleasing touch on the platform, and his Socialism was of the Blatchford-Bellamy

7. The *Pilot* (Boston), October 3, 1896; October 9, 1897.
8. Boston *Sunday Herald*, January 4, 1903.

school. Martha Avery thought the priest brought hundreds of New England Catholics into the party, in spite of his fuzzy economics. When other Catholics questioned the propriety of his political activity, McGrady published a bristling defense that furnished excellent copy for the Socialist press. He became an authority to cite when Catholics blistered the Socialist cause. The *Haverhill Social Democrat,* for instance, quoted McGrady's accusation that economic ignorance was widespread in the hierarchy. When a Catholic journal denounced one of Mc-Grady's pamphlets, he felt free to blast the review as "a triumph of banality that would disgrace a schoolboy . . . ," and the reviewer as "a consecrated bumpkin." The work in question—McGrady's pamphlet, *Socialism and the Labor Question*—was derived from Blatchford's *Merrie England* and was not worth the excitement.[9]

The point, however, was not so much the pamphlet as the profession of its author. Increasing identification with Socialism and the immoderation with which McGrady expressed his new conviction exhausted the tolerance of his bishop. Driven to a choice in December, 1902, McGrady gave up his pastorate rather than retract an offensive statement. The *Appeal to Reason* suggested a nation-wide lecture tour, and for about a year McGrady cashed in on his notoriety. No longer did he limit his indictment to individuals; increasingly he attacked Catholicism as a faith. He also displayed an entirely capitalistic desire to take his lecture fees while he could. A letter to the *People* noted that McGrady was charging $100 for an appearance and bankrupting local after local in the Bay State. He refused

9. Robert E. Doherty, "The American Socialist Party and the Roman Catholic Church, 1901–1917" (Unpublished Ed.D. dissertation, Teachers College, Columbia University, 1959), 128, 136; *People*, October 19, 1901; David Goldstein, *Autobiography of a Campaigner for Christ* (Boston, 1936), 23–24; *HSD*, August 17, 1901; February 23, 1901.

to surrender control of his tours to the national Socialist office because the standard fees were too low. Not surprisingly, national secretary Mailly lost interest in marketing the former priest. When the New Orleans local asked for financial assistance from Mailly's office to pay McGrady's stipend, Mailly quoted a member of his governing board: "What is the matter with Com. McGrady assuming some chances himself? . . . I see no reason why the national organization should incur any liability for his support, . . . especially in view of the princely fee he invariably demands." Mailly did not think $175 for three evenings demonstrated much of a "spirit of sacrifice" for the cause. Although many Socialists still warmed to McGrady personally, without his clerical collar his ability to draw audiences diminished, and he soon dropped into obscurity. In spite of a rumor that McGrady had abjured Socialism and rejoined the Church at his death in 1908, Brockton Socialists draped their charter in black in his memory. "Whether he had recanted or not," writes Robert E. Doherty, "McGrady would have liked that." [10]

McGrady was one of two priests who left the Church for Socialism.[11] The other, Thomas J. Hagerty, was more radical than McGrady and ultimately renounced the conservatism of mere Socialism for the radical militance of the Industrial Workers of the World. McGrady appeared more often in Massachusetts than did Hagerty, but the latter also helped combat the socialists-are-atheists line. In Brockton, Hagerty claimed that his understanding of Socialism made him a better Catholic than the Pope. "If it is atheism to say the workingman is entitled to the full

10. Goldstein, *Autobiography*, 25; *People*, April 11, 1903; Mailly to E. Vidrine, April 16, 1903, Mailly Letterbook III, SP Papers; Doherty, "American Socialist Party . . . ," 138, 140, 148.
11. A third Socialist priest, who had a small parish in South Dakota, apparently did not attract the attention of either the party or the hierarchy.

product of his labor," he said, "I stand here an avowed atheist." The same test, he maintained, would make an atheist of Jesus Christ. Since Socialism preserved the great moral traditions of Christianity, it was no threat to the faith.[12]

Yet Hagerty's bishop suspended him for deserting his parish, and in 1903 neither he nor McGrady were practicing priests. And so, as Socialists eventually realized, the presence of either apostate on their platform did not demonstrate that Socialism and Catholicism were compatible creeds. Either career seemed rather to prove conclusively that Socialism and the Church were in sharp conflict.

David Goldstein and Martha Moore Avery, who had first brought McGrady to Massachusetts, discarded him at once. Anyone "publicly designated as an ex-priest," Goldstein recalled, was "of no further use to our group in its endeavor to attract Catholics to the Socialist movement. . . ." Mrs. Avery returned to the Church in which she had been raised; her example and instruction led to Goldstein's formal conversion to Catholicism in 1905. After years as prominent, if troublesome, Socialists, they shifted causes after 1902 and sought to attract Socialists to the Church.

At the Massachusetts Socialist convention in 1902, Goldstein moved to amend the state constitution. The party's rostrum, he said, should be denied to speakers "who attack theological doctrines or dogmas, who advocate violence, free love, or other doctrines in opposition to the principles of Socialism. . . ." William Mailly hotly denied the implication that such speakers were disgracing Massachusetts Socialists. The proposal, he shouted, was wholly unnecessary. Frederic MacCartney eventually

12. For a sketch of Hagerty, see Robert E. Doherty, "Thomas J. Hagerty, the Church and Socialism," in *Labor History* (Winter, 1962), 39–56; see also Brockton *Times*, October 30, 1902; October 19, 1903.

found the compromise resolution that mollified both Goldstein and Mailly. MacCartney moved "that the Socialist party disclaims any attempt to regulate the religious or other private opinions of the members on the ground that the Socialist movement is a political movement, whose aim is to usher in by peaceful and constitutional methods an equitable economic system based upon the collective ownership of the means of production and distribution." Goldstein admitted that most of the membership did not believe in free love or advocate an assault on Christianity, and he seconded MacCartney's compromise proposal, which then passed.[13]

The patch did not hold long. Early in 1903, Mrs. Avery published an article in *Irish World* attacking Socialists for advocating immorality and atheism. Mailly, now the party's national secretary, branded Mrs. Avery's piece "an absolute slander. . . ." The Massachusetts movement, he continued, had "suffered for several years through the actions of Mrs. Avery and David Goldstein, and it would be a very good thing, in my opinion, if they discarded it. . . ." By the end of April, the Boston local had suspended Mrs. Avery for two years with the face-saving suggestion that she was so disappointed after being trounced in a race for school committee that she was too actively courting Catholic support for her next campaign.[14]

Suspension was another patch that satisfied no one. Mrs. Avery publicly signified her reaffirmation of Catholicism in a righteous letter of resignation: "I have taken upon myself the task of making amends, as far as I may, to my country and to Almighty God for working to give

13. Goldstein, *Autobiography,* 26, 32–33; *Gazette,* September 8, 1902; *Worker,* September 21, 1902; Carey to ?, n.d. Box I, SP Papers; copy, letter from Debate Committee, local Springfield to A. H. Hancock, January 26, 1914, SP Papers.
14. Mailly to Hagerty, March 6, 1903, Mailly Letterbook I, SP Papers; *Worker,* April 26, 1903.

power to that philosophy which I now clearly see to be an abomination—to be a blare of false gods, which leadeth to destruction rather than to the benign light which leadeth to wisdom." [15] Mrs. Avery was still having trouble with her prose, but the message was loud and clear.

David Goldstein was not far behind. No longer, he proclaimed, could he be associated with a movement that muzzled his long-time friend Martha Avery. She had devoted "her knowledge and her critical ability, not to speak of her life," to bringing the socialist dream to reality. Party officialdom rewarded her by trying to still her eloquent voice. Goldstein also announced that he was at work on a book, which came from the presses during the campaign of 1903. The title, *Socialism: The Nation of Fatherless Children,* raised interesting biological questions, but the thesis was less ambiguous. Goldstein argued that socialism would break up homes and families, subvert religion, and establish tyranny in the land.

Socialists were privately amused though publicly silent. As Mailly wrote an inquiring Socialist from Dallas, the party could have retorted, but the resulting publicity would have proved nothing. "It is only a few years . . . since Mrs. Avery was a pronounced 'free lover' and did not hesitate to say so from the platform, while her name and Goldstein's have been associated for years in a way not at all in keeping with the standards they are now vehemently upholding. . . . It makes all our people in Massachusetts snicker to see these two pose as defenders of the home, marriage, and the church." The *Social Democratic Herald* could not resist the observation that Martha Avery had "reached the period when women do unaccountable things." Thereafter silence descended on the Socialist press.[16]

15. Goldstein, *Autobiography,* 47–48.
16. Mailly to J. Kerrigan, July 23, 1903, Mailly Letterbook VII, SP Papers; *SDH,* June 20, 1903.

Goldstein and Mrs. Avery joined the staff of the *Wage Worker,* a periodical which promoted reform and the Democratic party. In the number for August, 1903, Mrs. Avery rehearsed her grievances in "Why I Left the Socialist Party." In an interesting twist, she criticized the Massachusetts party because it was untrue to Socialist orthodoxy. Public ownership and labor legislation, she wrote, was not the essence of the doctrine. Rather, Socialism sought the "destruction of the present social order." For Mrs. Avery, the social order meant church and marriage. Socialism had "no positive design" to "work toward the power of chastity, towards the beauty of holiness." Socialism even opposed motherhood, since Socialists argued that "women who sell their bodies" were "as good as any man's mother!" The absurdity was too much: "Great God!" exclaimed the pious Mrs. Avery.

The *Wage Worker* stayed on the offensive. F. G. R. Gordon, who had also deserted the Socialist cause, told trade unionists that the party leadership had once defended industrial unions and the Socialist Trade and Labor Alliance. Catholics could read a five-page excerpt from *Rerum Novarum* that stressed the Church's support for private property and its opposition to Socialism. Progressive change had the periodical's editorial support: trade unionism, better education in better schools that were equipped with fire escapes, the free use of state armories for civic purposes, legislation requiring that all banks pay equal interest on savings accounts, and the Democratic party were all worthy causes.[17]

Goldstein used the first receipts from his book to buy posters and rent halls to carry on the crusade. To meeting after unruly meeting, all over the state, he and Mrs. Avery carried the gospel of anti-socialism. They did not have to

17. *Wage Worker* (Boston) August, 1903, 12–21; August–October, 1903, *passim.*

bear the burden alone. In Haverhill, a group of Domini-
cans, conducting a series of meetings for Irish Catholics,
took a firm anti-Socialist posture. In Brockton, where Mrs.
Avery and Goldstein had encountered raucous heckling
earlier, the Reverend William Stephens Kress, a Catholic
priest from Cleveland, gave a series of free lectures that
concluded a few days before the municipal election.[18]

Although Father Kress arrived in the middle of a tough
campaign, and although he had come partly at the urging
of a Republican alderman, the priest did not endorse any
political party. He gave a reasonably balanced presenta-
tion of the economic program of the moderate American
socialists, though he rather overemphasized the Marxist
content of their faith. He suggested that the socialist proposals would not work. Does all labor, Father Kress wondered, really have the same value? If labor received the
full value of its production, where would investment capital accumulate? What was the substitute for initiative?
He acknowledged that economic and social problems existed in the United States, but asserted that socialism was
not the solution. He also examined the ethical dangers.
Fear that confiscation of capital would violate the com-
mandment against theft constituted his primary objection
to socialism. He thought the antagonism between the
Christian's spiritual view of human nature and the socialist's emphasis on materialism was clear. Clergymen who
flirted with the doctrine would end as had McGrady,
"with the loss of their Christian faith." The Christian, according to Father Kress, accepted inequality as a fact of
life in the spirit of Christ's remark that " 'the poor you
have always with you.' " The Christian earned merit on
earth beyond his wage in the pay envelope. "The great reward is hereafter. . . ." A reawakened faith, a practical
application of the Golden Rule would solve the social

18. *Worker*, July 12, 1903.

question. "Bring about . . . a reawakening of . . . faith," he pleaded, "which will make the poor more content and the rich more considerate." More practically, he extolled the moral virtue of work. Yet the community must, as a matter of moral justice, pay labor a living wage. Before the series concluded, Father Kress hit the familiar theme: Socialism endangered marriage and family life. Under Socialism, he foresaw "a loathsome saturnalia of lust." [19]

Socialists counterattacked in Brockton, using Hagerty to follow Goldstein and Mrs. Avery, and Carey in the middle of Father Kress's week of lectures. Both rebuttalists drew big, enthusiastic crowds; both belittled the opposition; neither could lay the issue. Charges clung and denials had to be reissued. A few days after Hagerty left town, a local Socialist leader had already inserted a new paragraph in his standard campaign speech: "If I couldn't be a Christian, I wouldn't be a Socialist . . . so you see the cry that is being put up . . . by other parties is all rot. . . . While I will admit that there are men in our party that are perhaps infidels, they must have been either democrats or republicans before they joined us." [20]

The Socialists would need more effective defenses, for the Boston *Pilot,* after years of virtual silence on the subject, enlisted in the anti-socialist forces. The opening blast was vehement. McGrady was lumped with spurious " 'ex-priests' and 'converted nuns' " who " 'exposed' the iniquities of the Church . . . for the delectation of a prurient public." The false prophets unmasked, the *Pilot* got down to cases. "That Socialism is inimical to revealed religion does not admit of discussion. . . . [E]ven Carey rejects religion. . . . Any modification in these extreme views

19. Brockton *Times,* November 23–30, 1903, *passim.* See also William S. Kress, *Questions of Socialists and Their Answers* (2nd ed., Cleveland, 1908).
20. *Times,* October 19, 24, 1903; November 25, 1903.

. . . is due solely to expediency." Socialist agitators, the paper warned, were up to no good:

Let not oppressed wage-earners . . . look to Socialism for the relief of their wrongs. There are, undoubtedly, good and sincere, if . . . misguided people in the Socialist ranks. But they are there because they do not know the elementary principles of the philosophy of Socialism.

. . . Socialism, striking at private property, strikes at the home, and at Christian marriage, and the sanctity of child-life.[21]

As the American Federation of Labor assembled in Boston for its convention, in late November, 1903, the *Pilot* pointed out the hostility to radicalism of Irish-American labor leaders. The presence of such able men gave the paper confidence "that the delegates of socialistic tendencies" would "make little impression on the toilers and home-builders who speak for the American workingmen." The *Pilot*'s satisfaction increased during the course of the convention. John Mitchell, the Catholic president of the United Mine Workers, who had achieved great prestige as a result of the coal strike of 1902, told the Boston Economic Club that labor and capital were not antagonistic; there was no class struggle. The convention defeated the resolutions of Socialist delegates, and the *Pilot* rejoiced: "Organized labor never did a better thing . . . than in this public and formal self-emancipation from even the slightest bond of socialism." Samuel Gompers' speech was "destined to live among the utterances of our great men," for he denounced Socialists for making the work of responsible union men much more difficult. Socialist legislators, Gompers said, were invariably hostile to trade union organizations. Finally he delivered a capsule denunciation of the Socialist movement that was eminently

21. Boston *Pilot*, August 19, 1903; November 7, 1903.

quotable: "I want to say to you Socialists that I have studied your philosophy. . . . I have studied your standard works in English and German. . . . And I want to say to you that I am entirely at variance with your philosophy. . . . Economically you are unsound; socially you are wrong; industrially you are an impossibility." "That address," David Goldstein remarked, "did a great service in further deadening socialism in Massachusetts."

During the convention, Goldstein himself had circulated among the delegates, distributing copies of the *Wage Worker* and of his book, which was dedicated to the American Federation of Labor. The *Pilot*, cheering the Federation's proof of its "patriotism and Christianity" and its forthright rejection of "the would-be destroyer of home, country, and Church," congratulated Goldstein: "We believe that no little credit for this memorable defeat of Socialism is due to David Goldstein's book, which was widely discussed and read during the convention."

Years later Goldstein recalled that the great campaign of 1903 had "put an end to the flourishing Socialist movement in Massachusetts." [22] Time and fond memory distorted the significance of the Catholic anti-socialist crusade and buried the party prematurely. Yet there was more than a little truth in Goldstein's expansive recollection. In a year when Socialists advanced elsewhere, the Massachusetts party lost both votes and momentum. Never again would the Socialists equal their record of 1902; never again would James F. Carey be a member of the General Court; never again would Charles Coulter be mayor of Brockton. It was too early for last rites, but the Socialist party was badly wounded. And the Roman Catholic Church, through Goldstein, Mrs. Avery, Father Kress, and the *Pilot*, had helped deliver the blow.

22. *Ibid.*, November 14, 21, 28, 1903; *Wage Worker,* December, 1903, 290; Goldstein, *Autobiography,* 67, 59–60, 66.

1903: COUNTERATTACK

In addition to Catholic opposition, Socialist politicians had other pressing worries in 1903. A bitter jurisdictional dispute among shoe workers in Lynn had ramifications in Haverhill and undermined Carey's support. Frederic Mac-Cartney's death removed a skilled speaker as well as a proven candidate. Democrats in Brockton borrowed part of the Socialist program; Republicans stepped up their anti-socialist effort; Socialists contributed handsomely to their own difficulty when a former city chairman accused Coulter of selling immunity to selected illegal saloons. And no longer could the party rely on the cordial, official support of the Boot and Shoe Workers' Union, for John F. Tobin's socialist ardor had cooled as his union prospered.

The *Monthly Report* of the Boot and Shoe Workers' Union for June, 1899, contained an official endorsement of the Social Democratic party. The same issue also reported that the organization's convention had adopted a new constitution. The preamble still declared for "the ultimate abolition of the competitive wage system" and the establishment of "collective ownership by the people of all means of production, distribution, transportation, communication, and exchange." The rest of the new document, however, was more concerned with the here-and-now than with the cooperative commonwealth. Tobin and Horace Eaton hoped to arrest a decline in membership, to achieve financial stability, to prevent debilitating strikes that could not be won, and to husband resources in order to support judiciously selected strikes. To these ends, the constitution increased dues substantially, established funds to pay sickness and death benefits, and set up a reserve for strikes. High dues, Tobin noted, "would take care of the sick and wounded of capitalism," but he did "not for one moment forget that something more is necessary before the emancipation of the working class" would become reality. "The final mission of the working class,"

197

said Tobin, "is . . . [to] educate the workers to the point that they will use the ballot for the total abolition of the competitive system, and in its place, through the working class political machinery, establish industrial democracy." [23]

The shoe workers ratified the new constitution; the flourishing treasury bred organizational caution. Within two years a trade journal reported that Tobin understood the problems of the manufacturers, made sensible propositions, and protected the employer through discipline over locals. The union's periodical warned against the impracticality of dreamy reformers who "in ten minutes . . . can prove to you that the world is upside down and that they know the only way to put it right side up. . . ." Such enthusiasts, lacking "all the practical and level-headed qualities that fit a man for leadership," were "altogether unfitted for any responsible, executive position, as the wreck of scores of unions" plainly demonstrated.

The ideal labor leader is not the one who can draw the best word-picture of the condition of wage workers in the 25th century, but the one who can obtain the best conditions here and now. The history of unionism shows that as long as workers demand the impossible, they fail to get the possible. . . . Trade unions need leaders with common sense and business ability, not orators, dreamers, and poets.[24]

The conversion to "pure and simple" trade unionism could hardly have been more explicit.

Before the presidential election of 1900, Tobin hedged

23. Boot and Shoe Workers' Union, *Monthly Report*, June, 1899, 19; *Proceedings of the Fourth Convention* . . . (Lynn, Mass., 1899) 8, 5; See also the *Union Boot and Shoe Worker*, May, 1902, 31. This periodical, which became the *Boot and Shoe Workers' Journal* in July, 1902, will be cited hereafter as *Journal*.

24. John Laslett, "Reflections on the Failure of Socialism in the American Federation of Labor," in *Mississippi Valley Historical Review*, March, 1964, 646–647; *Journal*, May 1901, 10; July 1901, 3; August, 1901, 6; February, 1902, 19, 25; August, 1902, 16.

his endorsement of the Socialists and resorted to the non-partisanship of the A.F. of L. The *Union Boot and Shoe Worker* decided "to let its readers formulate their own views on political and other mooted questions," since the editors did "not feel qualified to do all the thinking for all the people on all subjects." While favorable references to socialism still appeared, the union candidly acknowledged that politics might be divisive. The editorial line was specifically established in 1901: "We have thought it proper to leave the discussion of political questions to political publications. This journal has a distinct economic mission, and . . . will not sacrifice this purpose to any other." [25]

As long as Haverhill and Brockton had thriving Socialist organizations, no ambitious shoe union leader would openly disavow his Socialist past. In 1902, for instance, when a Brockton shoe worker won a seat in the legislature as a Socialist, Tobin led the cheers at his victory rally. At the union's convention earlier in the year, Tobin declared he probably would always be a Socialist, though he vowed not to allow political convictions to interfere with the work of his union.[26] Throughout 1901 and 1902, while the union was emerging as a conservative craft organization, an occasional item or turn of phrase in the *Union Boot and Shoe Worker* betrayed the Socialist heritage. Labor must recognize the "Solidarity of Labor," and act on the principle of " 'all for each and each for all.' " (The syndicalist Industrial Workers of the World later echoed both slogans.) In 1902, the publication pushed municipal ownership as "the cure for municipal poverty." Capitalists were described as "the scientific slaveholders of our present era. . . ." Unions were a dialectical necessity arising from "capital's insatiate demands" and would

25. *Journal,* March, 1900, 2; January, 1901, 3.
26. *Times,* November 5, 1902; *Proceedings of the Fifth Convention* . . . (Detroit, 1902), 43.

endure until "a more practical and speedier method of emancipating . . . mankind from wage slavery" appeared. Even before Socialists seized on the coal strike during the election of 1902, the periodical suggested nationalization. When injunctions were employed against strikers, the editor wondered how long it would be "before the workers of the world think and act?" On the same page, another article made it clear that the Boot and Shoe Workers' Union was not dangerously radical. While political action would help advance the cause, "the working class" could make no important strides without the trade union movement.[27]

And that trade union movement preached class cooperation. During 1903, the incidence of socialist terminology gradually dropped, or the words were used to promote exclusively trade union ends. The union label, for instance, was "organized labor's prescription for capitalistic ills" and "the only remedy guaranteeing a cure." The "treadmill of capitalistic gain" did not allow the weary laborer time rationally to analyze his plight. But the conservative trade unionist, who understood that labor must not interfere "with the legitimate interests of . . . business," would help the oppressed find the proper solution. Organized labor would bring about "economic justice" by "evolutionary means"; the goal could not be achieved "by revolutionary means." The union had faith in progress: "We believe the world is getting better. . . ." There were no artifical barriers: "Try to be somebody and you will succeed."[28]

The tone of the *Journal* for 1903 indicated that John F. Tobin was about ready to stop trying to please everybody from shoe manufacturer to Socialist. His periodical went

27. These quotations, in order, are from the *Journal* as follows: December, 1901, 8; September, 1902, 8; June, 1902, 16; August, 1902, 13.
28. *Ibid.*, February, 1903, 7, 11; June, 1903, 7; September, 1903, 3; February, 1903, 9; May, 1903, 12.

to employers as well as members. Expedience dictated that radicalism be subordinated. Expedience also dictated the socialist touch to which shoe workers, especially in Haverhill and Brockton, were accustomed. Tobin's association with Socialism helped him establish himself in his union and the union to attract members in two of the most important shoe manufacturing centers in the country. As late as 1901, Tobin argued that good Social Democrats ought to abandon other shoe unions for his own. But times changed; the union stamp contract required a union shop, and widespread adoption promised an increasing membership. By 1903, Tobin had less need for the Socialists, and after balancing skillfully for about two years, he climbed off the tightrope. The lead story in the *Journal* for December, 1903, was an enthusiastic report of the recently concluded convention of the American Federation of Labor. The debate on a series of socialist resolutions, according to the report, was ably conducted. Then, without editorial comment, the *Journal* reprinted the last few sentences of Gompers' speech, noting that he "has been and is irreconcilably opposed to Socialism." [29] While James F. Carey, an official delegate of the Boot and Shoe Workers, voted with the minority that had opposed Gompers' re-election to the presidency of the Federation, John F. Tobin and the rest of the delegation were in the majority.

That vote for Samuel Gompers was a final piece of evidence that the paths of Carey and Tobin had diverged. Early in January, 1903, rivalry between the Boot and Shoe Workers' Union and the cutters affiliated with the Knights of Labor matured into a jurisdictional war in Lynn. The A.F. of L. shoe workers held that their union stamp con-

29. Mailly to Editor, *ISR*, August, 1912, 184; *Journal*, March, 1900, 13; October, 1901, 11; December, 1903, 7.

tract obligated the cutters to join them. The cutters retorted that they were already union members. When
manufacturers decided to stand by their contracts with
Tobin's organization, the cutters walked out, and the Boot
and Shoe Workers' Union not only crossed the picket lines
but also began to fill the vacant jobs. From Wisconsin,
Missouri, Ohio, and nearby New Hampshire, the union
summoned cutters, who were pelted with jeers, eggs, and
rocks as they went into the Lynn factories. Michael Berry,
himself a shoe worker and the foremost Socialist Laborite
in the state, appeared on the scene to extract what he
could for his party. The Socialist party, on the other hand,
would collect only political problems in Lynn.

The Boot and Shoe Workers had always had trouble in
Lynn. Since the imposition of high dues at the convention
of 1899, independent unionism had also spread to Haverhill. Thus a Haverhill Socialist politician had to be wary
of an outright endorsement of Tobin's union. Further, the
activity of the Boot and Shoe Workers, while perhaps required by the union stamp contract, lent credence to the
charge that the organization was a "scab outfit" and "in
the pockets of the bosses." In March, the Haverhill *Gazette* reported that Socialists were frantically trying to
effect a compromise. Since both labor groups were afraid
of being victimized, conciliation failed.[30]

James F. Carey, busy in the legislature, stood above the
battle. It was, he said, "a family row between two sets of
workingmen and should be settled without political inter-
ference." Meanwhile, from the party's national headquarters in Omaha, William Mailly tried to keep track of the
situation. The national secretary shared his intelligence,
which came from "Sandy" Hayman in Haverhill, with
John Chase, who was recruiting for the party in the

30. Boot and Shoe Workers' Union Scrapbook I; *Journal,* February–
July, 1903, *passim;* "Haverhill Labor Problems," clipping book in local
history collection, Haverhill Public Library.

South: ". . . Sandy tells me that the politicians are after Jim's scalp for fair down in Haverhill, taking advantage of the trade union fight, and Sandy says things look mighty squally." A week later, Mailly wrote to Haverhill pleading vaguely for any action to prevent political ramifications:

> I understand that the union squabble is making it look bad for us and I hope you boys will get things in shape before the next election. . . . [T]he boys ought to all work together and help get the best results. If you fellows in Haverhill could only realize how much the election of Carey meant to the movement at large, you would do anything to secure his reelection.

The national secretary's spirits revived and dropped all spring as Hayman's reports arrived in Omaha. By mid-April, Mailly was optimistic that the party had survived the crisis without much permanent damage.[31]

His optimism was unjustified. A similar dispute broke out in Haverhill in spite of Mailly's pleas for solidarity. Many of the striking members of the independent union were residents of Carey's district and had supported him steadfastly for five years. Rival politicians did not miss the opportunity. And Carey, perhaps overconfident, or perhaps, as Mailly sadly observed, "too lazy to be depended upon," did not keep his political fences in order. Carey avoided his own district to campaign for the state ticket. He preserved public neutrality in the union dispute, a task complicated by his candidacy for delegate to the Federation convention from the Boot and Shoe Workers' Union. The popular assumption, of course, was that he favored Tobin's faction, which was the less politic choice.[32] He did not please the A.F. of L. with a forth-

31. *Wage Worker,* November, 1903, 236; Mailly to Chase, March 1, 1903; Mailly to P. Langway, March 7, 1903; Mailly to Chase, March 23, 31, 1903; April 7, 17, 1903. Mailly Letterbook I, II, SP Papers.

32. Mailly to Hillquit, May 8, 1903, Hillquit Papers; *Worker,* April 12, 1903; October 25, 1903; *Times,* November 4, 1903; *People,* November 14, 1903.

right endorsement and he alienated some independent unionists anyhow.

Before 1903, Carey's straddle might perhaps have worked. In 1903 there was no margin for error. The *Million*, a free anti-Socialist weekly published in Haverhill, kept up a constant bombardment. Two former Socialists, F. G. R. Gordon and Herbert Casson, were among the principal contributors to the sheet. Two other renegades, Martha Avery and David Goldstein, singled out Carey as the demon they most wanted to exorcise. The *Gazette* reported that Samuel Gompers had sent an emissary to Haverhill to encourage union leaders throughout the city to work for Carey's opponent. Gompers, the *Gazette* said, wanted to be sure Carey was shorn of his political eminence before the Federation opened its convention in Boston. Employers were said to have cooperated by firing and blacklisting prominent Socialists who then had to move to find employment. The resulting drain of leadership markedly lowered the efficiency of the party.[33]

Mailly did what he could. He sent speakers and funds to aid the cause in Haverhill. In the absence of a local paper, the national Socialist press gave the campaign extensive coverage, and collected and forwarded funds. But when the returns were in, Carey's district, the "Gibraltar of Socialism," had fallen to the Republicans by some 150 votes. Socialists consoled themselves with the belief that the opposition had had to mount an extraordinary effort: business, the Roman Catholic Church, a subsidized press, Samuel Gompers, and a combination of both parties had all worked together, in a year when a factional dispute divided the working population. Elation at Carey's defeat cost DeLeon's *Weekly People* control of its metaphor: "His malodorous connection with the still more malodor-

33. Goldstein, *Autobiography*, 56; *Worker*, November 22, 1903; October 25, 1903.

ous labor fakirs at last opened the eyes of the working-men. . . ." The Worcester *Catholic Messenger* was equally pleased: "The defeat of Carey . . . a man who turned his back on his church, to stand on an infidel platform whose chief doctrine is antagonism to the Catholic Church . . . is a matter for great congratulation." But the Lawrence *Sun*, no socialist organ, was less convinced Carey's loss was a boon: "Now that he is gone, the House will breathe easier, for many a legislative scheme never saw the light of day merely because Carey of Haverhill would be sure to shout at it, and he had the faculty of hitting the bullseye pretty often."

"Everything will happen for the best," was Carey's resigned comment. He authorized William Mailly to begin booking his national tour of Socialist locals and caught the train to the A.F. of L. convention in Boston.[34] It was nearly a decade before he tried to renew Haverhill's success by seeking local office.

The death of Frederic MacCartney in the spring of 1903 provided opponents of Socialism with an opportunity to reclaim a second legislative seat. Charles Drew, a baggage master and member of the railroad brotherhood, was the Socialist nominee to succeed MacCartney. The nearby Brockton *Times* noted that the contest would reveal whether MacCartney's success in the district was due to political skill, socialist doctrine, or to his own charm. Though Drew lost, the election was too close to permit such discrimination. His defeat only proved what the So-

34. See Mailly's extensive correspondence with George Keene in Letter-book VII, and letters to John Brown (July 29, 1903), J. W. Slayton (June 22, 1903) in Letterbooks VI, VII, SP Papers; Chase to Hillquit, November 14, 1903, Hillquit Papers; Chicago *Socialist*, October–November, 1903, *passim;* Seattle *Socialist*, October–November, 1903, *passim; Wilshire's Magazine*, December, 1903, 23; *SDH*, November 14, 1903; *People*, November 7, 1903; *Wage Worker*, December, 1903, 293; *Worker*, November 15, 1903.

cialists already knew: Frederic MacCartney's death had seriously weakened the party. Wallace Ransden, Brockton's Socialist representative, alone survived the election. The vote, reflecting a strenuous campaign, totalled more than two thousand votes in Ransden's district. His plurality was thirty-six.

Brockton's Socialists did not have to contend with the trade union quarrel that sapped Carey's support. Tobin's Boot and Shoe Workers were virtually unchallenged in the city. Socialist support in the union remained firm. So strong were locals of the A.F. of L. that Brockton was entitled to more than fifty delegates to the Federation's state convention, a quota second only to Boston's. Of these delegates, about nine of every ten were Socialists. A few days before the November election, the Central Labor Union selected a Socialist to represent that body at the Federation's national convention.

Socialist strength in the unions did not intimidate either major party. Both waged active campaigns. William L. Douglas, whose factory turned out more shoes with the union label than any other in Brockton, prodded and financed the Democrats to new life. Douglas hoped to defeat the Socialists at their own game. He urged a positive labor program as the proper campaign strategy.

In mid-September, Douglas sounded the keynote in an address to the local Democratic club. The manufacturer recalled his own terms in the state legislature nearly twenty years before. He was, he said, proud of his support of measures encouraging arbitration in labor disputes and of his bill requiring weekly pay. He thought the state's contemporary arbitration boards slighted organized labor. In early October, Douglas published a large advertisement inviting everyone to join the local Democratic organization and containing his own statement of faith. The Democracy, wrote William L. Douglas, was the party of the common people. During "its entire career" the party had "advocated the interests and defended the rights of wage earners." It favored political democracy: the direct election of senators; home rule for cities; initiative, referendum. It opposed the tariff that fostered trusts, protected the coal barons of Pennsylvania, and raised the price of hides and thus of shoes. It favored public ownership of public utilities. Finally, Douglas was a Democrat because ". . . When I act with a small political organization that is in the process of formation and having only local existence, I sacrifice my opportunity to make my influence effective or to secure a change in those conditions which I feel are not for the best interests of the republic, in which case my vote becomes an empty protest.[35] The Democrats, in short, could implement all the best planks in the Socialist program. And Democrats pursued this line until election. A candidate for state senator courted the workingman's vote with the assertion that Democrats had sponsored all the effective labor legislation on the statute books. John A. Sullivan, an imported Democratic Congressman, hammered the theme: "Socialism cannot presently remedy the evils that oppress the people. . . . A socialist ballot is the pointing of an unloaded gun; a democratic ballot is a straight shot at the enemy. . . . As our party is drawn largely from the working people, we cannot help feeling sympathy with the wage earners who strive to improve industrial conditions."

Republicans, under the spirited direction of W. A. ("Billy") Boyden, could not advertise their record on labor issues, since the Republican state administration had a reputation for opposing labor legislation. Bereft of a positive appeal, Boyden fell back on anti-socialism. Any "man who goes into the voting booth and votes for socialism," he charged, "votes against his home!" Goldstein and

35. *Times*, September 18, 1903; October 1, 3, 7, 8, 9, 29, 1903.

Mrs. Avery, while not under Republican sponsorship, contributed their bit in a Brockton appearance. Every week Boyden bought and distributed 5,000 copies of the *Million*, the anti-Socialist paper published in Haverhill. As the campaign closed, Boyden and other G.O.P. spokesmen stressed Socialist atheism. Boyden was confident that "the enlightened intelligence" of Brockton's aroused citizens would prevent their voting for a social system of which "free love" was "an integral part," and for "the party whose fundamental principles are against the Creator of the universe, against the home, against religion. . . ." [36]

Socialists could not ignore the Republican charges lest silence be interpreted as agreement. John C. Chase, again the nominee for governor, advanced the usual Socialist defense in an early Brockton appearance. Socialism, he asserted, would enable women to stop working and make Christian homes more blissful. The local Socialist campaign paper vainly hoped to concentrate on the party's program; Socialism was a political movement, unconcerned with religion. It was also, incongruously, a creed of "universal love exemplified in law and government— the religion of Christ . . . put in practice."

Socialists waged a hard campaign ending with an election eve rally attended by some three thousand people. Less than two thousand Brocktonians, however, voted for John C. Chase, who ran about 1,200 votes behind his Republican opponent and about three hundred ahead of the Democrat. It was some consolation that Ransden won. Still an editorial in the *Times* thought the results were "a sad disappointment to the Socialists." [37]

The announcement that Father William Kress would be in the city during the following municipal campaign indicated that opponents of the Socialists believed that lode

---

36. *Ibid.*, September 21, 1903; October 10, 16, 31, 1903.
37. *The Champion* (Brockton), October 16, 1903; see also *Times*, September 21, 1903; October 24, 1903; November 4, 1903.

could still profitably be mined. The *Million* still circulated; "Billy" Boyden now spoke for Edward H. Keith, a supervisor in the Keith shoe factories, who had once been a member of the Common Council and was now the nominee for mayor. Keith himself was silent, portraying the responsible businessman, disclaiming partisanship and personalities. Other Republicans kept up the anti-Socialist momentum of the state campaign. Audience after audience heard of the Socialist threat to moral values. John P. Meade, a trade union official and the Democratic nominee, tried another tack. Like the Republicans, he promised an efficient administration; in addition, he pledged unflinching enforcement of Brockton's prohibition ordinance, thereby raising an issue that hurt the Socialists badly.[38]

On November 14, there were indications of unusual friction in the Socialist camp. Edward M. Henry and George Monk, both prominent in the local organization, were rumored to be ready to oppose Coulter's bid for renomination; James Cox, a Socialist alderman, was threatening to lead his personal supporters into another party if unspecified demands were not met. Two days later the cause of the internal squabble was clear. Charles T. Laird, once chairman of the city committee and still a member in 1903, broke silence with a vengeance. At a committee meeting Laird charged that Coulter and Carlton Beals, the city marshal, were not enforcing prohibition. Another member of the committee, in turn, accused Laird of acting from spite. Gossip had it that Laird had once sought immunity for an illegal saloon but that Coulter had ordered a raid instead.

Laird decided to show all the skeletons in the closet. He declared that, while chairman of the city committee in 1901, he had acted for Coulter and Beals in a deal with the saloon in question. According to the alleged agree-

38. *Times,* October 5, 1903–December 4, 1903, *passim.*

ment, he was to be informed in advance of any raid in order to warn the bartender. But a hitch developed and Beals ordered a raid without notice to anyone. Naturally the saloon owner reproached Laird, who paid the fine, he said, to hush up the whole affair.

The city committee summoned Coulter from his bed, received his denial, voted to sustain him, and wearily adjourned at 3:15 A.M. after a nine-hour session. A day later, the party made an official statement admitting that Laird had several times tried to influence Coulter, but maintaining that the mayor had always denied such requests. The statement had the ring of truth. The party tried to turn the incident to advantage. It showed, said a Socialist release, that the party would go to any length to insure honest administration. But Laird would not keep still. Coulter, he claimed, had decided early in the first administration that the liquor traffic could not be wholly stopped. Laird then suggested that it might be regulated with an informal fee to defray the party's campaign expenses. He had minute books that purported to prove parts of his statement, though there was no evidence of the central charge.

This documentary evidence gave the party no pause. The city committee condemned Laird's alteration of the records in a formal motion. But Laird asked one question that no one ever answered: if he was as crooked as the party's statements alleged, why had he been kept for two years on the city committee, and why had the committee elected him secretary where he had access to the records? Why, in short, had the party not expelled him and reaped the political credit when he had first attempted to influence the mayor? If the Socialists tried to buy silence by keeping Laird among the hierarchy, they used wretched political judgment.[39]

As if to demonstrate the administration's zeal, a raid

39. *Ibid.*, November 14–20, 1903.

soon brought in a few culprits and some contraband liquor. Coulter then stood on his record, defending it against charges of shoddy school construction and graft in procurement. He sarcastically attacked his opponents for hiding behind the religious issue because they could not besmirch the solid Socialist record.

The Socialist record, in fact, was not bad. But the party's main claim to political prominence was that it was the instrument of labor and honest government. John P. Meade, the Democratic candidate, was a respected labor leader, and his party emphasized its labor program; Laird's charges smudged the Socialist claim to honest administration. Coulter lost by about 500 ballots to silent, responsible Edward H. Keith. Meade ran a distant third, even while doubling the Democratic vote of 1902. The liquor scandal did not affect the entire Socialist ticket, for two aldermen and three councilmen were elected. Keith paid off his chief campaigner by installing "Billy" Boyden in the city marshal's office, and acknowledged the help of the anti-Socialist statements of Samuel Gompers and John Mitchell. Nonetheless, the mayor-elect was puzzled that so many voters still lacked "a love of liberty, patriotism, and . . . God." The election, said the *Times*, "was a Waterloo for the Socialists." [40]

The election of 1903 was not really the Socialist Waterloo in Brockton, although the party was never again to elect a mayor of the city. The campaigns were disastrous for the Socialist movement in the rest of the state. Parkman B. Flanders, the incumbent mayor of Haverhill, lost to a fusion candidate by nearly 400 votes; the party in Haverhill was reduced to one office-holder, an assistant assessor in the fifth ward. John Chase polled 25,000 votes for governor, down 8,000 from his effort of 1902. Never again would a Socialist candidate do so well.

Losses at the polls were only part of the problem. The

40. *Ibid.*, November 20, 21, 1903; December 1, 3, 9, 19, 1903.

setback interrupted a record of steady gains and seemed to belie the faith in inevitable victory. Loss of momentum led to sagging enthusiasm. When Mailly, Chase, and Mac-Cartney were permanently removed and when Carey temporarily left Massachusetts, the movement had no experienced leaders to replace them. The stern opposition of the Roman Catholic Church and the estrangement of the Boot and Shoe Workers' Union indicated that retrieving the losses would be difficult. The movement in Brockton, which did not face all these trials, was able to live down the liquor scandal and revived, though it did not achieve its former prominence. The state organization had passed its prime.

One battle, as Socialists often told themselves, was not a war; one loss, not a calamity. And after the election of 1903, the anti-Socialist forces felt the same way about victory. The Socialist losses, wrote the *Wage Worker,* were important and gratifying, but 25,000 Socialists were still too many. Defeat must be turned to rout.

There seemed little point in changing a winning formula. Through 1904 and beyond, when the enemy's weakness made the effort seem increasingly pointless, anti-socialists reiterated the slogans of 1903. Socialists were against religion, the family, the home; Socialists advocated immorality, infidelity, atheism. Trade unions, major political parties, and churches could accomplish any reform that was within the bounds of American traditions, natural rights, and Christian ethics.

The anti-Socialist crusade held the attention of the Boston *Pilot* until mid-1904, when coverage began to drop off. Still Massachusetts Catholics did not lack reminders of the Church's continuing antagonism in the years after 1904. A Newton priest printed excerpts from Marx in his weekly bulletin and pointed out that the quotations were incompatible with Catholic doctrine. A Socialist from Springfield reported that a local daily had run an article by a Jesuit with the usual objections to Socialism. The *Pilot* attacked Congressman Victor Berger for an anti-Catholic speech. Indeed the party's exasperation with Catholic opposition provoked anti-clerical remarks, which in turn brought redoubled disapproval from the Church. One Massachusetts Catholic dejectedly wrote that Catholic workingmen were leaving the party, and that replacements could not be recruited because "a hodge-podge of Darwinism, atheism, anti-clericalism, and other nauseous theories not having the slightest connection with the Socialist party platform" barred the way.[41]

In 1911, Thomas Gasson, S.J., president of Boston College, spoke to an overflow audience on the "Dangers of Socialism." As James Carey later conceded, the speech was "courteous, kindly, and manly," neither "bigoted" nor "vicious." While Father Gasson sympathized with Socialist attempts to make the world better, he deplored the means and the philosophical invasion of the realm of the Church. Reform was necessary and possible within the existing framework of society. Socialists, in spite of their pretensions of scientific objectivity, were really utopians in their view of human nature; their system could not deliver either a better today or a perfect tomorrow.

A few weeks later, Socialists hired Faneuil Hall for Carey's rebuttal. Carey defined his creed: "SOCIETY SHOULD OWN AND OPERATE DEMOCRATICALLY THE SOCIAL TOOLS OF PRODUCTION AND DISTRIBUTION. . . ." And that, said Carey, was all he would defend. If some Socialists had wild religious ideas, that was an individual matter, not Socialist policy. Neither he nor Mrs. Carey, he ob-

41. *Wage Worker*, December, 1903, 311; New York *Call*, September 10, 1908; October 2, 1910; October 22, 1911; November 20, 1909; Doherty, "The American Socialist Party. . . ." 103.

served dryly, believed in free love or easy divorce. And
certainly Socialists were not responsible for prostitution
as some scurrilious stories had it: "If every Socialist in
this city were to frequent those places, the total income
. . . would not pay the rent." Nor were Socialists materi-
alists to the exclusion of a God. They did believe that economic and material forces influenced history. But Massachusetts Socialists were not German philosophers "who
talked about force and matter until your hair stood on
end." Finally, the Socialists were not opposed to some
kinds of private property.

> I want private property; I want a home and . . . I recognize
> that in order to get these things I must own the means of getting
> them. I cannot produce property alone. . . . And thus I join
> with my brothers. I say to them, let us collectively own these
> things and collectively operate them in order that wealth may
> be increased and returned to us in proportion as we have pro-
> duced it, in order that we may have private property. This is
> essentially the position of the Socialist movement.[42]

In 1912, the most important Catholic in the Bay State
spoke out. To the Socialist, said William Cardinal O'Connell of Boston,

> . . . nothing is sacred, neither God, nor His altars, nor His
> ministers, nor home, nor native land, nor wife, nor family. . . .
> No fatherland, no banner, no fireside, no altar, no law, no
> ruler, no God. Thus are summed up all the damnable nega-
> tions of this Satanic doctrine . . . which overturns with one
> fell blow all the holiest principles of human life.

At the end of the year, O'Connell wrote a pastoral letter
to be read in all the parishes under his jurisdiction. He asserted flatly that Catholicism and socialism were so mutually repulsive that a Catholic socialist was "an utter impossibility." Only the spread of true Christianity could

42. James F. Carey and Thomas Gasson, *The Menace of Socialism*
(Boston, 1911), *passim*.

calm "the clamor of those noisy hawkers of poisonous panaceas. . . ." Control of the state would prove nothing. Employees must be frugal and diligent. And employers must, in accordance with the teachings of Leo XIII, treat labor with justice and humanity. O'Connell defined these ideals so as to include the right to unionize and to require payment of a decent, living wage. The secretary of the Socialist party of Massachusetts once said that seventy per cent of the Socialists in the state were Catholics, and of these, nine-tenths practiced their faith.[43] By 1912, one or the other of these figures must have been declining.

David Goldstein and Martha Avery had enlisted in this fight to stay. After the election of 1903, they remained on the editorial staff of the *Wage Worker* and of *Mellen's Magazine* which succeeded it. The periodical buttressed its usual fare with articles explaining the religious objections of Roman Catholics to Socialism. It also promoted Goldstein's *Socialism: The Nation of Fatherless Children,* by reprinting the enthusiastic reviews of Catholic periodicals elsewhere.

Goldstein's book attracted more important endorsements. Early in 1904, Samuel Gompers wrote that he had read the work with "keenest interest." He found it "timely, . . . an excellent contribution to the literature on the labor question. . . ." The book tore "the mask of hypocrisy" from the faces of labor's false friends. Later, in the *Outlook,* Theodore Roosevelt especially commended the chapters on Free Love, Homeless Children, and Socialist Leaders. In 1911, a second edition of the book came from the presses with the imprimatur of the Archbishop of Boston. The proud author said he sold 50,000 copies, and that hundreds of other books, articles, and pamphlets had been based on his research.

43. *Call,* January 16, 1912; Brockton *Times,* December 2, 1912; Goldstein *Autobiography,* 380.

In 1905, Goldstein took the offensive. Disgusted by talk of official approval of the Socialist party by the state A.F. of L., he prepared a series of resolutions expressing the Federation's hostility. He shrewdly emphasized the participation of important Socialists in the recent formation of the Industrial Workers of the World, and hooked a condemnation of the new union to his carefully drawn anti-Socialist motion. The "Whereas" clause dealt with attempts of Socialists to distract labor from trade union pursuits; but the "Resolved" clause did not explicitly condemn Socialism. Goldstein's subtlety was probably unnecessary, for the motion passed 80 to 29, and the margin may even have exaggerated Socialist strength.[44]

Try as it might, the party could not really shake off the constant harassment of Goldstein and Mrs. Avery. Eventually, the two renegades put their show on the road, to the discomfort of Socialists beyond the Bay State. There was always a hint of bravado in the claim that the party's refutation was so effective that membership rolls swelled. Correspondence with national headquarters, however, was less confident. Officials there prepared material to help beleaguered locals meet the challenge of the team Daniel DeLeon dubbed "Brother David and Sister Martha."[45]

William Stang, the Roman Catholic bishop of Fall River, read David Goldstein's "very instructive" book soon after it appeared. Stang too attacked Socialistic atheism and immorality. But a glance at his own diocese told the bishop that there was, as the Socialists said, a "social

44. *Wage Worker,* March 1904, 394 ff.; May, 1904, 445 ff.; 477; Goldstein *Autobiography,* 53–55, 65, 72–73.

45. The SP Papers contain several items pertaining to Goldstein and Mrs. Avery. See undated material collected by Carl D. Thompson, Box 2; A. M. Simons to Thompson, December 5, 1913; Springfield Debate Committee to A. H. Hancock, January 26, 1914. See also James O'Neal to Comrades, a circular letter to the Indiana Socialists from the state secretary, June 4, 1912, O'Neal Papers, Tamiment Institute Library of New York University.

problem." The Church, he believed, ought to do more than reject the solutions of others; the writings of Leo XIII gave the foundation for a positive answer. Socialism never made much headway in Fall River. In 1903, for instance, John C. Chase received 233 votes of nearly 11,000 cast in the city. Socialist weakness reflected in part the lack of organization among Fall River's textile workers. William Stang was also a major obstacle.

Stang described the impersonality of the factory and the human costs of spreading industrialism with a frankness and an ardor that many a Socialist orator might have envied. The bishop did not deny the importance, even the necessity, of modern economic organization. But progress involved costs, and labor was paying the bills:

Look at the machines, the soulless antagonists of the workingmen; hear them whirring and clicking, humming and shrieking like a legion of devils, let loose from the abode of eternal woe. Hearts are bleeding to death under the cruel horrors of the sweatshop; minds are rebelling against the infamous injustice of employers, and are growing desperate under the yoke of trusts and capitalists. The filthy conditions of so many homes in our large cities, human dwellings without air and sunshine, should make us loathe to sing the praises of our great civilization.

. . . At the shriek of whistles, unsightly buildings, more like prisons, are belching forth masses of unhealthy, wizened and shrivelled men and women, who pass through the sulphurous and smoke-smothered streets, paved with cinders and dust, into the dark alleys, and into still more cheerless, crowded and ill-ventilated tenements, to gulp down a badly cooked dinner, and then throw themselves on a hard pallet, or spend the evening in a saloon, in wicked company, to begin a wretched morning in the same dreary way, until consumption, pneumonia or typhoid fever frees them from a bondage worse than death.[46]

Daniel DeLeon could hardly have improved the bishop's prose.

Stang's proposals were another matter. Since earthly

46. William Stang, *Socialism and Christianity*, 4–6.

hardship was the result of original sin, only a spiritual renewal would effect a lasting change. Universal Catholic
Christianity was "the complete solution to the social question." Factories under the management of enlightened
Christians would become "schools of refinement," where
virtue vanquished vice and the pure converted the way-
ward. Meanwhile the Church did not advise labor "to
bear in patience and holy silence . . . the heartless exac-
tions of the capitalists." No need, said Stang, to wait "for
the good things until we get to heaven. . . ."

What I claim for the workingman is not alms; for those that
starve and pine from the lack of the necessaries of life are not
beggars; they are honest men, willing to work. We demand for
them justice in distribution, the right to live, sufficient wages
for themselves and families to be properly fed, clothed, and
sheltered, and to have leisure for their religious and social
duties.[47]

And there were specific suggestions. Employers must
"come to terms with organized labor" and must not "de-
prive the workingman of his just and proper share in the
product." Legislatures must be freed from the corrupting
hand of capital in order that social legislation might be
enacted. Women and children should be barred from the
mills. Employers should indemnify workers in the event of
industrial accidents. A broad insurance program to protect labor against the hazards of sickness, unemployment,
and old age, would give workers security, and keep them
"from drifting to Socialism." Stang even appropriated part
of the Socialist program. Public ownership was an acceptable means to acceptable ends, and differed from immoral
Socialism. "The agitation for public ownership" did "not
seek the upheaval of society or the fall of government;"
rather it advocated "the enlargement of government power
and duty." The state might well own and operate gas,

47. *Ibid.*, 41, 47, 8, 25–26.

light, water, transportation, and communication facilities, and perhaps forests as well, without moral danger.[48]

Thus the Catholic attack on Socialism was two-fold: the doctrine endangered immortality; and other, more suitable institutions—trade unions, the Church, the Democratic party—could right undeniable wrongs more effectively. Socialists in Massachusetts had pitifully inadequate defenses. Two out-of-state defrocked priests were hardly a match for William Cardinal O'Connell and the rest of the hierarchy. Denials of atheism and immorality sounded hollow as David Goldstein dug up a mounting mass of contrary quotations from Marx, Engels, Bebel, and even a comrade or two in Massachusetts.[49]

Yet it is possible to overestimate the Church's responsibility for the decline of socialism in the Commonwealth. Though Catholics repeated the assertion that the Church was the last barrier to the Socialist triumph, the boast staked too big a claim. Socialists in fact could not break down Catholic opposition; nor could they break down the opposition of most trade union members, Protestants, Jews, Republicans, Democrats, Prohibitionists, and vegetarians. A mass of evidence attests the Church's hostility to Socialism; the same mass of evidence indicates the extent to which the Church overestimated the menace.[50] The active opposition of the Church in Massachusetts in 1903 was vigorous and timely; certainly it deserved credit for slowing the Socialist surge. But whatever the Church's attitude after 1903, the Massachusetts Socialists were not really going anywhere.

48. *Ibid.*, 56, 65, 69–72, 49.
49. See David Goldstein and Martha Moore Avery, *Socialism: The Nation of Fatherless Children* (2nd ed., Boston, 1911), 252–255; 258–259; 312–313, for material on the Massachusetts movement.
50. Stang, *Socialism and Christianity*, 33; Marc Karson, *American Labor Unions and Politics, 1900–1918* (Carbondale, Ill., 1958), has assembled much evidence that the Church opposed Socialists. See particularly Chapter 9.

C H A P T E R V I I

"Educate and Organize"

After 1903, the Socialist party of Massachusetts drifted. Without the certainty of an agreed ideology or the prospect of political success, the movement lacked purpose and élan. Divisions, debts, and a leadership that was intermittent and never vigorous restricted the party's effort. Rival parties wooed the votes of laborers and reformers. Participation of prominent Socialists in the formation of the militant Industrial Workers of the World estranged political moderates as well as trade unions. Most locals made the gestures expected of them: they enrolled members, paid dues, sold party publications, discussed socialism, and nominated a few candidates for office. Such was the pretense of life. Membership rose and a candidate occasionally won, but no longer did outsiders confuse the Socialists with a vital political party.

The legacy of the election of 1903 was a debt of $850 and pervasive, weary discouragement.[1] Both hobbled attempts to recover. John L. Bates, the Republican governor, handed his opposition an opportunity when he vetoed a first legislative step toward the eight-hour day. Outraged labor organizations vowed revenge. A few years earlier Socialists would have profited from the situation. In 1904, Democrats did.

Both wings of the Massachusetts Democracy united behind William L. Douglas. The Brockton manufacturer, a

1. The *Worker* (New York), March 6, 1904.

fiscal conservative, was the embodiment of the rags-to-riches American dream. Yet Bryan Democrats could support him as a fair employer who hired only union labor, paid good wages, established and financed a program of medical care for his employees, and had a reasonably liberal record in the state legislature in the 1880's. Although uninterested in the tariff, which both candidate and platform proclaimed the major issue, organized labor was very much interested in trouncing John L. Bates. Within a few days of Douglas' nomination, labor leaders were organizing a "Douglas Flying Wedge" of union officials to deliver the workingman's vote. Frank Foster, legislative lobbyist for the state American Federation of Labor, called Douglas "the ideal candidate of the workingman of Massachusetts." George Fred Williams, leader of the liberal Democrats, called the nominee a humane employer who had not forgotten his experience as a worker or outgrown his earlier political radicalism. Political advertising claimed that not a dollar of Douglas' fortune had been "wrung from the overworked and underpaid." He had "blazed the way for industrial peace and prosperity for the worker as well as for himself."

This Democratic strategy, incidentally designed to capture the votes that in 1902 and 1903 had gone to John C. Chase, put the Socialists on the defensive. The state organization made ridiculously optimistic predictions which convinced editor A. M. Simons of the *International Socialist Review* that Massachusetts had made "an almost complete recovery" from earlier "lethargy." National headquarters sent both Eugene Debs and Ben Hanford, his running mate, to tour the state. Debs admitted that Douglas, as an individual, was "above reproach"; he opposed him as the representative of an economic system and a social class. After Douglas' victory, a Democratic analysis of the returns concluded that he had attracted about 20,000 voters who had once been Socialists. Later, when John Chase confronted another labor reform ticket, he would refer to it as "a repetition of the Mass. affair when Douglas was elected." [2]

Douglas was the only Democrat to win a state-wide contest, and most observers found the explanation in the labor vote. "*Labor omnia vincit,*" remarked the Brockton *Times,* which called the result "a triumph for . . . the laboring interests of the state. . . ." [3] Less than 12,000 voters supported John Quincy Adams, the Amesbury physician who was the Socialist nominee. His total was about half Chase's vote of 1903. Yet so personal was Douglas' triumph that it failed to revive his party even in Brockton. He carried the city with 5,177 votes; a month later the Democratic mayoral nominee received less than four hundred.

Charles Coulter, once more the Socialist candidate for mayor, won most of the ballots that had gone to Douglas in November by reversing the Democrat's appeal. Douglas was the conservative friend of the workers; Coulter was the Socialist friend of the property-owner. Running against Edward Keith, the businessman who had beaten him in 1903, Coulter promised a "business administration" that would "guard the financial interests of all the people, especially the tax-payers. . . ." It was peculiar Socialism, but it almost worked. Coulter lost by fifty-three votes and polled about 3,500 more than had Adams in November. Two Socialist aldermen and three candidates for the Common Council won. [4]

While Socialists in Brockton could recapture local shoe

2. Brockton *Times,* October 7, 10, 15, 18, 1904; November 1, 10, 1904; *ISR,* October, 1904, 211; Chase to Dan White, Chase Letterbook, Papers of the Socialist Party of New York, Tamiment Institute, New York University Libraries.
3. *Times,* November 9, 1904. Italics added.
4. *Ibid.,* November 23, 1904; December 7, 1904.

workers with a blend of fiscal orthodoxy, radical vocabulary, and candidates from the shoe shops, the Massachusetts party's declining strength in the Boot and Shoe
Workers' Union was irretrievably lost. Early in 1904, the
union's *Journal* proclaimed in boldfaced type that "The
Policy of the Boot and Shoe Workers' Union is Conservative. . . ." The membership was periodically cautioned to
avoid schemes for social reform, which ought to be left to
"specialists in perpetual motion, air ships, and pipe
dreams. . . ." Unemployment, for instance, could best be
solved by the unions; Socialist proposals were either "im-
practicable . . . utopian schemes," or "palliatives" offering no permanent change. The *Journal* found Douglas'
candidacy "quite in order" and reported that shoe workers
throughout the state had given him "a splendid vote."

Although John F. Tobin, the union's president, did not
endorse Douglas officially, his position was never in
doubt. The S.L.P. often referred to Douglas as "Tobin's
friend" and correctly reported that Harry Skeffington, a
close associate of Tobin, was aiding Douglas' political
effort. Tobin sent the governor-elect a glowing congratulatory message, an act that merited a stanza in a partisan
S.L.P. ode:

> Even Tobin, our brother and chum, Douglas,
>   Our champion supplier of scabs,
> Has declared himself proud that you . . . won, Douglas,
>   Such conduct our craven heart stabs.[5]

Douglas' course in the State House fell short of labor's
expectations, but the Socialists forfeited any slight chance
of regaining Tobin's support when Eugene V. Debs and

5. *Boot and Shoe Workers' Journal,* February, 1904, 3, 9; October,
1904, 9; November, 1904, 11; December, 1904, 21; *People,* October 15,
29, 1904; November 19, 1904; *Times,* October 31, 1904. In 1905, Douglas
appointed Skeffington to the Harbor and Land Commission, a state job
with an annual salary of $2700. Even in a good year, a skilled shoe worker
might have made about a third of that amount (*Times,* October 25, 1905).

other party members helped launch the Industrial Workers of the World in 1905. Massachusetts Socialists were not responsible for the new industrial union that soon took such belligerent pride in uncompromising radicalism. No matter; the *Journal* of John F. Tobin's union promptly deplored the party's apparent complicity in the creation of a rival union. The I.W.W., said the *Journal*, discredited Eugene Debs and "his followers . . . in the eyes of the labor union world. . . ." The new organization was the product of "out-of-a-job men of the Debs stamp," who had never made a success of anything they touched. For the sake of "Mr. Debs and his friends," the *Journal* hoped that the new organization would open "some lucrative field of endeavor. . . ." The *Journal* later acknowledged that "Socialist publications from coast to coast" had denied "even a second cousin relationship" to the I.W.W. Still hostility never moderated. Summarizing Samuel Gompers' report to the A.F. of L. convention of 1905, the *Journal* quoted some of his invective. The I.W.W., said Gompers, was "a tail to the kite of a political party, the head and front of which are out of touch and out of . . . sympathy with the struggles, the hopes, the real aspirations of the toiling masses. . . ." Debs and his followers were either "incompetent derelicts," or in league with the employers. Their vision of a workers' revolution was a "fool hope." [6]

The conservative policy of the Boot and Shoe Workers' Union, especially the centralization of authority, was the chief issue in a bitterly fought contest for the union's presidency in 1906. The insurgents, led by Thomas Hickey of Brockton, seemed to have beaten Tobin, but the incumbents alleged irregularities in balloting, and the dispute dragged on for nearly a year. Finally, a convention expelled Hickey and declared Tobin's leadership vindicated. The dissidents, particularly in Lynn, were soon dickering

6. *Journal*, June, 1905, 23–24; August, 1905, 29; December, 1905, 11–12.

with the I.W.W., a flirtation not calculated to revive Tobin's radicalism. In 1908, the *Journal* printed large chunks of the Democratic platform, and advised members to demonstrate effective opposition to the "Taft-Injunction-Corporation ticket" by voting for the Democrats. We believe, noted the editors, "that every wage-earner should make his vote effective . . . even though on principle he would rather vote for a minority party." [7]

Socialists, for their part, decided that Tobin's union was a poor sort of labor organization anyway. In 1910, the Socialist New York *Call* quoted the remark of a disgruntled Brooklyn shoe worker who said the union was "nothing but a dues collecting and office sustaining institution . . . to keep the workers in submission." Two years later, the *International Socialist Review* ran two articles about "The Tainted Shoe Label." These articles denounced the union's policy of importing workers when a local conducted an unauthorized strike. The policy was not new; the same problem had led to the strife that contributed to Carey's defeat in 1903. But the rebuke was extremely harsh: the union allegedly was owned "body and soul, boot and breeches by the bosses and a little gang of union officials . . ."; the union label was "one of the rankest frauds ever put over on an innocent . . . public"; Tobin had converted the organization into "a scab-recruiting agency. . . ." By 1912, both John Tobin and Charles Baine, the union's secretary, had held office in the National Civic Federation, and their union had lived down its earlier commitment to economic radicalism. [8]

Those Bay State Socialists who were not too numbed by the election of 1904 tried to stiffen their tottering organi-

7. Boot and Shoe Workers' Union, Scrapbooks 2, 3, Archives of the Boot and Shoe Workers' Union, Boston; *Journal*, August, 1908, 19–20.
8. New York *Call*, November 23, 1910; Phillips Russell, "The Tainted Shoe Label," *ISR*, April, 1912, 633, 634; see also *ISR*, June, 1912, 845 ff. and August, 1912, 184.

zation. A. M. Simons, who had once remarked on the intelligence of the state's proletarians, now discovered that Massachusetts had been "one of the most backward states in the union in the thorough training of its membership in the principles of socialism." George Roewer, an attorney whose rise to party prominence was just beginning, suggested that Socialists stop engaging in Tippecanoe campaigns and start making thoroughly trained Socialists. Roewer's panacea had a familiar ring: "educate and organize." The *Worker*, the New York weekly that had assumed the subscriptions of the *Haverhill Social Democrat*, concurred. The Massachusetts comrades, "flushed by their early success," had depended too heavily on "a few prominent individuals." They had concentrated too heavily "on the purely political side" to the neglect of "education and organization." Henceforth, they must teach Socialism, "not brotherly love and 'new thought' and the 'reflection of humanity' and so forth. . . ." [9]

Not everyone agreed. One Bostonian made the common-sense observation that Douglas' candidacy was perhaps responsible for Socialist weakness; if one had to discover internal causes, perhaps the lack of money and the consequent closing of state headquarters would serve. Howard Gibbs, a Worcester Socialist, denied that Massachusetts Socialists were more politically oriented than their comrades elsewhere. After 1902, he explained, too many heads had become swollen; party headquarters grew too plush, and too many people drew salaries. Opportunists swarmed around the treasury and their antics disgusted the self-sacrificing Socialists who had built the movement. (Subsequently it became evident that Gibbs was referring in particular to Franklin Wentworth, a lecturer who was rumored to be interested in a place on the payroll, and to John C. Chase, who held a salaried job in the New

9. *ISR*, December, 1904, 340; *Worker*, November 20, 27, 1904.

York organization while neglecting less lucrative responsibilities in Massachusetts.)

David Goldstein looked on with satisfaction. Haverhill, he noted, had been "deserted by its luminaries. . . ."

Carey is now hanging on to . . . his pipe, reading dime novels in the Maine woods, waiting for sufficient funds to turn up to send him on another national tour. Ex-mayor Chase is holding down an organizer job in New York, while the Socialists of Massachusetts are struggling to pay the indebtedness incurred by the "bad bookkeeping" of the state secretary.

Goldstein was correct at least about Carey's inertia, for the vacationing Carey had warned Morris Hillquit to disregard any report of his undertaking a summer lecture tour. He would stay in Maine, Carey wrote, "garbed in the raiment of a bucolic citizen." [10]

In the fall of 1905, Carey was once more on the stump as the nominee for governor. The party optimistically reported its "organization . . . in better shape than ever." Rising membership and payment of indebtedness would permit an active campaign. After the election, when Carey polled less than 13,000 votes, a very modest improvement over 1904, it became clear that the debt had not quite been extinguished. And the moral, as before, was that the party must organize new branches and work harder to spread the Socialist message.[11]

"Educate and organize" became a post-election refrain among the Massachusetts Socialists. From 1906 through 1911, gubernatorial candidates averaged less than 11,000 votes, with a high in 1908 of 14,430, and a low in 1907 of 7,621. After the party's dismal performance that year, Carey blamed the lack of agitation during the summer

10. *Worker*, December 18, 1904; September 30, 1905; *Mellen's Magazine* (Worcester), March, 1905, 48–49; Carey to Hillquit, June 7, 1905. Hillquit Papers.
11. Chicago *Socialist*, September 30, 1905; October 14, 21, 1905; *Worker*, November 18, 1905; December 9, 1905.

months, when "hardly a place held a meeting. . . ." Although the party rebounded slightly in 1908, the *International Socialist Review*, which was well to the left of the Massachusetts movement, contrasted early political promise with present futility. The *Review* pointed to the slump in Massachusetts as the inevitable fate of Socialists who put politics ahead of principle. The Seattle *Socialist*, one of the party's most militant publications, simply found the Massachusetts party "too tame." [12]

A comrade occasionally questioned the emphasis on education. M. J. Kornikow, a Bostonian whose wife held party posts, wondered whether the instructors were teaching the right doctrine. Noting the competition of the Independence League, the political reform group backed by William Randolph Hearst, Kornikow narrowly skirted doctrinal heresy: "We are so anxious to establish the Cooperative Commonwealth, that we forget . . . we are dealing with human beings, whose natural impulse is to improve their present condition, whatever the future may be." He saw too much theory and not enough practical reform in the party's program.[13]

Within the limits of a beleaguered treasury, the state committee tried to follow the conflicting advice. Activity early in 1905 was almost frantic, as locals organized, educated, pondered, and reorganized. The national committee sent M. W. Wilkins, an experienced party organizer and lecturer, to help. During January and February Wilkins' audiences averaged forty-six people, but attendance improved to 130 in March. Work among immigrants was stepped up. The Finns, especially in Fitchburg, became party stalwarts with their own weekly newspaper. In 1906, Fitchburg was reported to be "without doubt the hot-bed of the organized movement. . . ." A month later

12. *Worker*, November 9, 1807; *ISR*, January, 1909, 533; *The Socialist* (Seattle), November 21, 1908.
13. *Call*, November 12, 1909.

311 voters there cast ballots for the Socalist ticket, a decrease of thirty from the previous year. At the same time, the party hired John MacLean, an energetic Socialist from Haverhill, to speak, organize, and sell literature throughout Essex County. MacLean sold 400 copies of Upton Sinclair's *The Jungle* and 600 subscriptions to various socialist newspapers. In the fall, the Socialist vote in the county declined sharply.[14]

Winfield R. Gaylord, a clergyman and state senator from Wisconsin, was imported in 1909 to add a sign of political success to the campaign. He only provoked internal controversy. C. L. Pingree, a self-styled "proletarian from the slum" of Lowell, was contemptuous of Gaylord's "middle class clap-trap and opportunism." Gaylord's address had certainly done "a lot of harm in Lowell." Pingree claimed that he had had to re-educate his friends, who had been "ready to jump the fence to Socialism," when Gaylord's speech "nearly knocked all the Socialism out of them." The Lowell local, on the other hand, voted approval of the lecture, which a Cambridge Socialist described as vigorous, revolutionary, and without a trace of middle-class compromise.[15]

The insistent demand for education assumed both ideological interest and ideological consensus. It assumed also that Socialists were themselves responsible for sagging political fortune. Neither assumption was valid. Moreover, the party could not afford unlimited education. Demands on a scanty treasury were always worthy and always too heavy. While the state organizer in 1907 was pleading for more funds to continue his work, he also had to dun the membership for unpaid pledges. Simultaneously, the Mas-

14. *The Socialist* (Toledo), April 22, 1905; *Worker*, January-February, 1905, *passim;* June 10, 1905; August 5, 1905; October 20, 1906; November 3, 10, 17, 1906.

15. *Call*, October 4, 24, 27, 1909; November 7, 1909. Gaylord's Socialism was in fact very moderate. In Brockton, he defined the creed as "social self-control" and said it was already being practiced by three million American trade union members (*Times*, October 1, 1909).

sachusetts party was urged to buy tickets to support the Chicago *Daily Socialist*. A speaker from Colorado passed the hat for the defense fund for imprisoned leaders of the Western Federation of Miners, and the Boston organization voted a per capita tax for the cause.[16] The party was never able to distinguish between generosity and diffusion of scanty financial resources.

Deterioration was so far advanced by 1910 that Dan White, the nominee for governor, confessed despair in a letter to his old friend William Mailly. White's campaign had encountered resounding indifference; five scheduled appearances had recently been cancelled. He suspected it would not matter if he skipped the rest of the schedule. "I am," he wrote, "surely discouraged with the way our work is being carried on." White thought the party valued fiscal prudence too highly: "With great possibilities right in front of us we sit tight and keep expenses down and even boast of our ability to write a check." The organization had become, he continued, "largely foreign-speaking" and the resulting "prejudice play[ed] a mighty part in holding back our movement." White had been in some towns where he could not find an English-speaking Socialist. In those places the party was a "huge joke." The whole organization was "blundering and impotent."

. . . it sometimes seems to me that if Socialism grows it will not be because of us but in spite of us. . . . If it were left to us to destroy capitalism it would not be destroyed. Were it not for the fact that it holds . . . the germ of its own decay, they might well laugh. . . .

"I do not look for a big vote," he concluded wistfully, and in fact White did not do well. The New York *Call* simplified the usual recommendation to "work, lots of hard work, and nothing else than work. . . ."[17]

16. *Worker,* March 16, 1907; April 27, 1907.
17. White to Mailly, October 27, 1910. Mailly Papers. Tamiment Institute, New York University Libraries; *Call,* November 13, 1910.

If the state's leaders were discouraged, many local leaders were totally indifferent. The shell of the party sometimes remained as a sort of fraternal lodge, but almost without exception local political activity slowed. In many communities, it stopped.

The radicalism of Boston Socialists had been suspect since the days of the Bellamy Nationalists. In 1905, the Hub local sponsored a Socialist dramatic society to raise funds and propagandize through its performances. One drama presented in 1906 concerned the unjust fate of a lady whose lover was "beneath her class." Franklin Wentworth, hardly a proletarian himself, privately referred to some Bostonians as "parlor Socialists." An unidentified correspondent was explicit in the pages of the *Worker*.

Boston is always radical, radical in religion, radical in politics and ideals, and radically divided into small, autonomous groups. In normal times these professional radicals are hard to find, but on gala occasions they appear as if by magic and applaud and cheer radical utterances and then disappear until the scenery is set to suit their fads. . . . [A] typical radical of Boston . . . will talk sometimes, but will forever refuse to do any constructive work. The radicals comprise Theosophists, Christian Scientists, flat-earth propagandists, municipal-ownership faddists . . . Single-Taxers, Spiritualists, Holy Jumpers, etc., etc., forever.[18]

Occasionally the city embraced a radical cause as in 1907 when thousands demonstrated to demand freedom for Bill Haywood and other imprisoned leaders of the Western Federation of Miners. More often the Socialist organization was "only fair," as May Wood Simons described it in 1911. Mrs. Simons, in Boston on a lecture tour, wrote her husband, A. M. Simons, that she had stayed with "some Back Bay aristocrat" and attended a dinner party in the city. Her reaction to her hostess and to the festivities was

18. *Worker*, January 6, 1906; December 8, 1906; Wentworth to Hillquit, December 6, 1908, Hillquit Papers.

an expressive "Ugh!" Always on the verge of upheaval, Boston Socialists had, she reported, recently experienced "a good deal of contention." [19]

The party had few elected officials to catch public attention after 1903. Nor were those few always constructive. Franklin Wentworth, briefly a member of the Salem Common Council, thought one of his resolutions "probably the most revolutionary ever passed by an elective body in this country." The measure denounced the use of injunctions in labor disputes, but no local strike occasioned Wentworth's action; the immediate cause was injustice to cigarmakers in Tampa, Florida. Wentworth also fought to establish skating rinks throughout the city to put recreation within the reach of the proletarians. [20]

Haverhill's lone Socialist office-holder, Charles Morrill, would never have described his actions as revolutionary. He was an unusually diligent party worker who served longer in elective office than any other Socialist in the state. Elected an assistant assessor in his ward in 1901, he was re-elected until 1909, when he won Carey's old House seat, which he held for nearly a decade. Once a shoe worker, Morrill had lost a leg at sixteen. Afterward, he worked at various jobs that required canvassing his neighborhood. He took the census, gathered information for the city directory, and sold a large quantity of Socialist literature. His campaigns were quiet, as befitted a cautious politician whose first term in the General Court was the result of a very light vote. Once in that office, Morrill compiled a respectably pro-labor record, attended all the roll calls, and did not unduly draw attention to himself. In his first session he introduced a measure to require companies against which a strike was in progress to report the fact in

19. May Simons to A. M. Simons, February 13, 15, 1911, Simons Papers, State Historical Society of Wisconsin.

20. A copy of Wentworth's resolution is contained in Official Correspondence, Box 2, SP Papers.

their advertisements for help. Morrill's bill was the only labor legislation to pass that session. He proposed a judicial investigation of pricing practices, but the resulting commission discovered only that the cost of living was indeed rising. The House passed his resolution to allow communities to begin a free lunch program in public schools, but the Senate killed the measure. Morrill's attempts to permit municipalities to own and operate transportation and utilities were buried, as was a bill asking an appropriation to be used for public works in the event of sudden industrial distress. Year after year, as had Carey, MacCartney, and Ransden before him, Morrill converted his platform into legislative language. Very little passed, but as the Boston *Herald* reported, both major parties had adopted parts of the Socialist program, and the legislature was passing bills that a decade before would never have been reported out of committee. Political action did have some impact.[21]

Morrill had almost no interest in the Socialist party beyond his own district. He admitted to May Wood Simons that "the votes of personal friends rather than Socialists put him in office." He paid careful attention to his labor constituency and de-emphasized his Socialist affiliation. When national headquarters asked him to submit copies of his bills and resolutions in order to assist less experienced legislators, Morrill agreed the idea was a good one. But he had an instinctive reservation, the result, he said, of "22 years experience in the Populistic and Socialistic movements. . . ." If word of assistance from national officers was "noised about in each legislative district . . . then one of the principal issues of the campaign in such district will be . . . that the member don't dare think, . . . or

21. *Call*, November 4, 1909; December 12, 1909; November 6, 1910; *SDH*, August 6, 1910. For Morrill's legislative record, see his campaign broadsides, in the Broadside Collection, Duke University; Morrill to Carl D. Thompson, undated, Box 8, undated correspondence, SP Papers.

act for himself, but is tied to the dictation of a . . . machine. . . ." After several prodding letters to Morrill, to the state secretary in Massachusetts, to the editor of the state's weekly paper, the national office eventually received a report of Morrill's activity. The Haverhill legislator apparently asked nothing in return. He sent back a hundred-dollar campaign contribution from the national committee, partly because of justifiable confidence and partly, perhaps, to avoid too close an identification with the national party. Morrill's effort, as he once noted in a letter to Carl Thompson of the party's national office, was a "lone fight. . . ." Charles Morrill preferred it that way.[22]

The Brockton Socialists had always been locally oriented. The state organization, in decline after 1903, did nothing to extend their horizons. Support for the party's nominee for governor from 1904 to 1912 would indicate the presence of about 850 Socialists in the city. Yet the Socialist vote for mayor could be nearly 4,000. Attractive candidates and a moderate reform program had always been the Brockton organization's recipe for success. Many of the most attractive Socialist candidates followed the most popular parts of the platform into other parties. By 1912, Socialists were left with Socialism, and the vote for mayor was nearly reduced to the vote for governor.

As the municipal campaign of 1905 approached, many Socialists thought the time had come to change the top of the ticket. The state election proved Charles Coulter's continuing popularity, for his 2,300 votes for the state Senate were about twice the total of the state ticket. Coulter had been the party's only choice for mayor since 1898, and other ambitious Socialists wanted a chance. Although

22. May Simons to A. M. Simons, February 22, 1911, Simons Papers; Morrill to Carl D. Thompson, December 20, 1912; Morrill to Thompson, September 3, 1913, SP Papers; *Call*, November 6, 1910.

Coulter blustered that the nomination was his, the caucus selected William H. Clifford. Claiming to be the victim of "political thugs," Coulter declared himself an independent candidate for mayor, an action that the party countered with immediate expulsion. Coulter nailed his red party card to a copy of the Declaration of Independence, called in reporters to view his handiwork, and launched his campaign with the charge that the major parties had connived at his loss in the caucus in order to get rid of a formidable foe.

Coulter's candidacy aroused surprisingly little enthusiasm and only 666 votes. Nearly 3,600 Brockton voters supported William H. Clifford, whom the Republican nominee narrowly defeated. And Coulter's defection did not destroy the party, which won a substantial representation in city government. One Socialist won election to the Board of Aldermen and five others won seats on the Council; all six were shoe workers.[23]

Clifford was again a losing mayoral nominee by small margins in 1906 and 1907. In the next year, when the party again decided to change the head of the ticket and nominated Dan White, Clifford followed Coulter's precedent and ran as an independent. The result was far different. Clifford's vote sank from 3,900 to 2,600, but White had only about half as many. Clifford obviously had helped the Socialists more than they had helped him. In 1909, without changing a detail in his campaign, William Clifford was elected Brockton's first Democratic mayor in more than a decade.

Like most Brockton Socialists, Clifford had never been "educated," as the party used the term. He promised better street railway service, but said nothing about municipally owned transportation; he vowed economy and fiscal orthodoxy; his solution to the city's economic problems in

23. *Times*, October 30, 1905–December 6, 1905, *passim*.

1909 was the slogan "trade at home." A successful lawyer of the community, reportedly backing the Democratic choice for mayor in 1906, hastened to announce his support for Clifford in a statement that explained why the Socialist vote in Brockton was not a solid, class-conscious bloc. He began with a reminiscence.

When I came to Brockton, among my neighbors was a "kid" . . . liked by all, and I learned to like him as well as the rest. That "kid" was "Billy" Clifford. In after years I played baseball with him. . . . The errors . . . I made disheartened him, and he gently told me I was a bum ball player. Of course, that hurt my pride, but Billy was . . . a good judge of ball players. . . . It is because of his good baseball sense, and his good sense in other matters that I am going to vote for him. . . . You say he is a Socialist? . . . Billy Clifford is the same individual to me whether he is running under the name of republican or socialist.[24]

Clifford's defection to the Democrats was only the most dramatic example of a fairly continuous process in Brockton politics. Socialists of proven political appeal often reappeared as nominees of one of the major parties. Frederick Studley, a Socialist alderman in the Coulter administration, was a losing Democratic nominee for city office in 1906 and 1907. George Monk, a Socialist alderman in 1904, was a prominent Republican in 1912. Andrew Clancy, a three-term councilman and three-term alderman as a Socialist, was beaten for re-election in 1907; in 1912 he played an important part in the directorate of the Progressive party. Thomas Lee, a Socialist member of the Council in 1905, was re-elected as a Democrat in 1906; a year later he moved up to the Board of Aldermen. The ultimate example of party flexibility in Brockton was the improbable career of Adelard Ledoux. Elected as a Socialist member of the Common Council in 1903 and 1904, Ledoux won another term as a Democrat in 1908. In

24. *Ibid.*, November 13, 1906; see also December 9, 1909.

1912, he resigned from the Republican city committee to help the Progressive campaign. Political ideology was clearly unimportant in Brockton.[25]

When Morris Hillquit asked the national secretary for membership statistics in 1903, it was embarrassingly apparent that no one knew how many active members the party had. Party headquarters subsequently published figures based on annual receipts from dues and estimates of state officials. In 1905, the Massachusetts organization included perhaps 1,000 or 1,200 members. Paradoxically, while the party's political support declined, dues-paying membership rose. By 1909, enrollment had about doubled, and the party claimed it had nearly doubled again by 1913, when a membership of 4,519 was reported. Socialists often pretended that the number of members was more important than the number of votes on election day. Massachusetts Socialists had looked too long to election statistics to hold such an illusion. Membership growth in the Commonwealth, furthermore, did not keep pace with the increases elsewhere. The seventh largest organization in the national party in 1905, Massachusetts dipped to eighth in 1907, climbed to fourth in 1909, and skidded to seventh in 1910, ninth in 1911, and eleventh in 1912.[26]

Other indices show the Bay State's diminishing importance to the national movement. While Eugene Debs's total vote more than doubled between 1904 and 1912, his support in Massachusetts slumped by 1,000 ballots. Of more than 250 English-language Socialist weeklies published in the United States in 1912, only one bore a Mas-

25. On Studley, see *ibid.*, December 3, 1902; December 3, 1906; December 4, 1907; on Monk, see *ibid.*, October 30, 1912; on Clancy, see *ibid.*, December 9, 1907; November 9, 1912; on Lee, see *ibid.*, December 5, 1906; December 4, 1907; on Ledoux, see *ibid.*, December 9, 1908; November 9, 1912.
26. See statistical summaries in January issues of *Socialist Party Official Bulletin*, 1906–1913.

sachusetts imprint. In 1911, more than a thousand American Socialist nominees won elections; victors in Massachusetts could have been numbered on one hand. While membership in the state quadrupled, membership in the nation zoomed from 20,000 to 150,000. Massachusetts had once led the party in success; the state now preceded the party in decline.[27]

And most Bay State Socialists cared very little what happened to the national party. James Carey was the only Socialist of national stature in the state. Dan White and Franklin Wentworth had some reputation, but were not party leaders of the first rank. Large friendly crowds greeted Eugene Debs when he toured the state. Yet Debs invariably trailed part of the Socialist ticket at the polls and sometimes ran behind all of it. As the Brockton *Times* reported after a big rally, Debs gave "an exposition of Socialism rather than an appeal for votes." In Massachusetts, a politician was supposed to be a politician, not a school teacher, no matter how lovable.

Questions of party policy roused little interest in Massachusetts. Declining election as national committeeman, Wentworth said it was an honorary post and that honors should be shared. Certainly the state's representatives on the national committee were indifferent, though this body governed the party between conventions. Recorded votes and comments of national committeemen on countless referenda choked the party's *Official Bulletin*. Massachusetts' members voted occasionally and commented infrequently.[28]

Aside from Carey and Dan White, delegates to national conventions were conspicuously silent. In 1912, for in-

27. Nathan Fine, *Labor and Farmer Parties in the United States* (New York, 1961), Chapter 8; Ira Kipnis, *The American Socialist Movement* (New York, 1952), 346, 364.
28. See, e.g., the file of the *Official Bulletin* for 1906–1907; *Times*, October 30, 1909; *Worker*, January 12, 1907.

stance, the nine-member delegation rated a mere sixteen entries in the indexed proceedings, and of these, eleven referred to Carey or White. By comparison, John Spargo, a New Yorker who was by no means the most important delegate there, had thirty-one entries. Bay State delegates could be stirred when the question might affect the ballot box. Dan White said the party's 1908 platform ought to suggest some governmental activity to aid the unemployed. Admitting such a plank contradicted theoretical socialism, he said the party in Brockton needed such a statement. "We cannot," declared White, "secure the aid of the working class in capturing the powers of government, unless we give them [sic] something tangible. . . ." Two years later another Massachusetts trade union delegate demanded that the party favor restricted immigration, whether or not such a plank would violate international class solidarity.

Carey too, bored by theory, was interested in political questions. When the 1904 convention discussed dropping a special appeal for the political support of trade unions, Carey was on his feet. What was he supposed to do, he asked, when a worker said: " 'Jim, let us take a stand for better conditions in this factory.' " Perhaps, he shouted over rising laughter, "I will hand over Karl Marx." In a seconding speech for Debs at the same gathering he poked fun at the party's intellectuals: "I care not," he said, "for the 'scientific analysis of the unity of the multiplicities'. . . ." In 1908, Carey wanted a discussion of religion stopped, for he knew the political repercussions that might result. The "working class members of the committee," he asserted, were not interested in the subject; ". . . intellectuals—the literary men" had brought it up. Carey decided to run for the National Executive Committee in 1909 because of a political question. Gossip in the party held that the N.E.C. wanted to convert the organization into an independent labor party, a political extension of the trade unions. Carey, who was opposed, decided to be heard on the matter.[29]

The uproar began when William English Walling made public parts of a private letter from A. M. Simons, who wrote that the A.F. of L. was more representative of working class aspirations than the Socialist party. The party ought to be changed, he declared, "to meet the demands and incarnate the position of the workers. . . ." Walling took a firm proletarian stance. The National Executive Committee, he held, was reactionary. Instead of catering to trade unions, the party must defend the unskilled workers without extending so much as a gesture to the skilled craftsman. Walling's letter made Socialists choose sides for an intra-party squabble. Walling called his opponents "intellectuals," and such writers as Simons, Victor Berger, Robert Hunter, and John Spargo were in fact on the other team. Walling's "proletarian" allies included author Gustavus Myers, millionaire J. G. Phelps Stokes, Eugene Debs, and James Carey.

The election of the new N.E.C. was the test. Victor Berger wrote Simons that together they ought to compile a slate for their followers as well as a list of candidates to be placed at the bottom of the preferential ballot. Berger was a skilled political manager: when the votes were tallied, James Carey finished twenty-seventh and last in Wisconsin. Carey had support elsewhere, finished seventh in the national balloting, and claimed the last seat on the National Executive Committee. And Carey himself was no political neophyte: in Massachusetts, Victor Berger ran twenty-seventh and last. The insulted Milwaukee boss wondered why Carey had not given Hillquit and others like treatment. Ideology had nothing to do with Carey's

29. See the published proceedings of the party's conventions as follows: 1904: 199, 220; 1908: 194–195, 216; 1910: 116; 1912: index.

support of Hillquit and his opposition to Berger. Carey and the New Yorker were simply close friends, while Berger had once disparaged Carey as a "ward politician . . . from Haverhill." The two had rarely agreed since the struggle for Socialist unity.[30]

Carey's stand in 1909–1910 seemed to stamp him as a member of the party's so-called "Left" or "proletarian" or "revolutionary" faction. Such "Leftists" as Walling and Charles Kerr, the editor of the *International Socialist Review*, regarded his election to the N.E.C. as acceptable, though Walling's approval was at best grudging. In 1908, Carey had been discussed as a presidential nominee, partly because of his presumed support among party radicals. Ida Hazlett, the delegate from Montana who made the nominating speech, noted that Carey was a real "working man," not a "candidate for the so-called intellectuals." In spite of his withdrawal, Carey received some support from the delegates.[31]

Yet it is difficult to pinpoint Carey in the Socialist spectrum. He was no more a "revolutionary proletarian" than he was a "bourgeois reformer." Morris Hillquit, who was as much of the "Right" as Victor Berger, actively intrigued for Carey's presidential nomination in 1908. In 1912, "Leftists" accused Carey of using his position as chairman of the national convention to ram through the program of the "Right."[32] His long connection with conservative trade unionism, his advocacy of specific reform

30. *ISR*, January, 1910, 598; March, 1910, 855; Walling to Comrades, November 26, 1909; Berger to Simons, December 6, 1909, SP Papers; Berger to Hillquit, February 13, 1910, Hillquit Papers. Carey's friendship with Hillquit can be traced in their correspondence in the Hillquit Papers; see letters of September 17, 22, 1910, and November 30, 1910. Berger's remark about Carey is quoted in Kangaroo *People*, April 15, 1900.
31. Walling to Debs, February 12, 1910, William English Walling Papers, State Historical Society of Wisconsin; see also *ISR*, March, 1910, 839; *National Convention . . . 1908*, 155, 160.
32. Hillquit to Mrs. Hillquit, May 11, 1908, Hillquit Papers; *ISR*, June, 1912, 821.

legislation, his interest in votes rather than doctrine were all characteristic of the "Right" wing. Carey was his own man; he belonged to neither faction.

Indeed, though broad generalizations about Socialist factions were possible, such labels constantly had to be changed. James Carey was not the only Socialist whose interest in many intra-party questions was minimal or who made *ad hoc* decisions on others without worrying about his factional standing. On some issues the Right-Left split was in fact a division between radicals and more moderate Socialists. On others, factional lines had no relevance and categorization has produced only confusion. Socialists changed sides not only in the course of years, but in the course of a single convention. American Socialists may have been concerned with ideology, but they were not obsessed with it. Differing views of Socialist theory help explain some party decisons. Personalities, ambitions, and the hometown voter also went into the balance.

Carey's conduct was a fair indication of the majority sentiment among Massachusetts Socialists. The usual party member felt even less concern than Carey about issues that stirred party moguls. In 1905, the recall of Victor Berger from the N.E.C. and a referendum obliging Wisconsin to apply for a national charter provided a test of factional strength. By a majority of three votes, Massachusetts voted with the "Left" to recall Victor Berger; recall failed. By a majority of a dozen, Massachusetts voted with the "Right" in favor of state autonomy; once more it was in a minority. Close divisions signified no bitter fight within the state organization. Rather the indecisive result was a function of apathy; less than a third of the membership bothered to register an opinion.[33]

During this tempest, Job Harriman, Debs's running mate in 1900, sent Morris Hillquit his remedy for the

33. *Official Bulletin,* September, 1905.

party's problems. "We will have to learn," Harriman wrote, that the "logic of events . . . determines our line of action." The party must remember, he continued, that "whatever we have power to do in behalf of our interests is right, and what we have not power to do is wrong— *dead wrong*—and don't let me catch you forgetting it." [34] The party, in short, ought to make a realistic assessment of the situation, estimate what feasible action would most quickly bring a desirable result, and act, without regard to Socialist doctrine.

Massachusetts Socialists had used Harriman's formula, without articulating it, long before Hillquit received it. Because Massachusetts Socialists tried to make realistic assessments, they were, on balance, on the "Right" side of the party. They knew that most Americans—even most American workers—were not Socialists. They could not give up reform measures for which they had fought for more than a decade. They could not attack trade unions, to which many of them belonged and from which came much of the party's vote. They could not disavow political action when their most glorious memories were bound up with campaigns and elections. They would not emulate Daniel DeLeon's insistence on ideological orthodoxy, for many of them knew of the purges and invective that went with doctrinal purity. Sometimes they were "opportunists," or "slow-cialists," or "fakers," or "reformers." Less often they were "proletarians," or "class conscious," or "revolutionary," or "Marxian." Usually they were just Socialists, which, like most political labels, had a variety of definitions.

34. Harriman to Hillquit, May 10, 1905, Hillquit Papers.

CHAPTER VIII

"... and Massachusetts Failed"

The great strike of textile workers that began in Lawrence in January, 1912, posed a cruel dilemma for the Socialists of Massachusetts. At last the phrases that had been mouthed for years—the class struggle, solidarity of the working class, capitalistic exploitation—had a clear and present relevance. Various systems of bookkeeping yielded different statistics regarding the weekly wages of Lawrence operatives, but almost everyone agreed that whatever the figure, one man's earnings would not sustain a family. Textile operatives, divided by craft, by nationality, and by religion, walked out of the mills together in an impulsive demonstration of class unity. From radicals all over the nation came support without which the strikers would surely have lost. Victor Berger, the first Socialist Congressman, forced a Congressional hearing that stirred public interest and sympathy.[1]

Yet the Lawrence strike was no unmixed blessing for Bay State Socialists. The strike seemed to prove the validity of an ideology that many of them had already ceased to believe and that others had always rather hoped was not valid. The phrases of Socialist orthodoxy had become slogans, reiterated out of habit as much as from convic-

1. The Socialist Party Collection in the Milwaukee County Historical Society, which includes some of the papers from Berger's first term in Congress, contains disappointingly little on the Lawrence strike.

tion. The class struggle of the cozy lecture hall seemed less appealing when transferred to the snowy streets of Lawrence, where fire hoses and bayonets put a price on enthusiasm.

Textile workers, furthermore, had rarely sustained a strike to victory and had been notoriously difficult to organize. Socialist attempts to generate an effective political movement in Fall River, New Bedford, or Lawrence had been equally futile. The Industrial Workers of the World, which never considered caution a virtue, was not inhibited by past failures. Joseph Ettor, an I.W.W. organizer, was soon in Lawrence, directing the multi-national committee that guided the strike; William D. Haywood, the most notorious "Wobbly" of all, followed Ettor to Lawrence. As membership in the I.W.W. rose, friction between the industrial union and conventional trade unions became bitter recrimination. And Massachusetts Socialists, caught between rival labor organizations, dithered. Many of their leaders were, or had been, members of trade unions, and the Socialist movement had once had a firm trade union base. Experience told Socialists that industrial unionism would divide the working population and alienate thousands of their supporters.

Their political instincts also told these Socialists that the I.W.W. would not help them on election day. The I.W.W. gave the Socialist party only a tepid endorsement, and ranked political action as an ineffective method of securing redress. Most of the strikers were nonvoting aliens. Though some of them later joined the party, their political impact was negligible.

If the advantages of association with "Wobblies" were uncertain, the risks were plain indeed. "Wobblies" did not temper radicalism with political prudence, and sometimes seemed to shock for the sake of shocking. Beyond the probable loss of the trade unions was the loss of the re-

245

form-minded voters who had made temporary success possible in Haverhill and Brockton. This group would never return to the Socialist ticket if the party grew disreputable by association with violence, atheism, and industrial sabotage.

"Wobblies" would also bring Socialists the burden of identification with recent immigrants, whom older ethnic groups in the Commonwealth resented. Better established Irish, Germans, and Scandinavians, for instance, tended to see Italians, Poles, and Lithuanians as inevitably unskilled, personally unwashed, and economically unfair because of their willingness to work for lower wages.[2] Social and national lines, in short, cut through the vaunted solidarity of the working class and forced the Socialists to make a choice when either alternative would be wrong.

Socialists watched events in Lawrence with hope mingled with fear, for, win or lose, the strike seemed sure to change the Socialist movement in Massachusetts. By most standards, the movement was not very impressive in January, 1912. But it was the only one these people had.

The Socialist movement in Lawrence began among the city's German immigrants in the 1870's. By 1884, a parade of the Socialist Labor party drew 900 marchers, most of whom were probably attracted less by the doctrine than by the drums and less by economic radicalism than by Socialist opposition to prohibition. Two renowned German radicals visited Lawrence in 1886, when both Johann Most, the anarchist, and Karl Liebknecht, one of the outstanding men in the German Social Democracy, spoke there. Most's fiery oratory (he suggested that "a rifle in the house" was "better than a thousand ballots. . . .") attracted only six new members to his branch of the International. On the other hand, the most respected members

2. Interview with Roland D. Sawyer, July 30, 1959.

of the German community turned out to hear Liebknecht distinguish socialism from anarchism. During the following decade Republican politicians were somewhat concerned that the Socialist Labor party might win part of the German vote that had traditionally been Republican. By 1899, the party promised a significant showing in the municipal election and indulged in a serious split that reflected the national division into DeLeonites and "Kangaroos."[3]

The Socialist Labor party bravely made the pretense of survival. The local expelled those members who deserted to the Social Democracy and maintained a small branch of the Socialist Trade and Labor Alliance. The state organizer hotly denied reports in the Lawrence press that he had been greeted with rotten eggs. True, he admitted, a few eggs had been dropped from a window above him, but they had been fresh. If the purpose was political, the activity was all pathetically futile. The vote for the Socialist Labor party dropped from 109 in 1900 to 70 in 1904 to a lonely 18 in 1908.[4]

The Socialist party was only slightly more successful than its arch rival. In mid-1902, William Mailly, the state secretary, complained that the Lawrence party lagged. The next year the Roman Catholic Church reacted in Lawrence as elsewhere. After Father Thomas McGrady had visited the area, Father James T. O'Reilly, the most influential local priest, countered his message. The bulletin of O'Reilly's parish, one Socialist reported, was "chiefly devoted . . . to falsified quotations from Socialist writ-

3. Donald B. Cole, "Lawrence, Massachusetts: Immigrant City" (Unpublished Ph.D. dissertation, Harvard University, 1956), 193; this dissertation, much edited, has been published: *Immigrant City: Lawrence, Massachusetts, 1845–1921* (Chapel Hill, N.C., 1963); see pp. 169–171. The dissertation will hereafter be cited as Cole, "Lawrence"; the book as Cole, *City.*

4. Cole, "Lawrence," 195; *People,* February 4, 1900; April 4, 1903; October 17, 1903.

ers, garbled reports of Socialist speeches, and platitudes about the sacred rights of property." Socialists continued to make sporadic efforts in Lawrence; Debs's campaign train, the "Red Special," stopped there in 1908, for instance. But in the election, Debs polled less than 300 votes in Lawrence, and dropped below his total for 1904.[5]

The struggle of organized labor was equally agonizing. The National Labor Union and the Knights of Labor had appeared and disappeared before the turn of the century. Neither left a significant mark on labor relations in the city. Various craft unions affiliated with the American Federation of Labor were only slightly more successful. Samuel Gompers himself came to Lawrence in 1905 to promote the National Union of Textile Workers headed by John Golden. Before 1912, Golden's union had spent "thousands and thousands of dollars," and had kept salaried organizers in Lawrence for months at a time. When the strike began, less than one-tenth of Lawrence's 30,000 textile workers were members of unions. Some months after the strike had been won, a local craft union published a booklet entitled *What John Golden Has Done for the Textile Workers.* Bound inside the impressive cover were several eloquent blank pages.[6]

Industrial unionism was no more attractive than craft unionism. The I.W.W. was first established in Lawrence in 1905. Five years later, the "Wobblies" held a convention in Lawrence, where the local chapter owned a building that included a lecture hall seating five hundred, plus adequate facilities for committees, a library, gymnasium, pool tables, and a brand new $700 furnace. Membership

5. The *Worker* (New York), May 25, 1902; May 17, 1903; Cole, "Lawrence," 195.

6. Cole, *City,* 134; *The Strike at Lawrence Mass. Hearings Before the Committee on Rules of the House of Representatives . . . 1912,* 62 Congress, 2 Session, House Doc. 671 (Washington, 1912), 75–76. This document will be cited hereafter as *House Doc. 671. Industrial Worker* (Spokane, Wash.), July 18, 1912.

fluctuated, with the Lawrence organization claiming up to a thousand members. When the strike began, the paid-up membership was about 300, roughly one per cent of the labor force.[7]

The I.W.W. made up in militance what it lacked in numbers. Once the Lawrence strike began, John Golden refused to refer to it as a strike, which might imply that it was a legitimate labor dispute. Rather, he said, it was "the revolution." "Wobblies" wore that badge proudly. Although organizers in Lawrence took a more moderate line, a national organ of the I.W.W. made no compromises for the sake of public relations. Even after it was obvious that William Wood, the president of the American Woolen Company, and other employers would meet most of the strikers' demands, an editorial in the *Industrial Worker* promised continued industrial warfare: "A slashed warp, a loosened bolt, an uncaught thread, a shifting of dyes, will make Billy Wood see the 'justice' of the men's demands quicker than all the votes cast since Billy Bryan commenced to run for office." And no worker should let a tender conscience inhibit his sabotage: "'To hell with capitalistic ethics.'"

Nor was the *Industrial Worker* restrained in dealing with the hostility of Father O'Reilly and the Roman Catholic Church. Priests were "weird things in black," who held up "uncalloused hands in [a] vain endeavor to shut out the light." The Militia of Christ, a Catholic labor organization to which Golden belonged, was scorned as an agent of "that great international whore—the Roman Catholic Church." Union leaders involved in this scheme to mislead the working class were "purgatory-scarred

---

7. *House Doc. 671, 75; Industrial Worker,* April 2, 1910; July 11, 1912; *Report on Strike of Textile Workers in Lawrence, Mass. in 1912,* 62 Congress, 2 Session, Senate Doc. 870. (Washington, 1912), 11. This report of the Commissioner of Labor will be cited hereafter as *Senate Doc. 870.*

pimps of the pope. . . ." When a few timid readers protested this characterization, the *Industrial Worker* fired
the other barrel under the lead "Oh Christ! What a Militia!" The organization had its American headquarters,
continued the I.W.W. paper, in Oberlin, Ohio. "The real
headquarters (or rather hindquarters) [was] to be found
on the dunghills of Rome." Small wonder that Lincoln
Steffens found a mill owner who belatedly longed for a
chance to bargain with Samuel Gompers. " 'Haywood
makes Gompers look like an angel,' " admitted the employer, and the " 'I.W.W. makes the mill men sigh for the
A.F. of L.' " [8]

The condition of the working population reflected both
the absence of unions and the determination of employers.
The executive secretary to the governor of the Commonwealth reportedly accused the manufacturers of being
"more solicitous for their machines . . . than for the flesh
and blood machines that work incessantly under conditions that are well nigh intolerable." By all the usual indices textile workers in Lawrence were less fortunate than
most other Americans. When mills ran full time, the average weekly wage was $8.76, with a third of the working
force receiving less than $7.00. A cost-of-living index
proved a more difficult statistic to secure, but rents averaged from $2.00 to $3.50 per week for quarters that were
by most standards inadequate. The Commissioner of
Labor, in a report submitted to the Senate of the United
States, concluded that "the full-time earnings of a large
number of adult employees" were obviously "entirely inadequate to sustain a family. . . ." Unless the head of a
family of five was "employed in one of the comparatively
few better-paying occupations," the family would have to
"supply two wage earners in order to secure the necessi-
ties of life." While he found Lawrence an underpaid and

8. *Industrial Worker*, March 14, 1912; February 22, 29, 1912.

unhealthy city, the Commissioner of Labor also pointed out that conditions there were "more or less typical" of textile towns. The strike, he concluded, was not "primarily due to any condition peculiar to Lawrence." [9]

Certainly management did not expect any significant difficulty when, at the end of December, 1911, preparation began for compliance in January with a new state law establishing a fifty-four hour week for children under eighteen and women. The reduction was only two hours and the owners expected to reduce wages in proportion. One official in Boston asked the staff in Lawrence whether the planned reduction would cause trouble among the employees. The reply was confident. Lawrence expected no difficulty, or "at worst" a strike that "would probably be confined to a . . . single mill."

While previous experience seemed to justify such confidence, the error was soon apparent. Early in January, various groups of employees tried without success to find out exactly how the reduction in hours would affect wages. The I.W.W. elected a committee to confer with local management. No local official would receive such a committee, however, since a meeting might imply recognition. Lawrence officials suggested the union might get an answer at corporate headquarters in Boston. When a letter to Boston brought no response, the "Wobblies" tired of the run-around. On the evening of January 10, the Italian branch decided to strike on January 12 if wages due that day were reduced; the next day, at another meeting, several hundred Poles, Lithuanians, and Italians took the same action.

At the end of the week, as pay envelopes were opened in mills throughout the city, machinery stopped. Asked by her supervisor why she had stopped her loom, a Polish weaver furnished the answer for what soon became thou-

9. *Senate Doc.* 870, 9, 19, 20, 25, 27; New York *Call,* January 25, 1912.

sands of strikers. "Not enough pay," she said simply. Violence quickly flared in the mills. Strikers ran from room to room persuading, sometimes coercing, others to leave their jobs. When switches did not stop machinery, an occasional slashed belt would serve; some machines and some unfinished cloth were damaged. Once picket lines were established in the mill districts, nonstriking workers had to withstand arguments, pleas, jeers, and sometimes a well-aimed fist in order to get into the mills. Early in the strike, factory windows made an inviting target for handy ice and snow missiles.

At the first sign of trouble, management called for the police. When a liberal use of night sticks did not stop picketing, Mayor John Scanlon sent for the militia. The presence of police and troops was supposed to produce order, which, by the interpretation of the authorities, precluded effective picketing. Mill owners expected the uniformed forces to make it possible for "loyal" employees to get into the factory; they expected hunger would do the rest.

Strikers clashed with troops and police. Several persons suffered minor bayonet wounds when a crowd did not disperse rapidly enough. Police reportedly returned to the station with blood on their night sticks. Women and children were not exempt. Two miscarriages were said to have resulted from beatings. John Rami, a young Syrian, died of a bayonet wound. A pistol shot that authorities maintained was intended for a policeman killed a bystander named Annie LoPezzi. Other witnesses held that the bullet was fired by a police officer, or an *agent provocateur,* or was the result of a personal quarrel that had no connection with the strike. At any rate, no one was charged.

When labor violence occurred, frightened citizens began to look for explosives. Acting on a tip from John

Breen, the son of a former mayor and an undertaker who was pursuing a political career on the Lawrence school committee, police found three caches of dynamite about a week after the strike began. But the plan to discredit the strikers was very clumsy. Within a few days the state police called the plot a "frame-up." The wrapping around the dynamite was paper like that used in Breen's undertaking establishment. Pages torn from an undertakers' trade journal covered another part of the cache; Breen's copy was minus those pages. Eventually Breen paid a $500 fine and was recalled from the school committee. The convenient suicide of a contractor associated with American Woolen forestalled a grand jury investigation of the general suspicion that Breen had been only a tool of the mill owners.[10]

The possibility of a social explosion in Lawrence was more dangerous than any dynamite. The working population gradually discovered that unity meant strength; some felt that only exercise would keep the new-found muscle hard. Employers began to appreciate that their control over their employees was tenuous. Moreover, law, order, and respectability no longer made strikers docile. How long, wondered one Socialist, would the Anglo-American tradition of property rights deter several thousand seething, hungry men who shared neither the language, nor the traditions, nor the property of those Anglo-Americans. Industrial conflict might well become pitched industrial warfare in the streets of Lawrence. Class struggle might become class warfare. And the struggle of immigrant op-

10. This account of the strike is based on material in the following sources: Cole, *City* and "Lawrence"; Justus Ebert, *The Trial of a New Society* (Cleveland, 1913); William D. Haywood, *Bill Haywood's Book* (New York, 1929); *House Doc. 671; Senate Doc. 870;* Sawyer Interview, July 30, 1959; Sawyer Interview, August 1, 1962; Sawyer Scrapbooks; New York *Call*, 1912, *passim; Industrial Worker*, 1912, *passim; ISR* March–August, 1912; Samuel Yellen, *American Labor Struggles* (New York, 1936), Chapter 6.

eratives against employers had most of the characteristics of what the early twentieth century called a "struggle of races" as well. The fittest might survive at a cost of a ruined city. Lawrence decided not to risk it. After about two months, the mill owners and the strike committee agreed on a schedule of wage increases that varied from five to twenty-five per cent, with the largest raises to the lowest salaried operatives. Overtime work was to receive another twenty-five per cent bonus. No worker was to be refused his job because of participation in the strike. It was, commented the London *Syndicalist*, the "greatest victory ever accomplished by labour in the United States." [11]

The magnitude of the workers' victory was as astonishing as the survival of the precarious truce that prevented full-scale industrial warfare. To be sure, violence occurred: a few damaged machines, some broken windows, several bruised and bloody pickets, and two deaths was the approximate total. But the cost might have been much higher. For ten weeks more than 20,000 workers had been unsalaried and unoccupied, while uneasy, inexperienced militiamen patrolled the streets with ready bayonets. The Commissioner of Labor told the Senate that "few strikes . . . have continued as long as the Lawrence strike with so little actual violence. . . ." He also knew how thin the margin had been: ". . . during the entire period the situation was . . . tense and threatening . . . , and there was hardly a time that a slight cause might not have produced the gravest disorder culminating in riot and bloodshed."

The Industrial Workers of the World, paradoxically, were partly responsible for both the tension that threatened violence and the discipline that prevented it. Superb

11. *Call*, May 28, 1912; June 2, 1912; London *Syndicalist*, May, 1912, 1.

leadership in the city not only steered the strike toward success, but also maintained some control over the restive labor force. Joseph Ettor, an I.W.W. organizer, helped establish the multi-national committee that actually conducted the strike. Although Ettor headed the committee, it was not a committee of the union; rather it represented all the strikers. Many committee members and most strikers never had any connection with the Industrial Workers of the World. Ettor made no mistakes. He cajoled, he pleaded, he threatened. He appealed to the immigrant against the native, to the worker against the capitalist, to the fortitude of wives and to the pride of husbands. After these efforts helped the strike through the critical first weekend, when, in the past, the urgings of clergy and the misgivings of family had turned fresh courage into sour acquiescence, Ettor breathed more easily.[12]

When the strike began, twenty-six year old Joe Ettor had been a Socialist for nearly a decade. At seventeen he had sent a nickel to national headquarters to buy his red button. By 1912 he was the veteran of labor battles in the construction, steel, and shoe industries. Later, when Ettor was brought to trial for inciting to murder, the I.W.W. stressed the peaceful content of his speeches. Although disciplined non-violence was not often associated with the "Wobblies," Ettor apparently did in fact temper his denunciation of capitalism with injunctions to keep the peace. "As long as the workers keep their hands in their pockets, the capitalists cannot put theirs there," he asserted. "With passive resistance, with the workers absolutely silent, they are more powerful than all the weapons and instruments that the others have for protection and attack." Or, more succinctly, on another occasion: ". . . violence necessarily means the loss of a strike." Ettor did not cringe. He could, and did, talk about industrial sabo-

12. *Senate Doc. 870*, 14, 16; Cole, *City*, 180.

SOCIALISM AND THE WORKERS

tage when he despaired: "If they starve us into going back to work, I say to you oil men, remember there is plenty of emery dust about." Nevertheless, Ettor directed the strike without some of the "I'm-a-bum" manifestations of the I.W.W. spirit. He unquestionably raised the possibility of class warfare, but he meant it to be a threat to force a settlement. The threat was enough. Ettor never had to try the last resort.[13]

Jittery authorities in Lawrence did not see Ettor as a bulwark of order and arrested him for inciting the unknown killer of Annie LoPezzi. Arturo Giovannitti, the editor of an Italian Socialist paper who had accompanied Ettor to Lawrence, was also charged and confined. The imprisonment of the two agitators, obviously intended to cripple the strike, furnished one more reason for continued resistance. When the courts refused bail for Ettor and Giovannitti, the action seemed a confession of fear. The prisoners became symbols of oppression; the need for oppression seemed to promise ultimate triumph.

So well had Ettor done his work in Lawrence that the strike never faltered. A second strike committee was established to be available in the event of further arrests. Elizabeth Gurley Flynn, Bill Haywood, and other I.W.W. organizers redoubled their efforts. The "Wobblies" planned to send children of strikers to the homes of Socialist sympathizers in other areas, an operation which not only relieved tight food budgets but also gained publicity and financial support that prolonged the strike. When authorities prevented some of the children from leaving the city, a bruising melee broke out, which caused a Congressional investigation. The hearings had no immediate legislative result, but they publicized the fact that textile workers in

13. Mailly to Ettor, June 19, 1903, Mailly Letterbook VI, SP Papers; *Industrial Worker*, May 23, 1912; Ebert, *Trial*, 61 (Italics removed), 50; *Call*, January 29, 1912.

Lawrence were not sharing all the blessings of the land of opportunity.

While public understanding certainly helped, sympathy without bread was useless. Perhaps the most important single factor that kept strikers away from the mills was the fact that loss of wages did not mean starvation. Radicals from all over the country sent contributions to the strike committee. Leftist organizations, predominantly the Socialist party, the Socialist Labor party, and the Industrial Workers of the World, accounted for eighty per cent of the amount raised. The grand total may have exceeded $45,000; primitive bookkeeping and a reluctance to put funds in banks where an injunction might block expenditure made an exact accounting impossible.[14]

Ideological disputes and internal bickering within the national party quieted as Socialists supported the Lawrence strike with all the money-raising techniques at their disposal. Not quite all the factional scars healed. When the Socialist mayor of Milwaukee evaded Elizabeth Flynn's appeal for support, she shared her fury with the readers of the *Industrial Worker*. Haywood's contempt for political action was notoriously undiminished. But, while the New York *Call*, for instance, mistrusted "Wobblies," the paper unstintingly supported the strike.[15]

While Socialists in Massachusetts hesitated to embrace the struggle as their own, they did organize protest meetings and collect money. Boston Socialists persistently solicited contributions that ultimately totaled perhaps $2500. An organization called the Cigar Makers Propaganda Club of Boston claimed to have contributed $200

14. *Call*, March 16, 1912; Ebert, *Trial*, 47; *Senate Doc. 870*, 502; Lester H. Marcy and Frank S. Boyd, "One Big Union Wins," *ISR*, April, 1912, 621.
15. *Call*, January–March, 1912, *passim; Industrial Worker*, March 21, 1912; Mary E. Marcy, "The Battle for Bread in Lawrence," *ISR*, March, 1912, 540.

per week for several weeks to the relief of the strikers in Lawrence. The Socialist Club at Harvard College raised $25, which did not prevent the Socialist press from emphasizing the participation of a few Harvard undergraduate members of the militia. A meeting in Saugus protested the refusal to allow the children of strikers to leave Lawrence in a series of resolutions to Governor Eugene Foss: ". . . you are making thousands of Socialists for us, Governor Foss, by your brutality toward the working class, but we . . . had far rather make converts in our own way of peaceful reasoning, than to have you make them with the sword." Haywood appeared in Salem to the consternation of the mayor and collected more than $100. Socialists in Brockton and Lynn offered to provide homes for children for the duration of the strike.[16]

From Haverhill came a timely $800 donation from the independent Shoe Workers' Protective Union. But the Haverhill Socialists were slow to fall into line behind the strike. Craft unionism, suspicion of immigrants, the disdain of the shoe worker for the textile worker all played a part in Haverhill's tardy and limited support of the nearby struggle. Proximity may also have been part of the reason for caution. Socialists in Haverhill had long been politically oriented. Suspicion of the I.W.W. and of direct action was habitual. Besides, Haverhill's thirteenth annual Socialist bazaar, which provided the funds for local campaigns, had just opened when the strike began.

The cheery account of Haverhill's fair on an inside page of the New York *Call*, contrasted sharply with the front-page headlines about events a few miles away in Lawrence: "SOLDIERS BAYONET HUNGRY STRIKERS." The Haverhill fair "opened very auspiciously . . . with a large collection of happy people." A large floral display, yards

16. *Call*, February 2, 16, 29, 1912; March 2, 6, 1912; undated typescript by Carl D. Thompson, "Who Won the Lawrence Strike?" Official Correspondence, Box 9, SP Papers.

of red, white and blue bunting, and "tastefully and prettily decorated" booths provided a handsome setting for games of chance and skill, and for the dancing that followed. Mottoes on the walls left no doubt about the brand of Socialism that was welcome in Haverhill.

"THE CHIEF WEAPON OF THE WORKING CLASS IS THE BALLOT. VOTE FOR SOCIALISM."

"THE BALLOT, NOT THE BULLET, OUR WEAPON."

"READ THE DAILY CALL, STUDY SOCIALISM, AND PREPARE FOR THE BETTER DAY."

In order to help strikers in Lawrence survive until that better day, the committee took up a collection on one of the fair's eight evenings; and the committee itself gave $25, a miserly share of the evening's expected profit. On the day of Joe Ettor's arrest, Haverhill Socialists had a party for some fifty children who had helped at the bazaar. The guests played games, ate ladyfingers, ice cream and popcorn, and heard a speech about the poor children of Lawrence, "which depressed them very much." [17]

Eventually Haverhill did face the disagreeable neighboring events. While New Yorkers emotionally welcomed children from Lawrence, a committee in Haverhill began to work on a mass meeting to aid the strikers. In holding such a meeting, the correspondent noted, Haverhill would be complying with a recent communication from the party's national headquarters. Conceivably such an action would not otherwise have occurred to the class-conscious local. The committee hoped to locate "some prominent out of town comrade to waken the people up to the necessity of systematic, energetic and persistent action in behalf of the strikers." The report implied that no Haverhill radical could stir the movement out of a lethargy that prevented action for the strikers. A meeting was eventually

17. *Call,* January 16, 26, 29, 1912; February 22, 1912.

held, and subsequent ones as well. Haverhill women sewed clothing for cold Lawrence children. A group of young girls from Lawrence came to Haverhill to solicit goods from local merchants; Socialists transported the donated merchandise to Lawrence. But somehow the effort seemed to lack spontaneity.[18]

Haverhill's Socialist representative in the General Court, Charles Morrill, seemed unsure how the workingman's spokesman should react to the crisis. He introduced a bill asking for a legislative investigation, but only an unofficial delegation was sent. The result was so inconsequential that Morrill's campaign literature in the fall never mentioned the incident. He introduced another bill that would have required all judges and legislators to spend five nights in jail and a month in the slums of Boston. Predictably, this measure also failed to pass. Morrill retreated to more conventional proposals, such as one to provide lunches for school children.[19]

All over the Bay State Socialists saw the need for action; just what ought to be done, however, no one seemed to know. And so they sent what money they could spare and went back to their customary activity. The party in Greenfield ran its usual March political campaign and was unusually optimistic about the usual defeat. Speakers from the national Socialist Lyceum Bureau explained "Why Things Happen to Happen." In Boston George Willis Cooke, a free lance Socialist lecturer, announced that crowds still attended his regular course of Sunday classes, where he discussed "Village Communism, Caste, and Industrial Guilds," or "Socialism and Evolution." Indeed, an "active Socialist, well informed as to party activities" had recently said "that these Sunday lectures were doing more

18. *Ibid.*, February 13, 18, 29, 1912; March 11, 15, 1912.
19. Marcy and Boyd, "One Big Union," *loc. cit.*, 627; see the collection of Morrill's campaign material in the broadside collection, Duke University; *Call*, January 13, 1912; April 26, 1912.

than anything else to call attention to Socialism."[20] Perhaps the strike in Lawrence had become a bore.

James F. Carey, the party's state secretary, was as much at a loss as anyone. Although some members of the party's "impossibilist" faction regarded Carey as a kindred spirit, he had never been an extremist. While he was a trade unionist by inclination and a supporter of political action by conviction, Carey could not ignore the upheaval in his own back yard. He shared the platform with Haywood and Ettor, but while they talked of industrial unions and collected money, Carey, ever the politician, assailed the tariff as an unjustifiable subsidy of the woolen trust. Carey might call the strike "one of the most hopeful things that has happened in this ancestral-soaked state for many years," but he was more in character when he told an I.W.W. rally: "The workers have the power, but by their votes they give that power to the American Woolen Company. . . . As long as the workers persist in voting the Republican and Democratic tickets, they will get what they voted for." Carey well expressed his position a few years later at a party conference that once more debated whether a political party could bear a revolutionary ideology. Drawing a line between economic methods and political methods, he made plain his preference for politics:

I have not the slightest objection . . . to industrial action, but I do object to those who believe in industrial action sticking a stick between my legs when I walk to the polls. . . . [The Socialist party has] many members who board in this country, but they live over in Europe. . . . I . . . want to have in this country a Socialist political party, and I . . . want it limited to those who believe in political action.[21]

20. *Ibid.*, January 15, 1912; February 9, 1912; March 11, 15, 1912.
21. *Call*, January 28, 1912; March 6, 1912; February 26, 1912; *Industrial Worker*, March 7, 1912, reports the same rally, mentions that Carey spoke, but does not include the quotation. "Minutes of Joint Congress of the National Executive Committee and State Secretaries, 1918," SP Papers.

The strike was about a month old when Carey announced that he would not be a candidate for re-election as state secretary. The mounting mass of paper work repelled him. "Neither by temperament, training, or inclination," he said, "am I a clerk." In his valedictory, Carey called attention to the growth of the party during his tenure and made an obvious reference to events in Lawrence when he suggested, without outlining a precise course for the party, that "prospects for even more rapid growth" were "exceedingly bright." [22]

New York Socialists prodded their Massachusetts comrades to take advantage of those prospects: "It is . . . time that the organization in Massachusetts was aroused to do its duty. The Socialist party should be conducting the fight in Lawrence." A few days later the *Call* found the silver lining in the cloud of hardship in Lawrence: ". . . there will be twenty Socialists in Massachusetts where there was one. . . . There is a magnificent opportunity for the most far-reaching work to be done for social revolution." The theme persisted. In May, the Socialists in Massachusetts read once more of the splendid chance they were not seizing: ". . . Massachusetts is backward. The workers have not really awakened. . . . A tremendous labor war has been fought. . . . Yet politically the workers are more blind and stupid than ever."

Eventually, Robert Lawrence, a member of the state executive committee, went to the textile city to promote the Socialist cause. The party established a Syrian branch and added more than a hundred members to the English-speaking organization in the city. As one Socialist remarked, a Socialist speaker before the strike was lucky to get a half-dozen curious listeners; afterwards he drew a crowd. Elsewhere in the state, however, no special program dramatized the Socialist gospel.

22. *Call*, February 29, 1912.

And the plain fact is that there was not much the Socialist party could have done. James F. Carey, a shrewder
politician than any editor of the *Call*, discovered no way
to turn the strike to the party's advantage. All the patronizing messages from New York demanded action, but
lacked specific advice. If votes were the object, the strikers of Lawrence were poor prospects. About fifteen per
cent of the strikers were children and perhaps half of the
remaining group were women. Of those men who were of
age, only about fifteen per cent were citizens who had
paid the poll tax and were entitled to vote. Of this group
—perhaps 1,600 voters—many were Irish Catholics who
might find Socialism unpalatable. In short, the strike did
not offer a rich harvest of votes in Lawrence. Nor did the
strike really offer an opportunity for the rapid acceptance
of Socialist ideas. A close student of the strike, Donald B.
Cole, has concluded that few strikers ever grew familiar
with radical ideas. The strike, he has written, was "for
property, not against it." [23]

Roland D. Sawyer believed events in Lawrence warranted more than indecisive pondering. For years a Socialist sympathizer, Sawyer had formally joined the party in
1908 and had dedicated himself to the cause with a zeal
equal to that he displayed on Sundays in the pulpit of his
Congregational church in Ware. Socialism was an active
creed; a Socialist must be a witness for his faith, not only
in the party's press, but in the industrial struggle.

At a time when members all over the nation were modi-
fying their socialism, the only prefacing adjective Sawyer
wanted was "red-hot." He reminded the *Call*'s subscribers
that once Christianity had been a powerful, united move-

23. *Call*, January 22, 1912; February 5, 1912; April 9, 1912; May 2,
14, 1912; June 2, 1912; Phillips Russell, "The Dynamite Job at Lawrence," *ISR*, October, 1912, 311; Report of the National Convention, *ISR*,
June, 1912, 823; Ebert, *Trial*, 75; Cole, "Lawrence," 365.

ment that "touched men by the power of its idealism." When the faith "fell into the hands of theologians and sectarians" it had lost its fire. Sawyer made the point explicit: ". . . our advance will be retarded by insistence on 'orthodoxy' and 'sects'. . . . [T]alk about . . . 'opportunist Socialists,' 'Marxian Socialists,' 'impossibilist Socialists,' 'revisionist Socialists,' is simply evidence of the theologians among us insisting upon his [*sic*] orthodoxy. . . ." During the Lawrence strike, Sawyer reiterated his conviction that revolutionary mass action must be complemented by evolutionary political action if the party was to advance. Factional squabbling, he held, would cause "a loss of twenty or thirty years. . . ." [24]

Roland Sawyer did not propose to lose a minute. Undaunted by the friction between the A.F. of L. and the I.W.W., he asked craft union members to defy their leaders and mail contributions to Lawrence. He pleaded for sympathetic appreciation of the wretched living and working conditions in Lawrence, for funds to continue the strike, for understanding of the villainy of the mill owners, the police, the militia. His indignation at the imprisonment of Joseph Ettor and Arturo Giovannitti triggered another chiding letter to the *Call*.

I know . . . that we have passed resolutions, contributed money—but these do not reach public sentiment—and it is the arousing of public sentiment that must save these men. The Socialist and labor bodies ought to send 200 men into Massachusetts to speak every day till these men go to trial; able speakers ought to speak in every town and city in Essex County.

The call for two hundred speakers was a fantasy, but Sawyer was a host in himself. He spoke wherever he could get an invitation, a hall, or an audience. Stereoptican slides added to the interest of the lectures, and the audi-

24. Sawyer Interview, July 30, 1959; *Call*, November 17, 1910; Roland D. Sawyer, "Socialism and Industrial Unions," *ISR*, May, 1912, 746.

ence invariably shouted approval of resolutions that deplored the unjustified imprisonment of Ettor and Giovannitti.

Sawyer sought more than resolutions. His reference to Essex County, where Ettor and Giovannitti would be tried, was calculated. After consultation with the defendants' legal staff, Sawyer set out to speak to every potential juror in Essex County. He hoped to present the emotional side of the strike that would never survive a judicial ruling, to create a compassionate comprehension of the conditions Ettor and Giovannitti were trying to remedy, to show that radicalism was not senseless destruction, but a rational response to senseless conditions. One determined member of the jury could force a new trial; several could permanently thwart an injustice. Socialists, Sawyer thought, could make a positive contribution to the effort.[25] He did more than his part.

Well before Roland Douglas Sawyer could vote, he had developed unconventional political opinions. At nineteen he displayed some familiarity with radical phraseology and began a life-long habit of writing to editors. In a letter to the *Game Bird,* a periodical devoted to cock fighting, Sawyer wrote of "bloated, gouty aristocrats" and "the dainty hands of society snobs." A fervent Populist at twenty, he proudly wrote in his diary that both "Sockless" Jerry Simpson and Senator William Peffer had replied to his letters and that he was reading three Populist papers. He also was writing to a paper that circulated in his own Kensington, New Hampshire, of the boss-ridden old parties, and arguing that "plutocracy's right Republican arm" and "its left Democratic arm" were impartially smiting the unprivileged majority. In the socialist *Coming Nation,*

25. Sawyer Literary Scrapbook, II, VIII; Sawyer Notebook 23, 24; Interview, August 1, 1962; *Call,* June 25, 1912.

he wondered why the "wage slave" would "fight . . . against the plutocrat" every day but election day.

Sawyer also tried his hand at practical local politics. In the winter of 1894–95, while the shoe strike a few miles away in Haverhill was converting Populists to Socialist Laborites, Sawyer converted Kensington Populists to Republicans in order to overturn the ruling Democratic clique in town. A year later, he was a delegate to the New Hampshire Populist convention. During the campaign he argued that no monopoly was defensible and that the monopoly of gold was the root of all other evil. "Shall we support Bryan and humanity against McKinley and plutocracy?" he asked in a letter to the Boston *Post*. "Shall we stand by the institutions of our fathers or submit to foreign Shylocks?" Roland Sawyer cast his first presidential ballot for Bryan and Watson.[26]

In 1897, Sawyer began his Christian ministry, expecting the pulpit to lead to politics as it had for many Populist orators. Gradually his growing genuine religious conviction fused with the social ideals of Populism in a mild Christian Socialism. His first parish was a small Congregational church in Brockton, where he noted that former Populists were organizing a Social Democratic movement in 1898. Sawyer attended the first formal Social Democratic gathering in Brockton, voted for most of the ticket, but rejected a proposal that he resign his ministry to run for the state legislature. When Mary Elizabeth Lease, speaking under Social Democratic sponsorship, criticised organized

26. Sawyer Literary Scrapbook, II; Roland Sawyer, *A Personal Narrative* (Farmington, Me., 1930), 43, 44, 54, 58; Boston *Post*, August 21, 1896, clipping in Sawyer Literary Scrapbook II. This last reference is one item of evidence in the historical controversy about Populist anti-Semitism. Sawyer was not a dogmatic anti-Semite and may well have used the word "Shylock" as a substitute for "banker." He had close Jewish associates in the radical movement. The Jewish heritage of his friends went unnoticed; a Jewish opponent was apt to be so designated. (Interview, July 30, 1959.)

Christianity, brash, young Ronald Sawyer evaded neither her dare to the ministry to combine religion and reform, nor the notoriety that he must have known would follow. He acknowledged Mrs. Lease's taunt that Americans had "substituted the almighty dollar for Almighty God" and admitted that the national mania for getting rich quick had affected the churches. But he asserted stoutly that Brockton Christians would respond generously to the needs of their less fortunate fellow men "within 24 hours." If Sawyer was bluffing, he was quickly called; if he was sincere, he was promptly disillusioned. He soon heard of several cases of acknowledged destitution, and neither his efforts nor those of the press brought any charitable response, let alone generosity, in twenty-four hours. Sawyer sent letters to seven clergymen about one case. He received one reply, from one of the city's leading Protestant congregations, which declined assistance because of calls from "our own worthy poor." The disappointed pastor pasted the letter in his scrapbook beside the clippings about his sermon. Then he wrote in the margin: "I was mistaken and acknowledge it. The church is more worthless than I had supposed. I take back what I said to the Socialists." [27]

But Sawyer did not join them. He voted for Charles Coulter in 1899 and served as chaplain at the inauguration of Brockton's first Socialist mayor. But he soon left Brockton and new places brought new causes. By 1906, when he was pastor in the Ward Hill section of Haverhill, Sawyer was backing John B. Moran, the reforming Democratic candidate for governor. Sawyer himself accepted a Democratic nomination for alderman, and, while losing, ran well ahead of the Socialist nominee. Yet the following year he preached a Labor Day sermon to the Haverhill

27. Sawyer Scrapbook 9, 11; Sawyer, *Personal Narrative,* 57, 58, 73, 74.

Central Labor Union that seemed almost to espouse syndicalism: ". . . I am not sure but that the union offers the solution to our industrial question; by and by the general strike and the taking over of great industries to be run by the workers may promise a better solution than political action. Labor organizations are then to be pushed with the aim of not alone regulating industry, but eventually directing and operating it." Sawyer later remarked that "the great event of 1907" was his reading of Lewis Morgan's *Ancient Society*, which made him a socialist as it had earlier influenced Daniel DeLeon.[28] But Sawyer's open avowal of the Socialist faith was delayed by the appearance of the Independence League.

William Randolph Hearst's Independence League movement appealed to the Haverhill minister for several reasons. Some reform Democrats whom he had supported had drifted to the League out of disgust with machine Democracy; the program, which opposed monopoly and promised political reform, was also congenial. Besides, the leaders of the organization, won by Sawyer's appearance at a legislative hearing in Boston, flattered him by printing his speech and asking him to nominate Thomas Hisgen, the League's candidate for governor. Following an impressive state campaign in 1907, it seemed conceivable that the League might supplant the splintering Democracy as the second party in Massachusetts. Sawyer's hankering for political success would not down. But neither Hisgen nor the League made a ripple in 1908, and after the campaign Sawyer announced his affiliation with the Haverhill local of the Socialist party. He supported Socialists in the Haverhill campaign of 1908. Within a year he decided to take a pastorate in Ware, since the Ward Hill congregation did not share his radicalism. From Ware he peppered the Socialist press with article after article until his expulsion from the party in 1913. He

28. Sawyer, *Personal Narrative*, 86.

wrote for the *Christian Socialist,* the *Masses,* the *International Socialist Review,* and constantly for the *Call,* which published his letters, his reviews, some poetry, an occasional fable, and a series of autobiographical pieces describing the development of his Socialism. His letters littered the editorial pages of papers all over eastern Massachusetts, every letter driving home the Socialist moral to be drawn from whatever recent event had caught his interest. And he spoke almost incessantly, on "Christ and the Socialists," on "The Relation of Temperance to Socialism," on "The High Cost of Living," on "The March of the Toilers," or almost anything that an audience would listen to.[29]

The tiny Socialist local in Ware was not accustomed to such activity. Though Socialist speakers had visited the town earlier, the organization was formally chartered in 1904 with about twenty-five members. During the following decade it rarely boasted ten members whose dues were current. Perhaps fifty names appear in the ledger of the financial secretary; usually there were few entries before a final "Suspended for non-payment of dues." Between 1904 and 1913, most of the members had jobs that would class them as "workers," but about a fifth of this number were clerks in the store of Charles C. Hitchcock, a merchant who was a frequent Socialist nominee for state auditor. Hitchcock was also the major source of funds for his local; he contributed almost half of the $216.89 that was recorded in the ledger before 1913. The local apparently met irregularly for a year. By 1906, it had become moribund. Records were kept as a matter of form, but entries consist largely of the reports of the caucuses and local conventions that were required to maintain the party's place on the ballot.

Early in 1910, Roland Sawyer joined the Ware local

29. Sawyer Literary Scrapbook II, Notebooks 8, 17, 21, 22, 23; Sawyer, *Personal Narrative,* 88–89.

and the level of activity picked up. Payment of dues to the state organization heralded a vigorous reorganization; for about two months dues stamps sold briskly. Hitchcock's proportion of the year's receipts declined. But the flurry of activity had no real base. As early as April, five members assembed at the regular meeting and voted to adjourn for a week to await a larger gathering. The same five members assembled once more and voted to combine the April meeting with the first one in May. The next entry is dated about eighteen months later. The minutes for 1911 once more consist of the records of required caucuses. The secretary for 1912 recorded three meetings, which, if the treasurer's records are accurate, was almost an average of one meeting per member.[30]

Official records did not note the activities of the Ware Study Club, which was not formally a socialist organization, but a circle of reformers to which Sawyer and Hitchcock belonged. Both frequently presented papers in the parlors of Ware that argued for the quiet, evolutionary variety of Socialism espoused by the most respectable American radicals. Hitchcock's papers, for instance, invariably began with quotations. One of his favorite sources was Theodore Roosevelt; others included Edward Bellamy, Reverend Charles Vail, Professor Richard T. Ely, and his friend Roland Sawyer. Hitchcock made a bow toward orthodoxy, mentioning Debs, Hillquit, and even Marx and Karl Kautsky. But Socialism, as Hitchcock saw it, was coming, step by step, through agitation for public ownership or through public construction of sewers, from which the public would learn the benefits of cooperation. The end of this process would be a new society in which labor would obtain the full value of its production, where

30. William Butscher to C. C. Hitchcock, August 18, 1900, Butscher Letterbook I, SP Papers; Ledger of Ware, Mass., local; Minute Book, Ware, Mass., local, Sawyer Papers; Sawyer Interview, August 1, 1962.

wealth would be justly distributed, where usury would disappear, and where the earth, like the atmosphere, would be the heritage of all. Hitchock did not use economic determinism or sociological analysis to prove his vision. Rather, he postulated the injustice of contemporary capitalistic conditions and relied on "self-evident truths," such as the principle that "every man is entitled to the product of his toil." [31]

Transition from the tranquil society of Ware to the bustle of immigrants striking in Lawrence did not ruffle Roland Sawyer's composure. He had early decided that Ware would not absorb all his energy. The slackened pace of the Socialist local in 1911 and 1912 reflected, among other things, Sawyer's full lecture schedule. Nor did the ideological gap gave him pause. Sawyer's path to socialism, after all, was not that of a dogmatic ideologue. He had persistently championed some sort of reform. The program changed periodically, and the political label tended to vary from one election to the next. These shifts may have been expedient; political office was always a temptation. Yet ambition and expedience did not fully explain Sawyer's career. His courageous acknowledgement of social and political radicalism jeopardized pastoral tenure and may well have blocked advance. His inconsistency was also the result of an idealistic, somewhat impulsive young minister's desire to achieve reform at once. Sawyer never understood a creed that demanded patience in righting injustice. His ambition was to make the world better; when his current political label seemed outworn, he changed it. His only ideology was his interpretation of the ethics of Christianity. The Christian defended those

31. C. C. Hitchcock, *Sanctions for Socialism* (Terre Haute, Ind., n.d.), 2; see also Hitchcock's *The Socialist Argument* (Chicago, n.d.); and "The Economics of Socialism and the Economics of Capitalism," in *ISR*, April, 1903, 581–586. All of these publications were first presented as papers to the Ware Study Club.

the world wronged, including the immigrant and the "Wobbly." And so Roland Sawyer began to stump Essex County in the hope of reaching the juror who might save Joe Ettor and Arturo Giovannitti.

Sawyer railed against the indifference of the ungrateful workers and denounced the envy of craft unions that precluded their support of the imprisoned heroes. Indeed, such men as John Golden and John F. Tobin were using their unions to "inflame sentiment against Ettor and Giovannitti." He quoted with contempt the secretary of the Haverhill Central Labor Union who had called Ettor a "damned skunk" and hoped for his execution because of the I.W.W. leader's earlier opposition to the Boot and Shoe Workers' Union. Sawyer spoke in Boston, Quincy, Rockport, Gloucester, Haverhill and Danvers, and from his meetings came resolutions and collections.[32]

When summer waned and the trial approached, defense strategists decided to stay threatened demonstrations in order to have a last card in the event the agitators were convicted. But thousands of sympathizers took an unauthorized twenty-four hour holiday that might more honestly have been called a strike. Then the trial dragged on until nearly the end of November. Six hundred men were examined to secure a jury. When the jury finally received the case, the prosecution's contrived charges did not long detain it. Joe Ettor and Arturo Giovannitti were acquitted after about nine months' imprisonment. A few days after his release, Ettor happily harangued demonstrators for two hours and a half during a snowstorm. It was, appropriately, Thanksgiving.[33]

And there was much to be thankful for. As a result of the settlement in Lawrence, textile workers throughout

32. Sawyer, "What Threatens Ettor and Giovannitti," ISR, August, 1912, 114–115; Sawyer Notebook 24; Industrial Worker, July 18, 25, 1912.
33. Call, October–November, 1912, passim; Ebert, Trial, 150.

New England received wage increases, often without more than mentioning a strike. Employees in Salem and Fall River accepted a ten per cent raise and stayed on the job. A few hundred strikers in Barre and several thousand in Lowell won increases under the direction of the I.W.W. Although the union's statistics were undoubtedly exaggerated, it claimed that 300,000 textile workers received $15,000,000 in wages in consequence of the triumph in Lawrence.

The Industrial Workers of the World demonstrated that one big union could effectively hold disparate elements together. Membership rolls climbed all over Massachusetts. By the end of 1912, the union had fourteen sections of textile workers and eight less specialized organizations in the Bay State and claimed a membership in Lawrence and Lowell of 50,000. Such swollen figures, if ever remotely accurate, could not last. But for the moment the union benefited by the gratitude and determination of employees like Josephine Liss. The Chairman of the Committee on Rules of the United States House of Representatives asked Miss Liss if she belonged to the Industrial Workers of the World. "No, Sir," was the firm reply, "but I intend to. . . ."[34]

The city of Lawrence and even the owners of the mills ought also to have been thankful. An almost unbearable tension was relieved; the city had a rotten reputation in the national press, a few smashed windows, and more workers in unions, even in craft unions. But the mills still stood and once more produced cloth; the militia had gone home; and the social volcano, which had threatened such sweeping destruction, produced only an occasional wisp of smoke. Civic boosters began a public relations campaign. The device was a parade dedicated to "God

34. *Call*, March, 1912, *passim;* Ebert, *Trial*, 83, *Industrial Worker,* July 4, 1912; *House Doc. 671*, 241.

and Country," with Father James O'Reilly at the head of 32,000 presumably pious and patriotic marchers. A radical counter-demonstration did not provoke violence, and the eventual return of good sense was heralded by the remark of a former mayor who opposed the march for God and Country as unnecessary and tactless.

The Socialist party of Massachusetts too could rejoice in the successful strike and the release of Ettor and Giovannitti. But there was no political dividend. In a year when the Socialist vote elsewhere in the nation climbed spectacularly, totals in Massachusetts dropped. While Socialists elsewhere faced the future, their best days in the Bay State were already a decade in the past. A disappointed party wondered why the investment in the strike in Lawrence had no visible return and asked impatiently what had gone wrong.[35]

Eventually the party found its answer in industrial unionism and its scapegoat in Roland Sawyer. The solution fit the prejudice of the national organization, which was concurrently shedding Bill Haywood. Socialists in Massachusetts, always hesitant to embrace the strike in Lawrence, ended by implicitly disavowing it. Socialism had never quite achieved respectability; the middle class was demonstrably uninterested in Socialist reform. Yet the party persisted in this impossible courtship, and thereby forfeited any political opportunity that might have existed in becoming in fact an organization of class-conscious workers. The party's course after the strike discovered no political base between bourgeoisie and proletariat, and the organization degenerated into a clique of English-speaking party functionaries in the eastern section of the state and the Finnish federations in the western part. That narrow path, bounded by reform and militance, led straight from futility to oblivion.

35. Cole, *City*, 195–196; *Call*, November 10, 1912.

At its national convention in May, 1912, the Socialist Party of America considered the divisive industrial unionism of the Industrial Workers of the World. A Committee on Relations of Labor Organizations in the Socialist Party hammered out a compromise that declared Socialist support for all labor organizations and disclaimed any preference for a particular type. The resolution passed unanimously, but the problem would not long remain under the rug. A delegate moved to amend the party's constitution to make advocacy of sabotage cause for expulsion. After an acrimonious debate, the amendment carried by 191 to 90, with all the delegates from Massachusetts voting in the majority. As a sequel to the new constitutional provision, a referendum recalled Bill Haywood from the National Executive Committee. Once more Massachusetts was in the majority.[36] Industrial unionism may have won the day in Lawrence, but it had not won the hearts of the Socialists of Massachusetts.

The party began again to crank up campaign machinery. James F. Carey, who had refused to continue as state secretary, also declined to run for governor. Instead Roland Sawyer ran at the top of the ticket and added the campaign circuit to his tour for the Ettor-Giovannitti Defense Committee. The party's connection with the Lawrence strike was further dramatized by the nomination for attorney-general of George Roewer, a lawyer on the Ettor-Giovannitti staff.

Sawyer announced a full schedule of speeches, mostly in the eastern part of the state. He promised to explain in detail the Socialist solution to social problems. But the detailed description never progressed beyond the usual suggestion that the workers would be better off by and by. The standard tactic was to deride the other parties rather

36. "The National Convention," *ISR*, June, 1912, 825–827; Typescript, "Weekly Bulletin," March 1, 1913, SP Papers.

than to spell out Socialism. Thus both Democrats and Republicans had been involved in dispatching the militia to Lawrence, or in white-washing the dynamite plot, or in railroading Ettor and Giovannitti. Both major parties only sought office to protect ruling capitalists.

Rival reforms were also sadly deficient. The Prohibitionists' idea that "taking down the beer sign" would "stop poverty" was too silly to refute. The Bull Moose Progressives, however, could not be dismissed so easily. A group of Harvard undergraduates argued ingeniously that only a large Socialist vote would scare the capitalists sufficiently to force enactment of the Progressive program. Therefore, the Progressive for whom the platform was vital ought to vote for Debs. A Socialist rally in Brockton heard that the Progressives stood "for honesty on a platform of stolen planks." Charles S. Bird, the Progressive nominee for governor, had been billed around the state as a "model workingman's candidate." Roland Sawyer had been to his dictionary and agreed that the phrase was apt. A model, he said, was "a small imitation of the real thing." The Progressive party was only a political diversion to maintain control by capitalists. Theodore Roosevelt was "like the boy in the cornfield ringing a cowbell to attract your attention while the capitalist boys are looting the melon patch."

Both Eugene Debs and his vice-presidential running mate, Emil Seidel, came to Massachusetts. Debs and Sawyer spoke to a reported 8,000 in the Boston Arena; more than a thousand marched to the Sawyer-Seidel rally in Brockton. But the smaller crowds Sawyer attracted without a national drawing card were more indicative of Socialist strength. Sawyer's total in the state sank about two thousand below Carey's vote of 1911, and the party dropped under the three per cent necessary to stay on the ballot without nominating petitions. Even in Lawrence the Socialists could muster less than six per cent of the ballots. While the rest of the state ticket, as usual, ran ahead of the gubernatorial nominee, the campaign was not a success. The Republican split, in Massachusetts as elsewhere, spelled victory for the Democrats. But while American voters gave Debs nearly 900,000 votes, only 13,000 came from Massachusetts. The tide of progressivism, which elsewhere gave Socialists a lift, left Bay State Socialists stranded instead.[37]

Harriet Raasch, secretary of the Boston organization, quickly dispatched an explanation to national secretary John M. Work. Charles Bird, she said, had made an effective campaign for labor's support. And the religious issue had hurt the cause in two ways:

In some places Catholic priests told the men if they voted for Socialism that they would be denied absolution.
Some of the Socialists . . . complained that a minister had no place on our ticket. We have not been able to ascertain how these men voted. Others or these probably voted for Bird. . . .
Though we have not been able to identify these party members, if discovered, they will be brought to task, most surely.

Harriet Raasch was the sort of officious party functionary that James Carey could not abide. His disgust with an organization that would elect her to office may have influenced his decision to leave Boston momentarily.[38] By December, Carey was in Haverhill running for local office for the first time since his defeat in 1903. Haverhill's nonpartisan municipal election minimized the split between Progressives and Republicans, and Carey, beaten in an exciting campaign, moved north again, to East Surrey, Maine, where he once more temporarily retired.

37. Sawyer Notebook 24; Harvard Socialist Tract #2, *Socialism and Present Day Politics* (Cambridge, 1912), 7.
38. Harriet Raasch to John M. Work, November 10, 1912; see Carey to Carl D. Thompson, February 12, 1914, for several references to Mrs. Raasch, SP Papers.

In Brockton, where the national split left local Republicans badly divided, the Socialists also failed to recover. Their platform invited all who believed life could be made better to join the Socialist crusade. As first steps, the party promised better schools, with free medical and dental clinics, free lunches, and free ". . . seaside colonies and summer outings for all children who wish to avail themselves of the opportunity. . . ." The adult was offered better parks and municipal ownership of utilities and market stalls. Joseph Poitras, making his third race for mayor, also sought votes as the only trade union member in the field. The Progressive platform revealed kinship with the Brockton Socialists. The Socialists had earlier made such proposals as a municipally owned market, free dental clinics in the schools, the initiative, referendum and recall, and bigger parks and better playgrounds.

But the Brockton election of 1912 belonged neither to the Progressives nor to the Socialists. Democrats won the mayoral race and a majority of both legislative branches. Progressives elected an alderman and five members of the Council. Socialists elected no one; their vote for mayor tumbled more than four hundred ballots. It just was not a Socialist year in Massachusetts.[39]

And disappointed Socialists elsewhere wondered why. "WHAT'S THE MATTER WITH MASSACHUSETTS?" asked the New York *Call.* The paper recalled past glories, contrasting them with the "awful" present. The problem, for the *Call,* was still that lost opportunity of Lawrence, where the vote was very small in spite of the fight that had "cost the Socialist party about $70,000. . . ." The editor cast about for explanations. Were the Socialists in the state at fault? Did the I.W.W. sabotage the vote? The campaign was obviously inadequate.

39. Brockton *Times,* October 30, 1912; November 9, 18, 23, 1912; December 4, 1912.

The comrades seem to be unable to do anything themselves and seem to be unwilling to allow anybody else to do anything. They neglected utterly the opportunity they have in the mill towns. They were entirely buffaloed by the presence in Boston of a cardinal. . . . The vote shows that they have failed all along the line. . . . They have let every opportunity be taken away from them. . . . They have not manifested any interest in anything.

The *Call* hoped that Massachusetts would "commence to get to work." [40]

Two weeks later the New York daily again prodded Bay State Socialists. In all New England, the *Call* could not find Socialists alert enough to make a noisy protest; they were, in fact, "sleeping." The official spokesman of the Massachusetts party confirmed the inertia. The Boston *Leader* complained that it could not get news reports from locals. From one hundred locals had come exactly five reports in a week. Since campaigns were in progress in some of these cities, surely locals had something to report. The *Leader* admitted that "a little more apathy" would turn the paper itself into "an honest-to-goodness corpse." The *Call's* criticism showed in the exhortation: "The eyes of all the Socialists in the country have been turned toward the old Bay State. . . ." The party must demonstrate renewed vitality at the next election. And the same article also contained the movement's epitaph: "Great things were expected of Massachusetts, and Massachusetts failed." [41]

Through November and into December the letters came into New York from Massachusetts, agreeing that something was wrong and offering varied excuses and explanations. Suspicious voters associated Socialism with religious faddists from Boston; the party was too intellectual, too orthodox, or maybe it was not sufficiently intel-

40. *Call*, November 10, 1912.
41. *Ibid.*, November 24, 1912; December 5, 1912.

lectual and orthodox; it was too oriented toward labor unions; it had too many foreign-born members; the I.W.W. was opposing political action; the locals were too autonomous, or perhaps the party had forced members into a mold resembling that of the S.L.P.

Some Bay State Socialists resented the patronizing chiding from New York. A Bostonian suggested that Massachusetts had contributed too generously of her money and talent to help build Socialism elsewhere. Henry Berowich listed fund appeals from Milwaukee, Los Angeles, Chicago, San Diego, Muscatine, Iowa, and even New York, to which Massachusetts had responded generously. Then came the drain of Lawrence, and, said Berowich, there was not much left for a campaign. Furthermore, experienced Bay State campaigners—Carey, Dan White, George Roewer—had been busy outside the state.

Roland Sawyer offered the *Call* no explanation, though he was making a comprehensive analysis of the Socialist failure. Instead, he asked the politicians on the *Call*, "What's the Matter with New York?" In Little Falls, Sawyer pointed out, a textile strike was going on, where police were re-enacting scenes reminiscent of Lawrence. "Where," he asked, "is the Socialist party in the state?" Sawyer reminded his New York comrades that votes were not the only measure of Socialist success. The movement must also "be measured . . . by the power with which it fights the battles of the working class." [42] Sawyer had been to Little Falls; he neglected to remark that George Lunn, the Socialist mayor of Schenectady, had also been there. But Sawyer correctly stressed the reluctance of many New York Socialists to be closely identified with an I.W.W.-directed strike. New York Socialists were always more ready to give advice than to receive it; the distant opportunity was easier to see than the one nearer home.

42. *Ibid.*, November 11, 28, 1912; December 3, 9, 1912.

Sawyer's formal rebuttal appeared in the *New Review* for January, 1913. He summed up national criticism: "It is generally felt that Socialism is not in a satisfactory condition here; that it was once in a flourishing condition. . . ; and that the decline is the fault of Massachusetts Socialists." While admitting that "the situation is not what it should be," Sawyer denied both the idealized past and the depressing view of the present. Comparison with "a former glory of Massachusetts" was inaccurate, since many non-socialists had then supported the party's candidates. Progressives had siphoned off this non-socialist reform vote, and the Socialist base was as firm and as large in 1912 as ever. Membership, he added, was at a record high, and prospects no worse than they had been before the election.

These prospects, Sawyer continued, did not seem very bright, if one were realistic, and the fault did not lie with the party.

1. All our industrial centers are filled with Irish-Americans, who give us a miniature Tammany Hall machine in every city; in addition they are loyal Roman Catholics, and the R. C. Church is not at the present time helping Socialism very much.

2. Our rural centers . . . are in the hands of the Puritanic Yankees; these people are smugly self-centered, and . . . have little interest in reforms.

3. Our working class is composed of many nations, all suspicious of each other, which suspicion is carefully fanned into flame by petty politicians and ofttimes by religious leaders.

4. There is no labor movement in Massachusetts. There are a lot of labor-leader politicians who play with the movement, but there is no united labor movement here. . . .

5. Massachusetts has been the field of more anti-Socialist propaganda than any other state in the union.

Illogically, Sawyer was hopeful. But his remedy was distasteful to his New York critics and his Massachusetts comrades. Had it been used, it would have been distasteful to Sawyer himself. For he argued that the party must eschew politics and instead work to build a militant labor organization. "A revolutionary, class-conscious labor union like the I.W.W. would be the greatest asset that Socialism could have. . . ." [43]

Such a declaration identified Sawyer as a member of the party's "Left" faction. The dispute between this group, which included Bill Haywood and the "Right" led by Victor Berger, was about to boil to a formal split. Roland Sawyer, as one of two members of the national committee from Massachusetts, would have an important vote in the intra-party tug of war. He left no one in doubt about his opposition to the attempt to remove Haywood from the party's councils. After "waiting for words of caution, of wisdom, of leadership" from the party's directors, Sawyer decided someone should try to calm the "petty squabbles." Haywood was certainly fit for office in the party and there was no question of his legal election; therefore attempts to remove him betrayed the ambition of spiteful, would-be party bosses. Sawyer believed Haywood "the most valuable man in a strike . . . in America today." Of course, if the party's purpose was simply "to fish for votes," then the "Haywoods and Ettors and Giovannittis" would have to go, for they were "a load to lug in a war for votes with the Bull Moose bunch. . . ." But if the party was going to "fight the battles of the working class," then it needed "a body of leaders big enough to lead. . . ." Sawyer did not add what every Socialist knew: virtually everyone called Haywood "Big Bill."

The rebuttal of the party's political leaders came from the pen of William J. Ghent, Congressman Victor Berger's secretary and an important Socialist in his own right. No other discussion of the Haywood case, wrote Ghent, be-

43. *New Review,* January 25, 1913, 115–118; Sawyer Literary Scrapbook VIII.

trayed "such . . . hopeless misunderstanding" as did Sawyer's. No one else was "so offensive." Sawyer's "zeal and . . . imagination" had led him to "canonize Haywood." He was blind to Haywood's violations of the party's constitution and indecently suspicious of the motives "of the men and women . . . whose work and sacrifice have built up the party, and who have instinct or sense or experience enough to realize that Haywoodism would soon make of that party a wrack and ruin." [44]

Roland Sawyer was neither so radical nor so opposed to political action as it appeared. Although the town government of Ware was officially nonpartisan, both parties caucused informally to nominate for local office. In March, 1913, both parties discussed Roland Sawyer, and the unofficial Republican list of nominees for selectman included his name. Although the Socialist constitution specifically prohibited members from accepting the nominations of other parties, the Ware local thought there was a loophole permitting such a combination if the local officially sanctioned the campaign. Three of the four members of the local, including Sawyer, met and duly registered approval. That nomination scrambled the terminology traditionally used to separate the party's factions and revealed once more the pitfalls of categorization. The "Right," the wing that relied on political action to spread the faith, virtuously opposed Sawyer's opportunistic political action. Sawyer supposedly belonged to the revolutionary "Left," which thought vote-chasing futile. And he was chasing Republicans. [45]

Sawyer lost the race, though one paper called him the candidate of the better class of voters. In Springfield, George Wrenn, a trade unionist who had once been the

44. *Call*, January 6, 1913; Sawyer Literary Scrapbook II.
45. Sawyer Notebooks 24, 25; Minute Book, Ware, Mass., local; Ledger of Ware, Mass., local, Sawyer Papers.

party's nominee for governor, moved to compound Sawyer's loss. On Wrenn's petition, the state committee voted
to suspend Sawyer for six months. The national committee was to meet soon, and the state hierarchy voted to replace Sawyer with Dan White, a known trade unionist.
White's selection, the committee said, was the result of
his placing behind Sawyer in the referendum for national
committeeman and was not a function of his stand on the
labor question.

Maybe so. But the coincidence of Wrenn's presidency
of a Central Labor Union affiliated with the A.F. of L. and
White's well-known support of the Federation, plus the
impending meeting of the national committee where industrial unionism was on the agenda, suggested that Sawyer's race for selectman was a convenient pretext. Although the party's constitution did not cover the specific
case, a referendum probably ought to have confirmed
Sawyer's removal. The committee acted without notice to
Sawyer or to his local. A streamroller was seemingly at
work. The *International Socialist Review* noted that
White was a "craft union rooter" and thought that fact explained "why Comrade Sawyer was illegally barred from
attending the meeting" of the N.E.C. *Wilshire's Magazine*
commented simply that Sawyer had been "'removed'
. . . for his Syndicalism." The *Industrial Worker* was sure
Sawyer's association with the I.W.W. was at the root of
the trouble. "Many of Sawyer's friends said he would get
into trouble with his Church," continued the *Industrial
Worker*, "but instead . . . it is the Socialist party; hence
the Socialist Party in Massachusetts is a more conservative institution than the Church." [46]

Following an investigation and the meeting of the national committee, the party expelled Sawyer and, for

46. *ISR*, June, 1913, 900; *Wilshire's Magazine*, August–September,
1913, 7; *Industrial Worker*, June 12, 1913.

good measure, the Ware local too. Although Sawyer sheepishly conceded that his action might have been improper, he maintained that he could be removed only after a referendum. An edge of sarcasm crept into his reference to National Secretary John M. Work: ". . . I grant that Comrade Work may honestly hold that the mission of the Socialist party is simply to conduct political campaigns and not to champion the cause of the workers. . . ." The state committee regretted the loss of Sawyer's talent and vigor on the stump, but did not propose to discuss the action further with those who would become Republicans, even for a single campaign. Sawyer's action "was a flagrant violation of all the concepts of [the] movement. . . . THERE CAN BE NO COMPROMISE, NO FUSION, NO POLITICAL TRADING." [47]

Charles Hitchcock, expelled with his friend, thought the penalty "ludicrous in the extreme" and reported the Ware Socialists "too much amused to feel spiteful." A Bay State editor remarked that most successful Socialist nominees ultimately committed some official sin. "Socialism in Massachusetts is over twenty years old, but it still seems to be in the kindergarten stage of development." The Haverhill *Gazette* thought Sawyer's main offense was "that he came near to being elected selectman in his home town. . . ." Sawyer himself announced that he would work for reform independently of the "petty minds" that controlled the Massachusetts Socialist party. The party had "developed no leadership . . . to help us in the problems of the day, nor . . . any capacity for a constructive program. . . ." [48]

By the summer of 1913, Roland Sawyer had finally thought his way through to the ambiguity that was at the

47. Sawyer Notebook 25; Sawyer to Comrades, in Sawyer Notebook 24; *Call,* May 8, 1913; May 13, 1913.
48. Sawyer Notebook 25, 26.

core of Socialist futility. "It is the claim of the Socialist Political Party the world over that it is a revolutionary party," he wrote. "Other political parties are scoffed out of court as being mere reform parties," while the Socialists stand "for revolution." For years, he continued, "I swallowed this, preached it—but now it at last dawns upon me that there can be no such thing as a revolutionary political party." Successful Socialist politicians were not revolutionaries nor even Socialists; they were "no better, no worse" than Robert M. LaFollette and other progressives. Revolutionaries would never be elected and would accomplish nothing in the nation's legislatures even if they were. Sawyer would himself continue to be active politically, but he did so with no illusion that his vote would "bring about a revolution." "I vote," he declared, "for reforms, not for revolution. . . ."[49] Roland Sawyer, reformer, had run for office in 1906 as a Democrat. In 1913, he returned to the Democratic party, announced his candidacy for the legislature, and won a seat he was to hold for more than twenty-five years.

Sawyer had never been a revolutionary, though he obviously was impressed with the I.W.W. Yet it was not the union's sabotage or syndicalism that caught the clergyman's respect; rather he admired its success in breaking through religious and national barriers to create in Lawrence a spirit of cooperative brotherhood. Cooperative brotherhood was the essence of Sawyer's socialism. He was as much at home as a Republican candidate for selectman as he would be as a leader of the Democratic minority in the Massachusetts legislature. He was politically ambitious, perhaps at the expense of the Socialist party, but not at the expense of socialism as he understood it. He discovered that the powers within the Socialist party did

49. *Wilshire's Magazine,* August–September, 1913, 7.

not understand the creed as he did, and he moved on to another party that would at least tolerate him. He was at once too radical and too conservative for the Socialists of Massachusetts. He was so committed to reform that he would help "Wobblies," Republicans, Democrats, or Socialists make the Bay State and the nation better.

Roland Sawyer's path in 1912 suggests that the gulf between the two major Socialist factions might have been bridged; his expulsion in 1913 indicates that the task was too much for the Socialist party of Massachusetts. He was a pragmatic idealist. He could applaud the increased wages the "Wobblies" secured for the Lawrence operatives without wondering whether he had thereby opposed political reform. He could simultaneously run for governor without feeling he was betraying his radical conscience. Realistic, non-ideological, Sawyer responded when he heard opportunity knock; he did not inquire suspiciously about heredity, associates, and beliefs. Massachusetts Socialists were not really more concerned with ideology than was Sawyer; they were just more timid, and perhaps less open-hearted. Sawyer had no stake in the party. He could, and did, move elsewhere if his impulsiveness led to "error." But some of his comrades had given more than a decade to a cause and to companions that they loved. Such Socialists would not idly watch syndicalists and opportunists discredit their movement. Even growth had perils. An influx of membership, either of ignorant textile workers brought by the "Wobblies" or of middle-class reformers brought by political action, would endanger the control of those who had long directed the party. Roland Sawyer suggested that with imagination and flexibility the party might stand with the working class and still run a respectable reform movement. His formula recalled the party's structure of an earlier, better day. While probably there was no permanent solution, as

Sawyer himself later realized, in 1913 no synthesis was even attempted. The party had reached the point where it always saw risks, never opportunities. Like the S.L.P., it could react decisively to expel, not to attract. It would not be revolutionary and had no capacity to reform. It was not a cell, nor a sect, and certainly not a political party. It was not significant enough to discuss, or worry about, or even laugh at. It was dead, and lacked the dignity to lie still.

Massachusetts Political Statistics, 1891-1912

	1891		1892		
	Governor	State [1] Ticket	President	Governor	State Ticket
Republican	151,515	153,119	202,814	183,843	181,954
Democrat	157,982	139,924	176,813	186,377	160,449
Prohibition	8,968	10,597	7,534	7,067	9,423
Populist	1,749	3,045	3,208	1,976	3,302
S.L.P.	1,429	1,872	649	871	1,521

	1893		1894	
	Governor	State Ticket	Governor	State Ticket
Republican	192,613	191,608	189,307	185,073
Democrat	156,916	145,511	123,930	116,260
Prohibition	8,556	8,850	9,965	9,200
Populist	4,885	5,887	9,037	8,306
S.L.P	2,033	2,433	3,104	3,890

1. This figure, an average of the returns for Lieutenant-Governor, Secretary of State, Treasurer, Auditor and Attorney-General, is often a more accurate indication of party strength than the vote for higher offices where ticket-splitting was more apt to occur.

APPENDIX

	1895		1896		
	Governor	State Ticket	President	Governor	State Ticket
Republican	186,280	181,889	278,975	258,204	241,611
Democrat	121,599	116,014	90,411	76,901	78,846
Prohibition	9,170	8,679	2,990	4,472	5,550
Populist	7,786	6,817	15,181	5,907	3,931
S.L.P.	3,249	4,474	2,113	4,548	3,545
National Democrat			11,749	14,164	18,941

	1897		1898	
	Governor	State Ticket	Governor	State Ticket
Republican	165,095	155,473	191,146	180,321
Democrat	79,552	75,671	107,960	102,966
Prohibition	4,948	5,480	4,734	5,393
S.L.P.	6,301	8,108	10,063	12,162
S.D.P			3,749	7,027
National Democrat	13,879	13,511		

	1899		1900		
	Governor	State Ticket	President	Governor	State Ticket
Republican	168,902	166,336	238,825	228,054	220,241
Democrat	103,802	96,659	156,982	130,078	147,241
Prohibition	7,402	5,270	6,196	5,950	8,150
S.L.P.	10,778	11,570	2,595	8,784	6,996
S.D.P	8,262	9,757	9,606	13,260	12,370

APPENDIX

	1901		1902	
	Governor	State Ticket	Governor	State Ticket
Republican	185,809	174,917	196,276	192,592
Democrat	114,362	104,794	159,156	132,644
Prohibition	4,780	6,051	3,538	6,018
S.L.P.	8,898	8,656	6,079	7,629
S.D.P.	10,671	12,410	33,629	36,259

	1903		1904		
	Governor	State Ticket	President	Governor	State Ticket
Republican	199,684	193,500	257,817	198,681	220,976
Democrat	163,700	135,909	165,729	234,670	158,076
Prohibition	3,278	5,467	4,279	3,156	5,252
S.L.P.	4,561	7,292	2,359	2,002	4,638
Socialist	25,251	27,188	13,600	11,591	15,364

	1905		1906	
	Governor	State Ticket	Governor	State Ticket
Republican	197,469	198,959	222,528	212,000
Democrat	174,911	145,592	115,764	160,150
Prohibition	3,286	5,280	25,636	11,539
S.L.P.	2,774	4,217	2,182	5,014
Socialist	12,874	14,482	7,938	7,552
Independence League			35,855	—

APPENDIX

	1907		1908		
	Governor	State Ticket	President	Governor	State Ticket
Republican	188,068	186,663	265,951	228,318	234,458
Democrat	70,842	84,897	155,538	168,162	130,994
Prohibition	3,810	5,376	4,374	5,966	6,837
S.L.P.	2,999	3,915	1,011	2,567	3,149
Socialist	7,621	9,432	10,778	14,430	11,678
Independence League	75,499	50,027	19,236	23,101	18,398

	1909		1910	
	Governor	State Ticket	Governor	State Ticket
Republican	190,186	196,793	194,173	204,944
Democrat	182,252	149,086	229,342 [2]	182,709
Prohibition	5,423	6,266	3,277	4,385
S.L.P.	2,999	3,928	2,613	5,277
Socialist	10,137	11,421	11,396	13,211

	1911		1912		
	Governor	State Ticket	President	Governor	State Ticket
Republican	206,795	207,075	155,948	143,597	163,903
Democrat	214,897 [2]	180,323	173,406	193,184	167,426
Prohibition	3,461	6,564	2,753	2,702	4,768
S.L.P.	1,492	5,309	1,100	2,212	2,829
Socialist	13,355	13,357	12,616	11,493	13,484
Progressive			142,226	122,602	91,454

2. Includes votes cast for Eugene Foss, the Democratic nominee, on other designations.

Bibliographical Essay

Although disappointing gaps exist, surprisingly vast resources for the history of American socialism have survived. Guides to this material are available, and make unnecessary a lengthy catalog here. The second volume of *Socialism and American Life* (edited by Donald D. Egbert and Stow Persons; Princeton: Princeton University Press, 1952) consists entirely of a bibliography compiled by T. D. Seymour Bassett. This reference, which is strongest on the intellectual aspect of the movement, should be supplemented by the bibliography in Ira Kipnis, *The American Socialist Movement, 1897–1913* (New York: Columbia University Press, 1952), which is more political in orientation. Walter Goldwater, "Radical Periodicals in America, 1890–1950: A Bibliography with Brief Notes," in *Yale University Library Gazette* (Vol. 34 #4, [April, 1963] pp. 133–177) lists nearly three hundred titles. Since radical publications changed names, places of publication, and omitted numbers, Goldwater's compilation is very useful. Gerald Friedberg has mimeographed his bibliographical notes on "Research Materials—Socialism in America, 1901–1920," and made them available to people working in the field. Portions of this guide have been published in *Labor History:* "Sources for the Study of Socialism in America, 1901–1919," VI #2 (Spring, 1965), pp. 159–165.

The Institute of Industrial and Labor Relations at the University of Illinois has issued two guides to writing on American labor history. *American Labor in Journals of History* (compiled by Fred D. Rose; Champaign: University of Illinois Press, 1962) is a sequel to *Labor History in the United States, General Bibliography* (compiled by Gene S. Stroud and Gilbert

BIBLIOGRAPHICAL ESSAY

E. Donahue, published in 1961). Maurice Neufeld has compiled *A Bibliography of American Trade Union History* (Ithaca, N. Y.: New York School of Industrial and Labor Relations, 1958). Lloyd G. Reynolds and Charles C. Killingsworth, *Trade Union Publications* (Baltimore: Johns Hopkins University Press, 1944) is a three-volume work of which the final two are an index to various trade union publications. Curators of several collections have described holdings of labor materials in articles in *Labor History*.

MANUSCRIPTS

Important collections for a study of American Socialism are those at Duke University, the State Historical Society of Wisconsin, and the Tamiment Institute branch of New York University Library. The Massachusetts party changed addresses and staff rather frequently, a practice which interfered with the accumulation of historical records. If early files exist, contemporary party leaders do not know of them; nor does the material seem to have found an institutional home. Roland Sawyer graciously made available his personal papers and scrapbooks. He has also preserved a few records of the Ware local of the Socialist party. There is some relevant manuscript material in the Archives of the Boot and Shoe Workers' Union in Boston. The manuscript records of the Lynn Lasters' Union are in the Baker Library of the Harvard Business School. The routine correspondence of Victor Berger's office during his first term in Congress, much of which was handled by W. J. Ghent, is part of the vast Socialist collection in the Milwaukee County Historical Society. The Yivo Institute for Jewish Research has many relevant letters of William Edlin, as well as other materials on American radicalism. Two diaries of the turn-of-the-century period in the Haverhill Public Library are disappointing; neither Mrs. John Crowell nor Nelson Spofford seems to have been politically inclined.

The Socialist party records at Duke University include letter-books of William Butscher for 1900 and 1901, and those of William Mailly from February to August, 1903. Evidently much material from the party's early years has been lost, but scattered correspondence, press releases, and minutes from committee meetings survive. A large collection of Socialist broadsides and campaign literature has been preserved.

The State Historical Society of Wisconsin holds several manuscript collections important for a study of American socialism. Two that reveal much of the history of the Socialist Labor party before 1900 are the S.L.P. Papers, which appear to be the files of Henry Kuhn, and the Daniel DeLeon Papers. Students of Populism and more radical movements have used the rich Henry D. Lloyd Papers. The Morris Hillquit Papers are particularly full on the controversy over Socialist unity and contain more letters from James Carey than any other collection. John R. Commons gathered miscellaneous material on radicalism, Populism, and labor that is part of the Society's labor collection. A few letters of A. M. Simons and his wife, and fewer of William English Walling were also relevant to this study.

The Tamiment Library, now a division of the New York University Library, inherited the collections of the Rand School of Social Science. Tamiment holds many records of the Socialist party of New York, including a 1906 letterbook of John Chase, then the organization's secretary. There are small files of varying value of many important American Socialists, including Debs, Berger, DeLeon, George Herron, Algernon Lee, and others. One important letter for this study appeared in the Mailly file. The correspondence of Henry Slobodin, secretary of the Kangaroo faction of the S.L.P., has not, I think, previously been used. The records of the New York City adjunct of the Lawrence Defense Committee, and a collection on the Ettor-Giovannitti case are relevant to the Lawrence strike. Tamiment's collection of broadsides is smaller than that at Duke, but is worth leafing through.

Scrapbooks in which the contents are adequately identified by source are rare, but even without such information, they may be useful. A dozen of Roland Sawyer's scrapbooks, already mentioned, revealed his interests and recorded his political career to 1913. Eugene Debs's scrapbooks are available on microfilm. Those of Henry D. Lloyd, Morris Hillquit, and Moritz Ruther are at the State Historical Society of Wisconsin.

BIBLIOGRAPHICAL ESSAY

Tamiment has a book of clippings about the wild Massachusetts Socialist Labor party convention of 1899. The Socialist collection at Duke includes a scrapbook of minutes and other official business clipped from the *American Socialist* in 1914–1915. The Haverhill Public Library has several clipping files, perhaps the most helpful of which is a five-volume set entitled "Haverhill Labor Problems." The Boot and Shoe Workers' Union has three very large books that partially cover 1899–1911.

NEWSPAPERS

The Socialist movement must also be studied from the press, for manuscript collections, while rewarding, are not sufficiently extensive. Use of the press, however, presents methodological problems. Often the non-Socialist papers noted the Socialists only to disapprove. Socialist papers, on the other hand, looked at the movement through a telescope, and rigged the news columns accordingly.

In the early stages of the Massachusetts movement, both the Haverhill *Evening Gazette* and the Brockton *Times* were remarkably fair to Socialists. The *Gazette* can be checked against other local non-Socialist papers: files of the *Bulletin* and the *Saturday Evening Criterion* are more complete and more fruitful than others. Similarly, the *Times* can be used with the Brockton *Enterprise*. Because of the prominence of Socialists in these cities, the local press gave the movement more extensive coverage than did papers elsewhere in the state. One exception to this rule is the superb five-page article in the Boston *Sunday Herald* (January 4, 1903). Another special case, the Boston *Pilot*, while not quite official, is a reasonably authoritative indication of thinking in the Catholic hierarchy.

The Massachusetts Socialists published several papers that have disappeared almost without a trace. The *Leader*, for instance, claimed a circulation of 5,000 and was the official spokesman of the party for some years after 1911. There is one mutilated issue at Tamiment; the Sawyer scrapbooks include perhaps three clippings. Extensive correspondence has discovered only one issue in private hands. The firm that printed the weekly believes it ceased publication about the time of the Communist split, and knows that a large balance was due the printer when the paper expired. The Brockton Socialists began a paper several times. The *Vanguard* lasted for a few months in 1901; the *Champion* and the *Leader* were successors in 1903 and 1904. One issue of the *Champion* is all that seems to have been preserved. The Brockton *Searchlight*, a labor paper, is in the collection of the State Historical Society of Wisconsin. A complete file of the *Haverhill Social Democrat* and its successor, *The Clarion*, is at the Massachusetts State Library in Boston and on film at the State Historical Society of Wisconsin. The Society also holds Moritz Ruther's *Holyoke Labor*, and a few scattered issues of the *Proletarian*, the Springfield weekly captured by the Kangaroos in 1899.

The Socialist Labor party must be followed through *The People*, files of which are reasonably accessible, among other places at the Boston Public Library. The Slobodin-Hillquit edition of *The People* has been microfilmed by the New York School of Industrial and Labor Relations. This weekly, in turn, was followed by the *Worker*, which assumed the subscription obligations of *The Clarion* and consequently circulated widely in Massachusetts. The New York Public Library has microfilmed the *Worker*. The New York *Evening Call* (also the New York *Call* or *Leader*) was the chief eastern Socialist paper after 1908; Tamiment, Yale, Duke, and the State Historical Society of Wisconsin have substantial runs of this daily.

The State Historical Society of Wisconsin also holds most of the midwestern Socialist press. The *Social Democratic Herald* was issued from Chicago and Belleville, Illinois, before it wound up in Milwaukee. The Seattle *Socialist*, which became the Toledo *Socialist* and then returned to Seattle, balances the moderation of the *Herald* with militance. The Chicago *Socialist* became the Chicago *Daily Socialist*; the file at Duke covers 1903–1909. The *Appeal to Reason* circulated very widely, and is less concerned with politics than are the more local papers. The Socialist party issued an *Official Bulletin*, the *American*

BIBLIOGRAPHICAL ESSAY

Socialist, and the *Party Builder,* among other publications. The *Industrial Worker* (Spokane and Seattle) presents the view of the I.W.W.

PERIODICALS

The bibliography in Ira Kipnis, *The American Socialist Movement,* already cited, is especially strong on periodical literature. There is little need to reproduce his list, which includes materials in *Outlook, Independent,* and the *Literary Digest,* for instance, that were useful to this study. *The Challenge* (which became *Wilshire's Magazine*), *The Comrade,* and the *International Socialist Review* circulated nationally. Articles in the latter helped fix the role of the Boot and Shoe Workers' Union. The *Nationalist,* the *New Nation,* and W. D. P. Bliss's *American Fabian* reveal the gentler part of the Socialist heritage. George Elmer Littlefield's *The Ariel,* of which a broken file survives in the Haverhill Public Library, is in the same tradition. The *Monthly Reports* of the Boot and Shoe Workers' Union were not issued that often, but show the membership, attitudes, and tribulations of the union before it adopted high dues. The *Union Boot and Shoe Worker* and the *Boot and Shoe Workers' Journal,* which succeeded the *Reports,* show increasing prosperity and a more conservative craft union.

The *Index,* of which there are a few issues in the Haverhill Public Library, was a local Catholic monthly. The *Wage Worker,* which became *Mellen's Magazine* in 1904, may have stimulated the Church to more vigorous opposition to socialism in 1903. The State Historical Society of Wisconsin has a broken file of this periodical, which provided an outlet for David Goldstein, Martha Avery, and Fred G. R. Gordon. Also important in this connection are two books by Catholic clergymen: William Stang, *Socialism and Christianity* (New York: Benziger, 1905) and William Stephens Kress, *Questions of Socialists and their Answers* (2d ed., Cleveland: The Ohio Apostolate, 1908). William Stang, the bishop of Fall River, was more directly concerned with the Bay State movement.

BIBLIOGRAPHICAL ESSAY

PAMPHLETS AND OTHER PUBLISHED
PRIMARY MATERIALS

Socialists published tracts by the ton. Libraries interested in radical material may have many uncatalogued pamphlets and much campaign literature. The S.L.P. has kept most of Daniel DeLeon's work in print. The following is only a sample of the available volume:

Appeal to Reason, *Appeal Army Picture Gallery, 1905,* Girard, Kansas: Appeal to Reason, 1905.
Casson, Herbert W., *The Red Light,* Lynn: Labor Church Press, 1898.
Carey, James F., *Child Labor,* n.p., n.d.
—— and Gasson, Thomas I., *The Menace of Socialism,* Boston: Socialist party, 1911.
—— and Hugo, George B., *Socialism, the Creed of Despair,* Boston: Socialist party, 1909.
—— and Stimson, Frederick J., *Debate on Socialism Held at Faneuil Hall . . . ,* Boston: Boston Co-Press, 1903.
DeLeon, Daniel, *Reform or Revolution,* New York: New York Labor News Co., 1961.
——, *Socialism v. Anarchism,* New York: New York Labor News Co., 1901.
——, *What Means This Strike?,* New York: New York Labor News Co., 1960.
Giovannitti, Arturo, *Address to the Jury,* Boston: Boston School of Social Science, 1913.
Harvard Socialist Tracts #2, Cambridge: Harvard Socialist Club, 1912.
Hawthorne, Julian, *The Soul of America,* Haverhill: The Ariel Press, 1902.
Hitchcock, Charles C., *Sanctions for Socialism,* Terre Haute: Standard Publishing Co., n.d.
—— *The Socialist Argument,* Chicago: Charles Kerr Co., n.d.
McGrady, Thomas, *The Catholic Church and Socialism,* Wayland's Monthly Pamphlet, #92, December, 1907.

BIBLIOGRAPHICAL ESSAY

————, *Socialism and the Labor Problem,* Terre Haute: Standard Publishing Co., 1903.

————, *Unaccepted Challenges,* Terre Haute: Standard Publishing Co., 1901.

The various Socialist parties published the proceedings of most of the national conventions. Major exceptions are the Rochester convention of the bolting S.L.P. faction in 1899, and the two Indianapolis unity conventions. Tamiment has a copy of the notes of the secretary of the Rochester meeting; typescript copies of the 1901 Indianapolis proceedings are available. Campaign books, with suggestions for local speakers, are also published. The *Socialist Annual for 1894* (edited by Thomas C. Brophy; Boston: S.L.P., 1894) is worth singling out because it was designed for use in Massachusetts. The *Social Democracy Red Book* (edited by Frederic Heath; Terre Haute: Debs Publishing Co., 1900) is more historical than later campaign books, and was intended for use as a reference. The Boot and Shoe Workers' Union has also published *Proceedings* of its conventions.

Bellamy's *Looking Backward,* available in many editions, is as good as Socialist fiction gets. Thomas McGrady, *Beyond the Black Ocean* (Terre Haute: Debs Publishing Co., 1901), and a sentimental play by Marion Craig Wentworth, *The Flower Shop* (Boston: The Four Seas Co., 1911) are the work of less talented authors. Robert Blatchford, *Merrie England* (London: Walter Scott Ltd., 1895), a collection of Fabian essays, is more entertaining than most Socialist fiction. *Socialism: The Nation of Fatherless Children* (2d ed., Boston: Flynn and Co., 1911) is the vision of the Socialist utopia by David Goldstein and Martha Moore Avery.

Histories of radicalism by radicals must be used with caution. The S.L.P. has published several historical accounts, including Arnold Petersen, *Bourgeois Socialism: Its Rise and Collapse in America* (New York: New York Labor News Co., 1951) which is mostly polemic, and Henry Kuhn and Olive M. Johnson, *The Socialist Labor Party During Four Decades, 1890–1930* (New York: New York Labor News Co., 1931), which is uncritical.

Biographies of DeLeon published by his S.L.P. disciples are reverent, but may be useful; the sketches by Henry Kuhn and Rudolf Katz in *Daniel DeLeon: The Man and His Work* (New York: New York Labor News Co., 1934) have some historical content. The party has also issued biographical sketches of De-Leon by Arnold Petersen and Olive M. Johnson. Morris Hill-quit, *History of Socialism in the United States* (many editions, New York: Funk and Wagnalls, 1903 ff.), has a much different perspective than the S.L.P. material. The history of the Lawrence strike can be seen through the eyes of the I.W.W. in Justus Ebert, *The Trial of a New Society* (Cleveland: I.W.W., 1913).

Most of the political statistics for this study have come from *A Manual for the Use of the General Court*, published annually in Boston. Other government documents of interest are those relating to the Lawrence strike, especially 62 Congress, 2 Session, Senate Document #870 (*Report on the Strike of Textile Workers . . .*) and House Document #671 (*Hearings Before the House Committee on Rules . . .*).

BIOGRAPHIES AND MEMOIRS

Most biographical information must be pieced together from accounts in newspapers and periodical literature; the series entitled "How I Became a Socialist" that ran in *The Comrade* is a case in point. Longer memoirs include Morris Hillquit, *Loose Leaves from a Busy Life* (New York: Macmillan, 1934); William D. Haywood, *Bill Haywood's Book* (New York: International Publishers, 1929); Roland Sawyer, *A Personal Narrative* (Farmington, Me.: D. H. Knowlton, 1930) and *The Making of a Socialist* (Westwood, Mass.: The Ariel Press, 1911). Different in outlook is David Goldstein, *Autobiography of a Campaigner for Christ* (Boston: Catholic Campaigners for Christ, 1936). The *Yearbook* of the Knights of Labor (Jersey City: A. Datz, 1898) contains some biographical data.

There are several biographies of Eugene Debs, of which Ray Ginger, *The Bending Cross* (New Brunswick, N.J.: Rutgers University Press, 1949) is the most satisfactory. Until Victor Berger's papers become available, Edward J. Muzik, "Victor L.

Berger, A Biography" (unpublished Ph.D. dissertation, North-western University, 1960) is the most convenient reference. Robert Iversen, "Morris Hillquit: American Social Democrat" (unpublished Ph.D. dissertation, State University of Iowa, 1951), makes surprisingly little use of the Hillquit Papers, to which he had access. Arthur E. Morgan, *Edward Bellamy* (New York: Columbia University Press, 1944) is definitive, as is Martin Ridge, *Ignatius Donnelly, The Portrait of a Politician* (Chicago: University of Chicago Press, 1962) on the mid-road Populist leader.

UNPUBLISHED SECONDARY MATERIAL

Duke University students have made some use of the Socialist party collection for graduate theses, more often in political science and economics than in history. William C. Seyler, "The Rise and Decline of the Socialist Party of the United States" (unpublished Ph.D. dissertation, 1952) has made more extensive use of the collection than have others. Martin Diamond, "Socialism and the Decline of the American Socialist Party" (unpublished Ph.D. dissertation, University of Chicago, 1956) has made almost no use of manuscript material.

Howard M. Gitelman, "Attempts to Unify the American Labor Movement, 1865–1900" (unpublished Ph.D. dissertation, University of Wisconsin, 1960) contains a perceptive chapter on the Socialist Trade and Labor Alliance. Donald B. Cole, "Lawrence, Massachusetts: Immigrant City" (unpublished Ph.D. dissertation, Harvard University, 1956) has been published by the University of North Carolina Press: *Immigrant City* (1963). Robert E. Doherty, "The American Socialist Party and the Roman Catholic Church, 1901–1917" (unpublished Ed.D. dissertation, Teachers College, Columbia University, 1959), has not used the collections at Duke or at the State Historical Society of Wisconsin, and overstates the importance of the clash between Church and radicals. The study is, nonetheless, a useful beginning. The Haverhill Public Library holds two unpublished studies by Albert L. Bartlett, "A Chronological Record of Historical Events with Notes," and "The Story of Haverhill in Massachusetts." The "Chronology" can be used as

BIBLIOGRAPHICAL ESSAY

an index to the Haverhill *Gazette;* the historical study is anti-
quarianism. John B. Nutter, "The Social Democratic Party and
the Brockton Municipal Election of 1899" (typescript in possession of Mr. Nutter) is based on the accounts in the Brockton
Enterprise.

ARTICLES

Socialist periodicals, as mentioned above, are a rich resource,
and non-Socialist periodicals occasionally noted Socialist activity. The following is a somewhat arbitrary selection of recent
scholarly writing, not cited in Kipnis, that is at least tangentially related to a study of Massachusetts Socialism:

Abrams, Richard M., "A Paradox of Progressivism: Massa-
  chusetts on the Eve of Insurgency," *Political Science Quar-
  terly,* 75 #3 (September, 1960).
Bedford, Henry F., "The 'Haverhill Social Democrat': Spokes-
  man for Socialism," *Labor History,* II #1 (Winter, 1961).
———, "The Socialist Movement in Haverhill," *Essex Institute
  Historical Collections,* XCIX #1 (January, 1963).
Blodgett, Geoffrey T., "The Mind of the Boston Mugwump,"
  Mississippi Valley Historical Review, XLIV #4 (March,
  1962).
Doherty, Robert E., "Thomas J. Hagerty, The Church, and So-
  cialism," *Labor History,* III #1 (Winter, 1962).
Laslett, John, "Reflections on the Failure of Socialism in the
  American Federation of Labor," *Mississippi Valley Histori-
  cal Review,* L #4 (March, 1964).
McKee, Don K., "Daniel DeLeon: A Reappraisal," *Labor His-
  tory,* I #3 (Fall, 1960).
Wood, Gordon S., "The Massachusetts Mugwumps," *New Eng-
  land Quarterly,* XXXIII #4 (December, 1960).

SECONDARY WORKS

The first volume of *Socialism and American Life,* already
cited, includes several stimulating essays, notably those of Sidney Hook and Daniel Bell. Bell's thesis that American Socialists lacked contact with the America in which they lived has in-

fluenced all who have since studied the movement. David Shannon, *The Socialist Party of America* (New York: Macmillan, 1955) is a sound survey, based on solid research, that summarizes the years covered in the present study. Shannon's suggestion that the Socialists were most successful where they emphasized local issues is borne out in this study. Ira Kipnis, *The American Socialist Movement*, as noted above, contains a comprehensive bibliography, with the surprising exception of the collection at Duke which he did not see. While Kipnis' impatience with the posturing of polite radicals is understandable, his thesis that a more militant Socialism would have been more successful is not entirely convincing. Howard H. Quint, *The Forging of American Socialism* (Columbia, S.C.: University of South Carolina Press, 1953), correctly emphasizes the indigenous contribution to the American Socialist movement, especially that of Bellamy and Julius Wayland. An older account, Nathan Fine, *Labor and Farmer Parties in the United States* is once again in print (New York: Russell and Russell, 1961), and is still valuable. Harry G. Stetler, *The Socialist Movement in Reading, Pennsylvania, 1896–1936* (Storrs, Conn.: The Author, 1943) contains some historical material and a good deal of sociological data.

A complete list of readings in areas related to this study would be pointless. The following may suggest lines of inquiry: John D. Hicks, *The Populist Revolt* (Minneapolis: University of Minnesota Press, 1931) has almost no material on eastern Populism, but remains the standard account. Norman Pollack, *The Populist Response to Industrial America* (Cambridge: Harvard University Press, 1962) is stimulating, and restores to the Populists the label "radical," though it does not succeed in making them "Marxists" as well. Other material on nineteenth century reform agitation can be found in Chester M. Destler, *American Radicalism, 1865–1900* (New London: Connecticut College, 1946) and Arthur Mann, *Yankee Reformers in the Urban Age* (Cambridge: Harvard University Press, 1954), which is concerned with Bostonians. Robert D. Cross, *The Emergence of Liberal Catholicism in America* (Cambridge: Harvard University Press, 1958) is a balanced and important study. Richard M. Abrams, *Conservatism in a Progressive Era* (Cambridge: Harvard University Press, 1964) is a useful account of Massachusetts politics, 1900–1912, although it is occasionally inaccurate in treating details of the Socialist movement.

A sampling of material on the shoe industry and its employees is Horace B. Davis, *Shoes: the Workers, and the Industry* (New York: International Publishers, 1940), Thomas L. Norton, *Trade Union Policies in the Massachusetts Shoe Industry, 1919–1929* (New York: Columbia University Press, 1932), and Augusta E. Galster, *The Labor Movement in the Shoe Industry* (New York: Ronald Press, 1924), which concentrates on Philadelphia but has relevance to Massachusetts as well. The Columbia University Press has issued two volumes on textile cities: Thomas R. Smith, *The Cotton Textile Industry of Fall River, Massachusetts* (1944) and Sidney L. Wolfbein, *The Decline of a Cotton Textile City, a Study of New Bedford* (1944). Marc Karson, *American Labor Unions and Politics, 1900–1918* (Carbondale, Ill.: Southern Illinois University Press, 1958) contains a detailed chapter on the trade unions, the Roman Catholic Church, and radicalism. The chapter correctly emphasizes Catholic hostility, while it may exaggerate the effect of this opposition. The Socialist party, as the present study suggests, had other problems as well.

Index

307

INDEX

INDEX

INDEX

3 1 1

INDEX

INDEX

129, 168, 171, 174, 192, 206, 218

Putney, Squire, 44-46, 59-61, 145-146, 149

Quincy, Josiah, 125
Quincy, Mass., 272

Raasch, Harriet, 277
Rami, John, 252
Rand, Frank, 89
Ransden, Wallace, 129, 169, 206, 208, 233
Raymond, Walter, 20
referendum, 15, 20, 23, 26, 38, 68, 105, 206, 278
Republican party, 9, 108, 219
see also elections
Rerum Novarum, 183-184, 192
Rochester, N.Y., convention (SLP), 1900, 146-147, 160
Rockland, Mass., 3, 8, 57, 132-136
Rockport, Mass., 272
Roewer, George, 226, 275, 280
Roman Catholic Church, 9, 108, 181, 204, 212, 247, 249, 281
opposition to socialism, 184-196, 212-219, 277
Roosevelt, Theodore, 97, 129, 215, 270
Roslindale, Mass., 23
Ruskin, John, 22
Russell, William E., 16
Ruther, Moritz, 39-41, 43-44, 49-50, 56-59, 64-65, 67, 71-73, 83, 92-95, 131

Salem, Mass., 82, 232, 258, 273
Sanford, Baalis, 116
Sanial, Lucian, 57
Saturday Evening Criterion (Haverhill), 162
Saugus, Mass., 175, 258
Sawyer, Rev. Roland D., 179, 263, 265-272, 274-276, 280-287
Scanlon, John, 252
Scates, Louis M., 26, 86-88, 98, 101
Seattle Socialist, 228
Seidel, Emil, 276
Seymour, William, 62

Shaw, George Bernard, 24
Shields, William J., 19
shoe workers, see Boot and Shoe Workers' Union
Shoe Workers' Protective Union, 258
Sieverman, Frank, 56
Simons, A. M., 140, 158, 170, 221, 226, 231, 240
Simons, May W., 231, 233
Simpson, "Sockless" Jerry, 265
Sinclair, Upton, 229
single tax, 42, 47
Skeffington, Harry, 223
Slobodin, Henry, 140
Social Democracy of America, 12, 65-66, 68, 71-72, 75-77, 83, 137
Social Democratic Herald, 88, 91, 139, 153, 154, 161, 191
Social Democratic party, 83, 87, 113, 133, 138, 146, 154, 201, 266
of Mass., 95, 138, 145; ideology of, 134-135
of Brockton, 108, 109, 111
see also "Springfield faction," elections, National Executive Board
Social Gospel, 182
Socialism and the Labor Question, 187
Socialism: The Nation of Fatherless Children, 191, 215
Socialist, Der, 34
socialist factions, unity of, 121-122, 141-160
Socialist Labor party, 3, 12-13, 23-24, 30, 33, 39, 42, 54-56, 67, 70, 80, 109, 140, 182, 186, 246-247, 257, 280, 287
organization, 34
campaign tactics, 36, 38-39
see also elections, "Kangaroos"
Socialist Labor Party (Mass.), 29, 32, 64-65, 83, 141
platform, 37-38
Boston, 35, 44-45, 47, 57, 140
Brockton, 110-111
Haverhill, 21, 31, 71-76
Holyoke, 93-95

INDEX

INDEX